PLAYING TO THE CROWD

D1636160

POSTMILLENNIAL POP

General Editors: Karen Tongson and Henry Jenkins

Playing to the Crowd

Musicians, Audiences, and the
Intimate Work of Connection

Nancy K. Baym

NEW YORK UNIVERSITY PRESS

New York

NEW YORK UNIVERSITY PRESS
New York
www.nyupress.org

References to Internet websites (URLs) were accurate at the time of writing. Neither the author nor New York University Press is responsible for URLs that may have expired or changed since the manuscript was prepared.

Library of Congress Cataloging-in-Publication Data
Names: Baym, Nancy K., author.
Title: Playing to the crowd : musicians, audiences, and the intimate work of connection / Nancy K. Baym.
Description: New York : New York University Press, [2018] | Series: Postmillennial pop | Includes bibliographical references and index.
Identifiers: LCCN 2017045025 | ISBN 9781479896165 (cl : alk. paper) | ISBN 9781479821587 (pb : alk. paper)
Subjects: LCSH: Popular music—Social aspects. | Music—Performance—Psychological aspects. | Popular music fans.
Classification: LCC ML3918.P67 B39 2018 | DDC 781.64—dc23
LC record available at https://lccn.loc.gov/2017045025

New York University Press books are printed on acid-free paper, and their binding materials are chosen for strength and durability. We strive to use environmentally responsible suppliers and materials to the greatest extent possible in publishing our books.

Manufactured in the United States of America

10 9 8 7 6 5 4 3 2 1

Also available as an ebook

"In the past bands could disappear for four years and live in a mansion somewhere, and people were just happy when they did come down from their Ivory Tower and release a record and allow you to go and buy it. Now I think that it's important that you engage with your listeners all the time."
—Roger O'Donnell, The Cure

"You can't just show up and be a rock star and not put the effort into showing your fans you care anymore. Before you were able to just be a rock star, be aloof, be a drug addict, go on tour and it was cool. You were cooler for it. Now you have to put in a lot of work to keep them interested."
—Sydney Wayser, singer-songwriter

"Now people expect you to reply to them. They expect you to respond to their tweets. It's not like 'Oh My God! She actually wrote back!' It's like 'of course you wrote back.'"
—Zoë Keating, cellist and composer

"In the old days pop stars, rock stars used to just drop out of the sky, didn't they? And now, they're tweeting about what they had for breakfast or, you know, whatever. Interesting days though. It's one of those things I suppose people are still trying to find out. Where to draw the boundaries and what works and what doesn't, you know?"
—Mark Kelly, Marillion

CONTENTS

LIST OF FIGURES

Introduction

The Intimate Work of Connection

The relationship between musicians and their audiences has changed. No more disappearing into skies or mansions, today's musicians are earthbound, under pressure to build connections with listeners. Audiences, especially those who came of age in a time of ubiquitous media, expect the musicians they follow to be "constantly accessible, especially on social media, offering unique and intimate moments to their fans."[1] Where once the audiences for mass music had no "real" relationship with powerful and distant performers,[2] today musicians relentlessly seek relationships with audiences, following listeners from platform to platform, trying to establish a presence for themselves and build connections. Day in and day out, the work of relating is never done. "People are so busy," says the savvy young songwriter Greta Morgan, "If you can't find a way to sneak into their daily routine, they'll miss your show."

The music industries of the second half of the twentieth century were never really stable, but for many working within and around major and independent record labels, they came to feel natural. The path for a certain kind of musician to make playing into a steady gig was unfair and unlikely, but it was clear. You got a band together, you made demos, you performed. If you were lucky, you got "discovered" by the A&R (artist and repertoire) guy from a record label. The label would pay you up front and then finance, distribute, and publicize your work. Fame and fortune would follow.

Brian Travers, saxophone player with the British band UB40, was one of the lucky few who made an enduring career in this system. In 1983, several years after they first started playing together, their cover of Neil Diamond's "Red, Red Wine," recast as a smooth reggae number, became a breakout hit. The band, two siblings and a bunch of friends from the working-class town of Birmingham, went on to sell more than 70 million records. To their shock and continuing confusion, they got rich. They don't have all their original members, but they're still going, and they still draw huge crowds.

Now, Travers wonders whether anyone can ever be as prosperous doing what he did again. "I'm probably part of that last generation that sold vinyl, and then everybody re-bought your vinyl on CD, and then the record company sold them your CD in a different packet 55 times and really milked an album," he reflects. "But that's not a bad thing," he adds quickly. "I mean, that's got nothing to do with music. That's got more to do with being an industrialist."

Few recording artists liked the old model—even Travers derides it as industrialism rather than music—but at least they felt like they knew the game. Music businesses were among the first to be upended by the internet, as audiences' abilities to create and distribute media and interact among themselves undid the centralized control that recording and related industries had long enjoyed. Recorded music sales have dropped precipitously from their 1999 heights and the industry has contracted. Where once there were only labels, radio stations, magazines, and face-to-face conversations with friends, now there are more ways to release, hear, read about, and discuss music than anyone could have imagined when people like UB40 were starting their careers.

As a result, everyone is winging it. People who've been making music professionally for decades are as confused about how to build a career as those just starting. "My friends and I have been having the same conversation for the last ten years," says Roger O'Donnell, who has had a forty-year career in music, sometimes as a solo jazz artist and most notably as keyboardist with the Cure. "We're now no closer to knowing what the answers are." O'Donnell worries that today young people who would like to turn music from hobby to career will split between a very few who become industrial stars and those left behind to "slug around." "You have a job. You work like a slave, and you tour and don't make any money. And you sell a few albums at gigs."

Canadian band Cowboy Junkies had a huge hit in 1989, coincidentally also with a cover, this one of the Velvet Underground's "Sweet Jane." Unlike UB40 and the Cure, they need the income that comes from continuous work. It's hard now to figure out where that money will come from. At this point in his life, their songwriter and guitarist Michael

Timmins reflects, it's "not like I'm going to go become a lawyer." It's a recurring topic of conversation with his music friends too. They lament "the fact that money's drying up and you can't get any money to do this or money to do that, and nobody wants to pay to do this, and everybody's calling on you to do stuff on spec and 'Come do my free concert' and blah-blah-blah." Ultimately, though, "it's just like 'Well, this is what we do, so we do it.' At least we have the benefit of really loving what we do, you know?" He laughs. "I mean, you kind of just sort of hope. How are you going to find food is a whole other question. You just do it because you love it, and that's what we do. That's basically what it comes down to at this point."

The cellist Zoë Keating was a child when Travers and O'Donnell found fame and fortune on major label contracts. Today, like Timmins, she is one of the many musicians trying to find a way to earn a middle-class living somewhere between the "slugging around" O'Donnell fears and the hit-centric industry machine Travers scorns. To say she is unusual is an understatement. Classically trained, she performed with the cello rock band Rasputin and collaborated with indie/alternative acts like Amanda Palmer and Imogen Heap before launching a solo cello career composing and performing uncategorizable instrumental music somewhere between new classical and alternative. She oversees the creation, production, distribution, and sales of her recordings, using the direct-to-fan platform Bandcamp, which allows her to sell her work at a minimum price she sets and allows buyers to overpay if they choose. She makes her money through album sales, live performances, performing with other artists, and licenses and commissions for film, television, and dance.

Though she is one of a kind, Keating exemplifies the entrepreneurial musician best suited to these new times. Having worked in information visualization at a San Francisco tech company during the 1990s, she's at ease with computers and with online interaction. She knows how to code and creates open source tools for other musicians. She is a frequent speaker at music conferences, one of the few who (pays attention to, let alone) shares the financial data from her career. She is a policy advocate who works on behalf of other musicians. She was an early internet adopter, webcasting concerts from the Bay Area artists' warehouse where she lived in 1996, long before most people had broadband. In the

Figure I.1. Zoë Keating, performing at the Intel booth, Consumer Electronics Show, 2011. © Jon Fingas, and made available under a CC BY-ND 2.0 license. https://www.flickr.com/photos/jfingas/5337722042.

early days of Twitter, an employee put her on a list that new users could use to populate their feeds with a single click. It got her more than a million followers, most of whom continue to follow. This is complemented by a loyal adoring audience on Facebook and hundreds of subscribers to her mailing list. She has posted to all regularly for years, sharing details of her daily life. When she tweets something like "There is a light at the end of the tunnel. My son just got up and POURED A BOWL OF CE-REAL AND MILK WITHOUT ME,"[3] dozens, sometimes hundreds, of people "like" it within hours.

Keating is the opposite of the 1980s rock star, rich not in money but in the business, technical, and social skills it takes to run her own career. She likens herself to "a small family grocery store" where shoppers realize that choosing not to pay "might actually hurt them." She conveys this message to her followers in part by saying so explicitly, and in part by building a more intimate relationship with them than any 1980s rock star ever could. She reaches out to her audience day continuously on social media, talking about topics like baking, child-rearing, and, when tragedy came, her husband's illness, death, and her ongoing mourning. "I need to let people know that I do live entirely on album sales," she told me: "I just need to be vocal about that. Once they know that, then they might actually buy a record. Because I know that these people might be listening already. I get these emails a lot, like people have been listeners for a while and then it wasn't until they got to know me on Twitter that they bought my album." Keating sells beautiful music in part by offering her audience her *self*. They listen to her music already. They *buy* it because they get to know her.

The Uncertainty of Connection

In 2009, I was asked to speak about connecting with online audiences for recording industry and artist representatives at MIDEM (Marché International du Disque et de L'Edition Musicale), Europe's biggest music tradeshow. Held in the French resort city of Cannes as the global economy crashed, the event featured champagne brunches and yacht parties. The theme that year was "connecting with" and "serving" audiences. "Monetizing" lay just below the surface, the implied and sometimes explicit point of connection and servitude. If musicians connect, the logic went, audiences will pay, artists will make a living, and so too will we. The musicians on stage at MIDEM, and events like it that I have attended since then, told compelling tales of how they had used the internet to run successful promotional campaigns or raise money directly from fans.

But when I heard the musicians in the audience ask questions, or talked with them after my own talks, I didn't hear confidence or enthusiasm.

"Do I really have to use *all* the sites?" they'd ask.

"I don't know what to post," they worried.

"I have nothing to say."

A musician's path to a sustainable career was being redefined as maintaining a never-ending, always-engaging, continuously innovative conversation with their audience, one self-promotional enough to remind people that they have something to sell, yet interpersonal enough to make listeners feel connected and eager to spend money on them. All they had to do, it seemed, was get on social media, post, respond, and let the likes roll in. It struck me as a bit like telling someone who's moved to a new town and has no friends to "connect and engage!" as though that were actual advice for how to go about doing it. No one was discussing the daily practices of engagement, let alone what it takes to build and live in relationship with audiences day in and day out, month after month, year after year.

I wasn't surprised to hear onstage pundits' uncritical enthusiasm about social media as a recipe for entrepreneurial success. Anyone familiar with the history of technology knows how common it is to succumb to utopian visions of new media, as though they offer simple mechanistic solutions to complex social problems. Similarly, their silence on the relational opportunities and challenges of these quasi-magical connections that could transform follower counts into cash was expected. Having taught courses in interpersonal communication for more than twenty years, I know how common it is to see relationship building and maintenance as common sense rather than strategic accomplishments. After all, we all do it every day. Give us a few good examples and we'll catch on, right?

No.

Teaching that class showed me that those most convinced relational communication is intuitive rather than scientific and artistic tend not to do it as well as those who take time to learn about it, understand its challenges, and make conscious choices about their practices. Every conversation, I'd tell my students, everything we say to someone or do in their presence sends messages that further support, redefine, or undermine our relationships.

When we ask musicians to be direct, unique, and personal with their audiences, we ask them to redefine a relationship that has been structured in particular ways for decades. We ask them to do more work, work that requires relational, communicative, self-presentational, entrepreneurial, and technological skills that music work had not previously demanded. Where once organizations and media created many boundaries for their relations with audiences, it's now musicians' job to "draw the boundaries of what works and what doesn't." No one was addressing the personal ramifications of this relational labor. No one was asking what those relationships and interactions look like or mean to the musicians who are expected to live them. What, I wondered, would musicians have to say if asked?

To find out, I began interviewing as many as I could get to talk to me. This book draws on those interviews, a variety of other materials, and my observations and experience over decades to paint a holistic portrait of the historical, cultural, and technological contexts that give rise to the expectations that musicians connect with their audiences in more intimate ways, the dialectic tensions this ongoing relational maintenance entails, and the ways that musicians make sense of and strategically manage their connections with audiences. Musicians are the focus, but this book is not only about them. Musicians are cultural forerunners. The tensions they face as they try to negotiate the boundaries of their relationships with audiences, and the strategies they devise to manage these tensions, have implications for workers in countless fields as they strive to build and maintain markets for their work. If anyone has insight into playing to the crowd, it's them.

Relating in the Gig Economy

Industry and government figures often consider musicians to be exemplary entrepreneurs. The U.S. Bureau of Labor Statistics, for example, started a 2016 blog post titled "Working in a Gig Economy" with this romantic description: "Ryan Heenan works whenever, wherever. He's a songwriter who sells customized jingles and videos online to clients worldwide. 'It's really a dream come true,' says Heenan. 'It gives me the freedom to set my own hours. And I can do what I do anywhere there's an Internet connection.'"[4] One need look no further to see evidence of musicians' leadership in the gig economy than the origins of the word "gig," a gift from American jazz musicians who adapted it from African American slang to describe work.[5] "Gig" made its way from music into wider parlance in the 1950s, "when the hipsters and the Beats adapted it to mean any job you took to keep body and soul together while your real life was elsewhere."[6]

The gig economy prizes many of the qualities that enduring musicians have. They're flexible, mobile, can take on a wide range of tasks, and they're used to working in teams assembled for short-term projects.

There are reasons to wax romantic about this. The autonomy and continuous change of gigging can be exhilarating and exciting. When so many feel alienated in their places of employment, the freedom from institutions and bosses can help "keep body and soul together" even at work. While many workers must stifle their feelings to get through the workday, creative workers like musicians draw on emotions, have more opportunities to experience emotion-provoking events, and have more latitude in how they express emotion in their work.[7] Yet musicians also exemplify the individualized risks, responsibilities, and precariousness of contemporary work.[8] Gig work is inherently unstable, and questions about where money will come from now and in the future cause anxiety. The threat of poverty is ever-present. This is the context in which forming and maintaining friendlike relationships in which artists share their "authentic" selves with audiences, online and off, comes to be seen as a potential means of maintaining their careers.

As steady jobs give way to the gig economy, people pursuing all kinds of careers now find themselves blurring lines between friendship and professional networking as they work to remain visible, stay marketable, and court audiences for their work. While a few generations ago, many workers in Europe or North America could expect to keep the same job for life, more workers are now like musicians, always on the lookout for the next gig, unsure where the money will come from, and bearing the risk of unemployment alone. Nearly 40 percent of American workers, a third more than a decade ago, are part-time, freelance, and contingent "gig economy" workers.[9] Mary Gray and Sid Suri estimate from a Pew survey of contingent workers that "by the year 2027, nearly 1 in 3 American adults will transition to online platforms to support themselves with on-demand gig-work."[10] Self-employment is "fundamentally different from wage labour"; it requires distinctive communicative and relational practices, and demands that workers invest their "entire human capital" to compensate for "the lack of any organizational structure."[11]

Getting a gig isn't just about finding colleagues and employers; it's about building relationships. To stay marketable, many people find themselves like musicians, commodifying their selves as well as their professional talent.[12] Developing a "personal brand" is supposed to provide us with stability, financial success, and career advancement.[13] Whether they are the creatives of New York's Silicon Alley, socializing late into the night at networking parties where dancing girls shimmy as they drink[14] or would-be Web 2.0 personalities seeking opportunity in the Silicon Valley nightlife,[15] workers use their time off work socializing, hoping to make a name for themselves, and create the interpersonal conditions through which they can find work. Building friendly relationships with crowds of strangers is essential to the "venture labor"[16] in which workers invest their time, selves, and relationships to grow their future careers.

Social media, from mainstream platforms like Facebook to bespoke apps, are central to building and maintaining these relationships and to acquiring and displaying the status markers that make people marketable.[17] One manager explained to me that musicians should treat reaching out to their audience and peers online "like a full-time job." But no matter how much they do, there is more to be done. And no matter how optimistic the dream of staying professionally afloat through personal connection, or how enriching the connections people form may be, as we'll see, the daily practices of relating can also be boring, confusing, unsettling, and a source of stress, anxiety, and fear. Relational labor often demands skills and practices different from the job you want to be paid to do, and it can take time away from that work and from leisure.

Intimacy has been mobilized to serve capitalism for generations, but the internet, particularly the loose collection of platforms known as "social media," brings a new twist. The "commodification of intimate life" that sociologist Arlie Russell Hochschild calls the "the great unnoticed trend of our time"[18] increasingly includes an expectation that people use always-on media to turn their selves into products and personal relationships into career opportunities. The internet's networking, data-sharing, and platforms have been used simultaneously in ways that undermine the labor structures that once shaped careers and push people toward making and maintaining professional connections that resemble intimate relationships in their frequency, ordinariness, and how personal they are.

The relationships people form through relational labor can be rewarding and pleasurable in ways that transcend the utilitarian frames that surround them. Aside from the practical benefits of being able to broadcast information, being in touch with the people who appreciate your work brings validation, interesting conversation, and genuine friendship. As Andrea Muehlebach wrote of Italians doing volunteer work for the Italian state, "the economy of good feeling is more than an ideological smoke screen or a psychological palliative. Rather, it is a profoundly indeterminate space of both love and loss, pleasure and pain, compassion and exclusion." She warns us not to underestimate the potency of the emotional ties this work generates: "The fact that the public produced through these acts is partial does not make the acts themselves so."[19]

In many ways, the relationship between musicians and audiences has always been intimate. Musicians often compose and perform from a very personal place. When that music affects audiences, it can feel like a direct line of heart-to-heart communication has opened. Nacho Vegas is a Spanish alternative folk singer-songwriter, known in Spain as a literary figure akin to Bob Dylan. Sometimes, he told me, music can "create in some people who like your songs the sense that you have important things in common, like feelings or experiences in life. Which is not always true. But it can be beautiful as well. Relationships with the audience can be beautiful and strange at the same time. And that's great, I think."

Once commodified, music was marketed in part by strategically crafting and selling artists' images so that audiences might feel a sense of identification, admiration, or awe (e.g., Richard A. Peterson on the fabrication of authenticity in country music).[20] Technologies such as microphones that can capture a voice no louder than a whisper and relay it directly into our bodies put us into close sensory contact with musicians even if they were worlds away. But until recently, these experiences of intimacy were ephemeral and largely imagined by listeners as they engaged with musicians' recordings. On the rare occasions musicians and fans were in the same place, their encounters were usually highly ritualized. Unless they were in the same social circles in the same towns, musicians and audiences couldn't have the kind of ordinary, friendlike interaction so common today.

That changed in 2002 with the launch of MySpace. It may be a punchline now, but MySpace was the first social network site to explode globally. Created and based in Los Angeles, MySpace seeded its network with people in the LA music scene, betting that musicians' need to build and reach audiences could serve the company's need to convert people, be they musician, fan, or anyone else, into users. For musicians, the potential seemed clear: make a profile, upload your songs so people can hear them, start collecting friends. Other musicians can also be used as friends. Get enough friends to up your friend count to where it demonstrates marketability and you can parlay that into gigs, recording contracts, and—if you are as lucky as Arctic Monkeys, early on described as "the first MySpace band" (a description they rightly rejected)— worldwide success. Getting and keeping friends on social network sites could be fun and really did create new opportunities, but rather than replacing what musicians had long done, these new media platforms "set up new (often completely unforeseen) musical relationships and activities."[21]

What musicians sought with MySpace after 2002, gig workers around the world seek today on sites like Facebook and LinkedIn where, with the right contacts and a well-maintained, engaging presence, you might find your next career opportunity. People who never thought of themselves as having "audiences" now find themselves trying to "connect" and "self-brand" in the hopes of following their dreams, living their passions, or, more likely, getting a paying gig that covers rent. Online and off, freelancers and entrepreneurs court social bonds in what used to be free time, blurring the boundaries between social life and work life, colleagues and audiences, friends and fans. Relational labor is now normal, yet we have barely begun to understand it.

Music

Musicians are exemplary workers, yet music work has distinct qualities. It is widely agreed that music fulfills "different needs and ways of being human" than language does.[22] Cultures vary in how they express and limit music, but there are no cultures now or known to history without it. Music allows us to communicate, process, and structure feeling, relationship, and social order in ways that language cannot. It is a highly structured, abstract, and complex information system, organizing parts into hierarchical containers and drawing extended contours that we recognize as melody.[23] It raises and subverts expectations in ways that arouse feelings. Yet even when it incorporates lyrics, it does not—indeed, cannot—impose meaning. It has unique power to mean precisely *because* it evokes without explicit reference.[24]

The musicologist Christopher Small argues that the interplay of notes and passages in music—raising, dashing, and fulfilling expectations—allows us to experience and reconcile the contradictions of relationships between people and metaphysical deities, one another, and the social institutions that bind and separate.[25] Musicking, he writes, using the Old English word to remind us that music is an activity, not an object, is "a tool by means of which our real concepts of ideal relationships can be articulated, those contradictions can be reconciled, and the integrity of the person affirmed, explored and celebrated."[26] Simultaneously personal, intimate, and collective, music has unusual power "in forging, fostering, solidifying and challenging values and attachments."[27] Music produces and inflects social relations "from the most concrete and intimate to the most abstract of collectivities."[28] It embodies nations, social hierarchy, and "structures of class, race, gender and sexuality" while supporting institutional forces like "elite or religious patronage, market exchange, the arena of public and subsidized cultural institutions, or late capitalism's multi-polar cultural economy."[29]

Musical instruments were among the first technologies our species created. In what is now Europe, and perhaps other places not yet discovered, approximately forty thousand years ago, early people carefully carved mammoth tusks and bones of swans and griffin vultures into sophisticated flutes. Designed to serve metaphysical functions, these ancient people carved holes and beveled them to best fit their fingers. They strategically placed the holes to separate continuous sonic ranges into a discrete, fixed pitch. Parts were carved separately and fitted together with adhesives. Although we can't know just how these flutes were used, in the surviving anthropological record of humanity, music always appears to be tied to religion, ritual, and their institutions. In his groundbreaking history, Gary Tomlinson argues that music was essential for the very creation of social institutions among early humans.[30]

Against the epic backdrop of history, the period in which "musicians" have performed for and been paid by "audiences" is a tiny blip in the recent past. Until recently, and still today in large swaths of the globe and pockets of gatherings in Westernized societies, music making has been a ritual communal event in which all those present take part. The ethnomusicologist Thomas Turino calls this "participatory music."[31] In participatory musical events, "there are no artist-audience distinctions.

Participatory events are founded on an ethos that holds that everyone present can, and in fact should, participate in the sound and motion of the performance."[32] Over the course of history, particularly in the last thousand years, participatory music, while never disappearing, has had to make room for (and sometimes has found itself replaced by) what Turino calls "performative music," something made by a special expert category of paid "musicians" for paying "audiences" whose role is to listen.

Since the European Middle Ages, music has been increasingly objectified, commodified, and industrialized, to the point where, even as it retains all of its personal, cultural, and human value, it has become entrenched in commerce.[33] As global cultural investment has shifted ever more toward market logics, especially since the 1970s, the community-enhancing values of music have been increasingly obscured by a focus on financial values. Governments and industrial actors have acted on the presumption that "the life enhancing properties of art and culture were less important than the goal of economic prosperity."[34] In mass music industries, for at least the last hundred years, value has been "gauged according to financial, not cultural or aesthetic, criteria."[35] Music workers thus find themselves between worlds that can have competing ideas about what constitutes appropriate relationships between those who make music and those who appreciate it.

Musicians

Music is an activity in which anyone can participate, making "musician" a fuzzy category. There is "no definition for 'musician'" or any "one organization that represents the majority of musicians," as the nonprofit musician advocacy organization the Future of Music Coalition notes.[36] In this book, I focus on career (or would-be career) music workers who, even when they find success within the industry, work in what Jennifer Lena describes as "scene-based genres." They perform in a variety of specific genres, including indie, singer-songwriter, jazz, Desi, afropunk, heavy metal, Electronic Dance Music (EDM), and others. Leno identifies four categories of music genre, distinguished in part by their economic positioning. "Industry based" genres seek to sell "musical products to as many consumers as possible."[37] Industrial musicians are supported and paid for by industry organizations. "Avant-garde" and "traditionalist" genres operate outside commercial markets. Musicians in these genres neither expect nor make money. Scene-based genres sit in between. Musicians may earn livings from music, but they usually draw financial and practical support from diverse sources, including "family members, friends, and nonmusical employment to support their creative labor."[38] In scene-based genres, musicians and audiences tend to prize "authenticity" over artifice, and audiences' sense of connection to the performers' personalities is essential to the music's appeal and marketing.

The forty-some professional and semi-professional musicians I interviewed lived in the United States, Canada, the United Kingdom, Germany, Sweden, Norway, and Spain (a list of those who agreed to be identified is found in appendix 1). I met many through events like MIDEM and other European conferences. Others I got to know on Twitter. Some were recruited through my own social networks. Because I wanted to know what, if anything, was actually new about social media, I spoke mostly with people who had built audiences before MySpace and had been through the shift from the age of aloof rock stars to the everyday connections of the socially mediated musician. As a result, I do not address how to build new audiences from scratch. I also spoke with younger artists, to see what transcended age and experience and what did not. While some people were eager to speak with me, I met countless dead ends trying to broaden the pool of interviewees, even when asking people I already knew. The time-honored method of snowball sampling rarely worked. Musicians, I quickly learned, protect one another, and friends who think their connection means they can offer others access are usually wrong.

The musicians I spoke with earned livings with varying degrees of success and varying reliance on selling music. Some were rich. Some were earning nothing from music and were only intermittently releasing or performing music. Most had been able to earn a living primarily as musicians, at least for a while. The money they did earn from music came mostly from live performances, although others lost money touring. Some made money from selling recordings. Several doubted there were still careers to be made selling recordings for anyone but a small set of stars. Many found other ways to make money in music. They compose and license music for film, television, and advertising; write musicals; teach music or songwriting; run recording studios; work as engineers or producers; and work with other musicians. A few had corporate sponsorships. Several found work outside of music. One produces a nationally syndicated sports radio show. Another sells his paintings. A Grammy-award-winning musician has since trained as a barber and opened a small barbershop he calls the Handsomizer. One has turned his Prince and Michael Jackson super-fandom into a professional sideline, working with their estates and running a popular tribute YouTube channel.

Only a minority of working musicians ever earned livings from recordings. The Future of Music Coalition spent 2012–14 collecting and analyzing surveys from 5,371 American musicians about how they earn money and how much.[39] They estimate that only 6 percent of musicians' aggregated income comes from music sales. Even in rock and hip-hop, where people were most likely to earn money from recording, less than 15 percent of revenue came from sales. Live performances accounted for 28 percent of aggregate revenue. Those who think t-shirt sales are the miracle cure for musicians' recession will be disappointed to hear that only 2 percent of revenue came from merchandising. Altogether, individual musicians cobbled together income from forty-two different sources, including advances, commissioned jingles and soundtracks, licensing, ringtones, salaried employment with an orchestra or ensemble, live and studio session fees, teaching, fan funding (5 percent had received that), speaking honoraria, awards, grants, and more. Those who spent at least thirty-five hours a week on music and who earned at least 90 percent of their revenue from music made on average $62,757 annually.

The interviews, eight hundred pages of transcripts in all, form the core of this book, but I draw on a variety of other materials to situate them in broader contexts. I spent seven years reading and following what musicians and other public figures did on social media. I paid close attention to news and social media coverage that touched on musicians' relationships with their audiences, collecting hundreds of examples. I followed social media accounts of digital music strategists and people in the music tech industries. I read biographies of musicians who differed from those I had interviewed.

I also draw on my own immersion in the field which, in addition to these daily rituals of media consumption, included attending music industry conferences, where I spoke, kept up on the changing state of the field, and listened to musicians and the questions they asked. Furthermore, I write as a lifelong music fan whose personal and professional histories dovetail conveniently with the internet's. I am the kind of music fan who defined much of my life in terms of which artists' work I was obsessed with at the time. I obsessed on music from a couple of people I interviewed as I wrote this book. I spent much of adolescence hanging out at the independent record store in the college town where I lived. I worked there as a graduate student. I saw hundreds of shows a year, dutifully logging them in a hardcover blank book throughout the 1980s. For a long time, nearly all my friendships were focused on music. Some still are. Many of my friends were in bands. I have an odd knack for befriending bands I love, perhaps due to my awareness of issues I cover in this book.[40] My experiences as a fan, as a friend of musicians, and as a person with access to musicians ground and shape this analysis. Music genres and social identities shape one another, so what you read here is inevitably informed and colored by my own social position. I came of age in an indie music scene in the American Midwest that was overwhelmingly white, educated, and cosmopolitan. I seek to move beyond this by including material from other scenes and sources, but rather than disappearing into a veil of feigned objectivity, I remain present in the book, as situated interpreter, fan, and participant in decades of technological and relational continuity and change. Please interpret my omissions as invitations to further inquiry.

Relational Labor

People often romanticize creative labor, forgetting that the people who do it are workers,[41] but sometimes the ugly truth shines through. In 2014 *Buzzfeed* posted a comparison of meet and greet photos with the pop stars Avril Lavigne and Rihanna.[42] If you were among the millions of people who read this article, you learned that Lavigne has a "no-touching" policy that leads to awkward photos in which "everyone looks like they're dying inside." The photos show Lavigne with weak smiles standing awkwardly beside fans in Brazil who, having paid four hundred dollars for the opportunity, try to look like they're having fun. Rihanna, in contrast, "has the best meet and greet pictures." She is all over her fans—groping their breasts, grabbing their butts, making kissy faces, vamping, and playing it up. Everyone, including her, looks like they're having a great time.

The article's message about how to treat audiences is clear. Rihanna, slipping easily into intimacy with strangers, is relating rightly. Lavigne, enforcing distance, is not. Humiliating coverage seemed to *Buzzfeed* an appropriate response. But what if Lavigne just really doesn't like to be touched by strangers? Why is that so bad? What would faking it cost her? Too much, it seems, for Justin Bieber, who in 2016 canceled fan meet and greets entirely, claiming they left him too drained and unhappy. Perhaps Rihanna is an excellent actress, but it's also possible that for her this kind of fan encounter is validating and pleasurable, while for Lavigne and Bieber it's an alienating part of their job.

In her groundbreaking book, *The Managed Heart*, Hochschild described the demand that we manage our emotional displays as part of our job requirements as "emotional labor." In work that demands emotional labor, the "emotional style of offering the service is part of the service itself."[43] Though the phrase's meaning has expanded considerably, Hochschild's original definition was quite specific.[44] Emotional labor occurs in jobs that (1) require contact with the public, (2) are meant to produce a state of mind or feeling in others, and (3) are supervised by organizational superiors. Later scholarship has shown that these measures to control emotion can come not just from supervisors but, perhaps more repressively, "from peers, customers, and the self."[45] Hochschild briefly mentions contexts in which contact with members of the public may recur frequently enough to form relationships, such as that between doctors and patients, but her analysis focused on one-shot encounters, such as the flight attendant seeking to calm a surly or frightened passenger or the bill collector trying to intimidate someone shirking payment.

Perhaps ironically, perhaps inevitably, the more technologically mediated society has become, and the more emotions have been commodified as part of labor, the more value is placed on public embodied performances of authentic, natural feeling.[46] "Impersonal relations are to be seen *as if* they were personal," writes Hochschild; "relations based on getting and giving money are to be seen *as if* they were relations free of money."[47] In parallel, "the increased global commodification of popular culture creates an even stronger desire among many consumers for that which seems

*un*commercial and therefore less affected by the strong hand of the mar-
ketplace."[48] Whether you're a country singer trying to pick the right shirt[49]
or a waitress taking an order, acting authentic takes work.

The growing emphasis on emotion, personal connection, and authenticity are part of what labor sociologist Lisa Adkins describes as
a "cultural feminization of work" that can be traced to the 1970s.[50] In
many ways, commercialized music, with its emphasis on aesthetics,
style, image, emotion, and creating a soundtrack for social gatherings,
was way ahead of this curve. As consumer culture has shifted toward
feminine aesthetics and practices of "style, surface, image, simulation,
and masquerade,"[51] even noncreative labor is valued in terms of how it
makes others feel. More work is like hostessing, demanding that people
manage friends' and strangers' social situations and needs.[52]

Emotional labor can be both rewarding and alienating, depending
in part on how workers interpret their practices.[53] Using our feelings
as commodities can be enjoyable, healthy, and fun if we feel them sincerely and appreciate their effects on others.[54] If Rihanna really enjoys
meet and greets as much as it looks like she does, it's probably good for
her, at least for now. Many of the musicians I interviewed took genuine pleasure in hugging their fans. But emotional labor also comes with
inherent risks to our well-being. Hochschild worries about the human
cost of managing our hearts for commerce, asking, "what happens when
a gift becomes a commodity and that commodity is a feeling?"[55] When
we can't separate job demands from feeling work, it's difficult to maintain clear lines between which of our practices are paid and formal, and
which are unpaid and informal.[56] Work and personal identities blur.
Are we performing our delightful social media personalities because we
enjoy it or because we are in search of income?[57] Even those who enjoy
emotional labor risk burnout, stress, and cynicism.[58] Lavigne and Bieber
aren't the only ones who run into trouble staying whole while giving so
much of themselves away.

Useful as it is, the concept of "emotional labor" does not get us all
the way to the relational work that musicians now do with their audiences. I use "relational labor" to emphasize the relationship building
and maintenance at stake in this work, while calling attention to the
"labor" context of work and the concerns about the self and alienation
raised by Hochschild and others. Joyce Bellous describes "relational la-

bour" as "effort expended to initiate and maintain connections to other people" in contrast to "productive labour (effort expended using abilities to get resources to live on)."[59] Muehlebach takes the phrase from Italian volunteers she studied, who referred to their work as "lavoro relazionale."[60] She describes it as an effort to re-create social bonds, diffusing and enabling the fact that it may be done in ways that both resemble and replace paid work. Though these works, and those cited above, use the word "relational," none defines what they mean by "relationship" or unpack the processes that make relationships work. Instead, not unlike the music industry pundits I described earlier, they use terms like "connection" and "bond."

Viviana Zelizer doesn't use "relational labor" in her book *The Purchase of Intimacy*, but she elucidates the "relational work" people do to differentiate categories of social bonds and to manage those relationships.[61] She describes people as having implicit matrices of relationship types, separated by dynamic boundaries that are made explicit in the legal cases on which she is focused. I understand relationships as ongoing communicative constructions.[62] People have formed a "relationship" when they have interacted often enough to form recognizable patterns and have expectations of each other. They agree there is a relationship (though they may disagree on its nature) that continues even when they are apart. They can draw on a shared past in current encounters, and those form the basis for their future encounters. A change in one person's behavior affects the relationship as a whole. Relationships change and require continuous, if often unnoticed, renegotiation. Each person in a relationship sees it differently, but the relationship involves feelings, knowledge, and understandings for all involved.

I define "relational labor" as the ongoing, interactive, affective, material, and cognitive work of communicating with people over time to create structures that can support continued work. This includes (1) the communication itself, but also (2) the time and effort it takes to develop the skills, knowledge, and other human capital such communication requires (from years of experience in the field to familiarizing yourself with new social media platforms or metrics); (3) the ongoing sense making needed to understand yourself, others, and the relationships you are building; (4) the development of communicative and relational strategies; (5) the boundary making and marking it takes to set limits on relationships; and (6) the never-ending revisiting of all of these things as each encounter can raise new dynamics. All relationships take work. I distinguish relational "labor" from relational "work" to emphasize that even if relationships become voluntary or pleasurable, this kind of relational work is done as part of a job (paid or otherwise) or in hopes of securing one.

The kind of relational labor musicians do differs from emotional labor in three significant ways. First, while emotion is certainly an important part of it, relational labor is about much more than the performance and creation of feeling. Musicians build and maintain enduring relationships, getting to know their audiences and letting their audiences get to know them. This kind of relational labor is common in many fields. The phrase "relational labor" has been invoked (sometimes too broadly for my tastes) in papers about mentoring and teaching, care work, and sex work, as well as to describe the work women do in romantic and domestic relationships.[63]

Musicians' relational labor differs from emotional labor, and from many of the other work domains in which relational labor is practiced, in that as gig workers their emotional and relational work are untethered from organizational rules and norms. Professions have codes of ethics to provide relational boundaries and differentiate personal relationships from professional ones.[64] Companies offer policies and training. Though some musicians may have recording contracts that shape their behaviors toward audiences to some extent, nearly all of them are left alone to figure out how to deal with their own and others' emotions and to create whatever kinds of relationships they will have.

Third, "emotional labor" is almost always applied to encounters between pairs of people. The kind of relational labor musicians do is with individuals, but also with crowds made up of people with whom they have any range of actual and potential relationships. They must simultaneously manage the relational demands of each person who reaches them and play to the crowd as a whole, with all of the diverse audiences of allies, antagonists, strangers, and others it contains.

Musicians, as we have seen, are pushed toward relational labor that takes friendship as its aspiration. Hochschild's work with debt collectors reminds us that friendship, with its routinized exchange of intimate information and affection, needn't be the only model for relational labor. However, in popular culture, it has become a dominant one. Intimacy is a fuzzy concept,[65] but common to languages sharing the Latin root *intimus* is "that intimacy means an awareness of the innermost reality of one person by another; it is a privileged knowledge of what is disclosed in the privacy of an interpersonal relation, while ordinarily concealed from the public view."[66] Zelizer defines intimate relationships as those that "depend on particularized knowledge received, and attention provided by, at least one person—knowledge and attention that are not widely available to third parties."[67] The kind of interpersonal intimacy I talk about in this book includes more than access to private information and personalized attention, although certainly these are important. Intimacy is also about how and with whom we co-construct our selves. Steven Beebe, Susan Beebe, and Mark Redmond, in the textbook from which I liked to teach, define "interpersonal intimacy" as "the degree to which relational partners mutually confirm and accept each other's sense of self. The closer the relationship, the more you depend on a partner to accept and confirm your sense of self; your partner does the same."[68]

The call to be more personal in professional interactions can be traced to a mid-twentieth-century transformation of "intimacy" as a feature of close relationships into a public and moral good, a shift with origins in the rise of capitalism, secularism, and urbanization.[69] In a fascinating historical analysis of intimacy in the United States, Howard Gadlin argues that since the early 1940s, "technological intimacy" has become common.[70] Intimacy becomes a tool when it is used to meet needs other than its own realization. Once "a respite from alienation at one's place of work, from isolation in the community, from the incomprehensibility of technology, and from social anonymity,"[71] intimacy was appropriated by the very forces from which it offered sanctuary. Yet even as (perhaps because) it was reduced from sanctuary to tool, the emerging twentieth-century "ideology of intimacy" repositioned closeness as morally superior to distance and formality.[72]

Marveling at the new ambiguities around "intimacy" that they saw in the early 1970s (around the same time Hochschild was in the field doing ethnographic research for *The Managed Heart*), Levinger and Raush write: "On the one hand we witness a quest for closeness; on the other hand, there is a breakup and distancing. Certainly traditional concepts of relationship are under question. We are no longer sure of the meaning of such words as friendship, marriage, love, intimacy, family, closeness or distance; the boundaries that once seemed to define such concepts have become diffuse."[73] Like the quest for closeness these authors describe, the desire for intimate connection that we see in fans' new expectations of musicians may be "best viewed as part of a larger historical quest for community and for a world in which all needs for intimacy and affiliation are satisfied."[74]

Relational Dialectics

Intimacy, as these thinkers describe it, is a pull toward interpersonal closeness that counters pulls toward distance, publicness, formality, and techno-capitalist alienation. To make sense of the intimate work of connection that musicians and so many others do, we need to account for both the pulls toward closeness and the pulls away from it. The relational dialectics perspective is particularly helpful for understanding relationships in terms of the inherent, irreconcilable, inseparable contradictions they pose.[75] Think of the yin-yang symbol, in which each side is defined by its contrast to the other and each holds the seed of the other within it. Dialectics may be in opposition, but they form a whole. Each end defines the other. Closeness means nothing in a world with no distance. Distance means nothing without closeness.

Philosopher Martin Buber's influential work *I and Thou*, first published in 1923, describes humans as necessarily moving between two dialectical stances toward the world and one another. When we approach others or the world in the I-You mode, we turn ourselves over to the intimate, ephemeral, emergent, participatory experience of whatever happens between us. "Whoever says You does not have something for his object," Buber wrote; "he has nothing. But he stands in relation."[76] The I-You approach is an ideal, rarely and fleetingly fully realized. It is essential to our humanity, to our personal evolutions, and to moral relations with others. But it can also "pull us dangerously to extremes, loosening the well-tried structures, leaving behind more doubt than satisfaction, shaking up our security—altogether uncanny, altogether indispensable."[77] In the I-It mode, we see people and the world as objects to be understood and used. I-It seeks control and so requires distance. I-It offers the potential to perceive structure, order, and a sense of who we are relative to others as we move through a complicated and messy world. It helps us identify and mobilize resources to navigate what would otherwise be an overwhelming sensory flow. These dialectic struggles are experienced individually, yet are culturally and historically shaped.

The challenge, as with all dialectics, is not which side to choose; it is to find an acceptable balance between them as dynamics of situations shift. Anticipating Gadlin's concerns about transforming intimacy into a tool, Buber warned that the human need for structure and order had been overtaxed for centuries. I-It relations threaten to overwhelm modern people's capacity to continuing relating to one another as Yous. It is "the sublime melancholy of our lot," he wrote, "that every You must become an It in our world," "assigned its measure and boundary" and losing "actuality."[78] "Without It," he warns, "a human being cannot live. But whoever lives only with that is not human."[79]

To build and maintain personal relationships, including those we'll see in this book, we must constantly negotiate dialectic tensions. Interpersonal relationships scholar William Rawlins has written extensively about the dialectics that characterize close relationships.[80] We need to love and be loved, but we also need to use one another. We want to express ourselves, but we also want to protect ourselves and one another. We want to accept and be accepted, but we judge and are judged. We want to be individuals, different from, and perhaps better than, others, but also to participate in a larger whole, relating to others through shared activities founded on commonality and equality. We have ideals of relationships and one another, yet we continuously confront the realities of their limitations. The dialectics we manage are "multiple, varied, and everchanging in the immediate context of the moment."[81] They clash and collide. Our relationships are always becoming, never done. "From the perspective of relational dialectics," write Leslie Baxter and Barbara Montgomery, "social life exists in and through people's communicative practices by which people give voice to multiple (perhaps even infinite) opposing tendencies. Social life is an unfinished, ongoing dialogue in which a polyphony of dialectical voices struggle against one another to be heard, and in that struggle they set the stage for future struggles."[82]

Dialectic tensions take form in daily interaction practices as people draw on psychological and communicative strategies to manage these and other contradictions. Every time people speak, as Mikhail Bakhtin described a hundred years ago, their words balance and anticipate countless opposing forces. He wrote poetically that "The word, directed toward its object enters a dialogically agitated and tension-filled environment of alien words, value judgments and accents, weaves in and out of complex interrelationships, merges with some, recoils from others, intersects with yet a third group: and all this may crucially shape discourse."[83]

What today is so often blithely called "engagement" is how we manage these challenging dialectics, make meaning, and make relationships. As contexts change, as they did throughout the twentieth century and still do, different dialectic forces gain and lose strength. The boundaries and norms on which appropriate and comfortable interaction depend become unsettled. We are in a time that calls us to use intimacy as a tool with strangers on an unprecedented, technologicially mediated, everyday scale. We are still trying to work out how much information is "too much information." Over time, across interactions, across people, across contexts, the ways we come to balance these dialectics through our communication will create new cultural boundaries and norms.

We don't get to change historical contexts or eliminate relational dialectics. We do get to choose how we manage them, and that can make the difference between satisfaction and discontent, between flourishing and withering, between good work and bad. The techniques workers used to resolve dialectics can have different personal and organizational effects.[84] In our least sophisticated moments, we may simply choose one side or the other. We may move back and forth between them, never finding balance for long. At our most mindful, we are able to attain the most rewarding approach, celebrating "the richness afforded by each polarity and tolerat[ing] the tensions posed by their unity."[85]

Music is itself dialectical and much of its value lies in its ability to trouble and transcend dialectics. As Georgina Born wisely puts it, music is "a medium that destabilizes some of our most cherished dualisms."[86] Music grounds our intelligence in our bodies and affects us as little else does. It is both end and means. It is universal, yet also cultural and still deeply individual. It is both product and process, pleasurable and profound. Musical endeavors, Reimer and colleagues argue, "represent a pinnacle of what the human condition exemplifies." Music's unifying transcendent experiences "inevitably have many positive effects on the quality of the interrelated mental, physical, and emotional dimensions of human life." [87]

Musicking, and all the social activity that happens around and through it, is a form of communication with ancient powers to build meaningful identities, help us find our place in the world, and help us flourish. "At every age," wrote Reimer and his colleagues, "a life being 'well lived' is a life being lived with the fullest possible richness of feeling. Whatever the quality of feeling music affords, from the amusing to the soulful, from the fleeting to the indelible, from the frivolous to the passionate, all are precious contributions to a central value humans seem to share—the value of life being fully lived because it is being abundantly experienced."[88]

Music's commodification—and the ensuing commodification of musicians' selves—strikes at the heart of the dialectical tensions between the life-giving potential of so much work and its utilitarian commercialization. Music's contribution to life can be impeded by "social, institutional, and psychic factors."[89] As much as it brings people together, music can contribute to inequality and suffering. It can help lead people to hate and to war. It may serve as a sedative that numbs us to conditions we should be fighting, or may become a vehicle for individualistic competition.[90]

When music is industrialized, and when it is swept up in new digital industries, it often becomes a source of inequity, driving a system in which a few—be they elite musicians or, more likely, well-paid executives and computing professionals—profit immensely while most cannot afford to devote their work life to music. In this regard, too, music shares much with other fields, in which the potential for work to contribute to human flourishing stands in constant tension with its potential to drive inequity, disparity, and alienation.

"The twenty-first century may well bring terrifying changes in social life," writes Zelizer, "but they will not occur because commodification in itself generally destroys intimacy."[91] Rather than seeking to extricate the intimate from the commercial, or to extricate money from close relationships, "the challenge is to create fair mixtures. We should stop agonizing over whether or not money corrupts, but instead analyze what combinations of economic activity and intimate relations produce happier, more just, and more productive lives. It is not the mingling that should concern us, but how the mingling works."[92] In an ideal world, all work would be meaningful and help people flourish, what David Hesmondhalgh and Sarah Baker call simply "good work." In place of alienation, workers might find their best selves.

Since music dwells in the social realms of feeling, relationship, and creativity, music work would seem to have tremendous potential to be the kind of ideal "good work" that leads to human flourishing.[93] Yet, as we will see, it is difficult. Music is a context in which all the tensions around feeling, relationship, intimacy, and work collide. What is at stake as musicians forge their way through the work of relating to audiences is more than how they can make a living; it is how they, their audiences, and ultimately all of us relating through commercial platforms in market systems can hold on to our basic humanity and help one another flourish.

Understanding Musicians' Relational Labor

This introduction has laid out the main issues the book addresses. Before ending, I want to give you a brief guide to the chapters ahead. The book can be read as a whole, in order, and you will get more from it if you read it this way, but some readers may find that some chapters are less interesting to them than others, or that some parts provide too much background information for their needs. Should you be such a reader, feel free to skip such sections. The rest will still make sense.

The musicians in this book are communicators, seeking to give and gain social meaning, and laborers, seeking to make money in contexts dominated by capitalist market logics. The book's first part, "Music," discusses these two sides of music. With an eye toward the ideal of flourishing, the first chapter asks what it is about the relationships with audiences that musicians find most rewarding. The answers, not surprisingly, have little to do with getting paid. It is about knowing what their work means and finding validation of its significance. It is about communicating feeling and fostering relationship.

Music is communication, but it is also commodity. The second chapter traces the history of music as a form of labor, showing how musicians became a professional class of sorts, one separate from amateurs and audiences, and how technological innovations, particularly in the twentieth century, continually upset and reset the relations between them and those audiences. Once close, musicians and audiences became separated by mass mediation. When the recording industry floundered as the internet rose, musicians were pushed to be entrepreneurs, reaching back to the audiences once again.

The book's second part, "Participation," turns to audiences, how the internet has changed their practices, and the dialectic tensions this raises for musicians concerning participation and control. The third chapter traces the history of music audiences following the commodification of music. Rather than giving up on participatory practices when mass media separated audiences from musicians, audiences created new kinds of participation through fandom. I show how fans developed cultures among themselves, replete with practices, norms of acceptable behavior, and hierarchies. From the earliest days of networked computing, music fans were there, shaping the technologies and cultures that emerged online, setting the stage on which musicians would later perform their efforts at connection. By the time musicians and industry figures realized they could use the internet to reach audiences directly, those audiences had already established their presences and social norms online, putting them in unprecedented positions of power.

The growth of audience power means that artists must negotiate a dialectic between maintaining control of their work and professional identity and acting as participants in the subcultures built around their music. The fourth chapter turns to their strategies for doing this. It outlines three common strategies of control—territorializing, invoking intellectual property rights, and datafying—and two strategies of participation—recognizing autonomy and collaborating with audiences. Within market systems, I argue, even the most participatory strategies necessarily incorporate elements of control.

Part 3, "Relationships," turns to the expectation of intimacy I've been discussing in this introduction. In chapter 5, I look directly at the impact of social media, showing how platform affordances reshape relationships between artists and audiences. I compare social media platforms to the stage and the merchandise table. Many of the dialectics raised in social media are seen also in these older modes of encounter, but the relational affordances offered by social media, in conjunction with the emerging norms around their use, push musicians to be more accessible and more engaged in mundane, daily personal interaction with their audiences. Relationships change from imagined connections with perhaps a brief moment of actual meeting, to ongoing connections, with the obligations and pressures those entail.

The final chapter asks how musicians manage to maintain distance when culture, economics, and technology push them toward "authenticity" and closeness. I consider how "authenticity" in music has shifted from meeting genre criteria to being your true self. I address the potential negative consequences of closeness, including its threat to mystique and the fact that it only takes a few people who think they are far closer to you than they really are to create both stress and danger. Relationships are built through both disclosure and restraint. I explore musicians' strategies for creating boundaries in their relationships with audiences by managing their availability and the topics they discuss.

The examples we'll see throughout the book speak to how, beginning centuries ago and culminating in the twentieth century, participatory experiences have been transformed into commercial objects, driving wedges between those who create and those who consume. We'll see the twentieth-century movement away from appreciating formality and distance toward viewing intimacy as a virtue to be deployed widely in all domains of life, including for commercial profit. We'll see workers move from systems that offered local and institutional support toward decentralized systems in which they are on their own to follow their passions, crash and burn, or muddle through, hoping nothing goes too terribly wrong. And with the rise of social media, we'll see creators and consumers brought back together in new ways, challenging boundaries that have long been taken for granted and reformulating relationships under new terms that have yet to be determined.

A dialectic perspective will never tell you that something is either good or bad. What it offers is a way to understand the dynamics that underlie relationships and the strategies people use to manage those dynamics in ways that work for them, and perhaps for others. The conclusion asks what we can take from musicians' experiences to help us understand relational labor, regardless of the field in which it is deployed. Relational labor has the potential to bring both revenue and meaningful connection. It can help people understand the value of their work and feel inspired to create more. It can create friendships and communities. But it can also alienate, overwork, and undermine the good work people are trying to do. It's up to all of us to help shape the world that lets people do their best work while holding on their selves. I hope this book gets us closer.

PART I

Music

1

Music as Communication

If you've ever seen Kristin Hersh perform, you know that music is her calling. She seems to enter an almost altered state. Her head moves like an owl's. She shrieks and screams. Her guitar emits an enormous amount of sound. It's beautiful, but it can be a little scary. As soon as Throwing Muses started, she realized "that music happened between people." "We weren't entertainers," she told me, "because we weren't entertaining. But there was something that was happening when we made noise and a room full of people got it. It was resonating with them, which resonated with us. We felt like at our deepest, we were the same, as lame as that sounds. Musically it seems to be almost physically true. It was quite clear to us that we needed these people in order to make music happen. And music was our religion for lack of a better word."

Music is a way of communicating that somehow, by evoking without referring, has extraordinary power to help people find their deepest selves, bring them together, and feel connected to what feels most important. Hersh describes a cycle in which people make music that resonates as sound waves, listeners feel those energetic waves and send them back, inflected with their own energies. When it works, music has unique powers to help people connect to themselves, to their deities, and to one another.

Music has always been about building, sustaining, and reworking social relationships and institutions. No matter how commercialized it becomes, it can "never be just a product."[1] In a history that manages to undersell its breadth even with the title *A Million Years of Music: The Emergence of Human Modernity*, Gary Tomlinson synthesizes evidence from fields as diverse as musicology, paleontology, cognition, philosophy of mind, and semiotics to show how music, technology, and human sociality emerged together in our species, stimulated by cognitive and sociotechnical skills developed over time spans far longer than human existence. Music emerged among our prehistoric ancestors as they

Figure 1.1. Kristin Hersh. © Derek Haun, and made available under a CC BY 2.0 license. https://www.flickr.com/photos/dhaun/30427327574.

worked together, co-present in ancient "taskscapes." Over hundreds of thousands of years in one another's presence, they developed some of the basic prerequisites for music: synchronized rhythms (or "entrainment") and cognitive capacities such as abstraction, the ability to think of things in the future or things that are not present, and the ability to combine physical and conceptual parts into hierarchical, forward-thinking combinations.[2]

Sometime in this ancient story, our predecessors developed vocal "gesture calls." These cries, grunts, growls, whimpers, howls, and who knows what other sounds had social functions, conveying information that helped co-present beings navigate encounters in which they needed to know whether to approach or avoid, submit or dominate, and otherwise establish social order quickly and effectively. As they shared and coordinated their activities, our ancestors developed shared cognitive patterns of expectation, violation, and fulfillment tied to sociality and sound, patterns that music continues to exploit for emotional effect. Slowly, gesture calls were refined, conveying ever subtler shades of meaning. Early humans gained control of their vocal chords.

Eventually, human gesture cries split. One branch became language, used to create shared meaning through the manipulation of symbols. The other, often now called "paralinguistics," continues to directly express the primal affective and social information central to coordinating our encounters. Our speech retains this musicality. Even as our words convey information about content, the way we speak—our pitch, volume, rhythm, and pace—nonverbally encodes messages about how to interpret both content and relationship. Are the words meant to be exciting, sad, boring, sarcastic, or angry? Are they said as a friend, enemy, bureaucrat? Music exploits the affective and relational realms of gesture calls, arranging sounds aesthetically to provoke resonant cycles of meaning that other modes of communication cannot.

The musicians I spoke with saw themselves as artists, creating work of aesthetic value, and, to varying degrees, as communicators, engaged in a form of social work. From its inception, music has been integral to the folk life of communities. For most of our existence, as Spanish singer-songwriter Nacho Vegas puts it while describing his own aspirations, people made music "while they were working or they were at funerals, or at parties. They made this music just for celebration of life, a way to communicate, one people to each other." They didn't want to "have a career or be a rock star or something like that." Like most of us, musicians hope for a life not just of creature comforts but of significance. Stephen Mason, of Grammy-award-winning band Jars of Clay, mused that if the time came that they didn't feel a "vibrant conversation between the audience and the music," it might be time to break up. "If it was just down to the music itself," he said, "I don't know if we'd still be doing it, because we want what we do to have more significance than just a financial engagement: we make a product and people buy the product, and then we make money."

At the heart of this book is the question of how artists and audiences can relate to one another in ways that help them flourish within the decidedly modern context that calls on them to exploit their feelings and selves for commercial gain. Though some surely dream of stardom, people rarely become musicians because they think it's a smart career move. To understand what helps them flourish, I start with the question of when the cycle of their communication with audiences feels most validating. Research suggests that people feel that their workplace is at its best when their individualism and uniqueness are recognized; they are challenged and achieve mastery; they feel belonging and connection, safety and security; and when they feel empowered, which includes having a voice, autonomy and flexibility, as well as being heard, needed, and able to help others.[3] I asked everyone I spoke with to give me an example of an interaction with their audience that they found "particularly rewarding." Most of the stories in this chapter were told in response. These musicians echo the workers Lutgen-Sandvik and colleagues surveyed, especially regarding their ability to help others. These musicians appreciate how their music helps themselves and their audiences articulate and process feelings. They are humbled and rewarded by the relationships their music fosters, from seeing how it strengthens others' bonds to forming new friendships of their own.

Seeking Meaning

Musicians need audiences. "I know I can play without anybody listening," Hersh tells me, but "it's unfinished then. It's almost like a kid. You don't want to keep it in the closet. You grow it up maybe, but then when it's grown up it goes out and makes friends and is effective in the world. And you're not done raising the kid until the world has accepted it." Only listeners can do the essential work of "accepting their kid" by imbuing musicians' work with meaning. Mikhail Bakhtin, pushing back against the idea that meaning resides in the mind, argued that whatever meaning an utterance may seem to have to its speaker, it only "reveals its depths" through engaging in "a kind of dialogue" with the meanings it encounters when real people hear and respond to it.[4] When an artwork is finished, as Martin Buber writes, it is "changed into It and frozen into a thing among things," yet it is "still endowed with the meaning and the destiny to change back ever again" through the dialogic encounters with its audiences.[5] Art "enters into the world of things in order to remain incessantly effective, incessantly It—but also infinitely able to become again a You. Enchanting and inspiring."[6]

Musicians are communicating in ways meant to produce feeling, but, like most culture workers, it is impossible to know in advance (and can be difficult to learn even afterward) whether and how their It became a You for audiences and with what consequences. The mass mediated music industries of the twentieth century separated and distanced musicians from their audiences in both time and space. Even though they could communicate to more people than ever before, they became less likely to interact with any of them. Recording artists have long had some clues as to how their music lands with their audiences. In a live performance, there is instantaneous feedback. Performers can tell whether resonance happens. They can see, hear, and feel their music encounter its audience. Recordings, however, "take on very different meanings" in people's home.[7] Once recorded, music becomes "open to reinterpretation over and over again as listeners create new contexts for their reception and their ritual use of it."[8] Audiences interpret music in many ways. They can be scholarly, synthesizing a diverse range of musical output, tracking themes through a body of work, or they can be personal, making aesthetic, political, and biographical associations.[9] In their interviews with creative workers in many fields, including music, David Hesmondhalgh and Sarah Baker found that "the often deeply affective and emotional nature of the response sought by creative workers in these distant, mediated audiences produces anxiety, ambivalence and even distrust."[10] To resolve the uncertainty, musicians need to hear from audiences after their music has gone out into the world. Only through communication can they learn the significance of their work. Opening themselves to hear their audience's experience can validate them as artists and as humans. But to become listeners they must be able to take criticism and withstand self-doubt.[11] What their audiences have to say may not always be what they want to hear.

One of the first things people did once they networked computers and created communication media like email and bulletin board posts was discuss music (see chapter 3). This has made audience meanings more visible to musicians than ever before. David Bowie, interviewed in 2000, predicted that the twenty-first century would be about "the gray space in the middle": "the idea that the piece of work is not finished until the audience comes to it and adds their new interpretation and what the piece of art is about is the gray space in the middle."[12] The internet has made that gray space more visible. Brave musicians can read what people write about their work in online discussion forums and on so-

Figure 1.2. Stuart Braithwaite, 2011. © Alessio Moffeis, and made available under a CC BY 2.0 license. https://www.flickr.com/photos/imaffo/6111455567.

cial media. They can run search alerts, bringing anything that mentions them to their attention.

But musicians don't have to look around to get feedback. Audiences now reach out to tell them on an unprecedented scale. "Our email address is on our website," says Stuart Braithwaite of the Scottish post-rock band Mogwai, "so people can email us without any trouble. And we get a lot of really nice emails, a lot of contact that's kind of just made me really happy about what we do and what our music means to people. People saying that our music means a lot to them and helps them. You know, just these kind of things."

"It's just more immediate," says Cowboy Junkies' Michael Timmins; "the internet makes everything right there at people's fingertips, and people feel they can reach out and it'll reach you somehow." The messages audiences send may speak to an artist's work as a whole, to particular songs or moments in their lives, or what they loved about last night's gig. "It's a nice touch," says Timmins. "It's almost like a thank-you note. 'I had a great time at the show last night.' And, again, it does help. Especially when you're on the road and you're grinding it out and you get a few of those, and it's like 'Oh, wow, okay. So we did. We touched some people last night.' That sort of stuff does help."

When I asked a younger artist, Sydney Wayser, if she ever thought about what it might have been like to be a musician before the internet, she responded initially with bemusement. "You mean I'd just make music?" Perhaps it would be nice to have more time to focus on music, she speculated. But then she remembered an email she received from a fan describing how one of her songs had opened long-blocked emotions and brought her release. If she were "so separated from the fans and from the listeners I would have never been able to know that I actually really affected someone like that," she concluded.

Timmins lurks on the Cowboy Junkies' message board to see what people say about the music. "Yeah, I listen. I do pay attention." He's been at it long enough that he has "a pretty thick skin," but he's still curious "as to how people are interpreting things or how they're hearing things. It's always interesting." Hardcore fans can be eerily accurate in reading what the song meant to him:

> They'll parse a lyric and figure it out, like where it's coming from. And I find that kind of amazing that people have the time to do that and the passion to do that. I think that's pretty fantastic. It always amazes me, and I'm always really gratified when I read somebody reviewing something on the message board, and it's like "Wow, you really got it. As far as from my angle, you really got it." But I don't think there's only one way to interpret things. I mean, I know how I want to interpret them, but that doesn't mean it's necessarily the right way.

Often, the meanings audiences make from music are personal. When Timmins meets his fans, they "want to express how a particular song or a group of songs or whatever have affected them. They want to talk about the music and tell their story. People usually want to just tell their story."

Stories are a particularly powerful speech genre for completing the communication loop between artist and audience. Timmins tells me that most musicians got into it

> because as fans they'd been deeply touched by music in some way or another, and usually by a handful of bands or musicians, and they have their

Figure 1.3. Michael Timmins. © Joe Loong, and made available under a CC BY SA 2.0 license. https://commons.wikimedia.org/wiki/File:Michael_Timmins_and_Cowboy_Junkies_at_State_Theatre,_51_(13686756163).jpg.

own stories as fans. So when that gets reversed and somebody's coming up to you and telling you their story and how your music and what you've written or sung or played has deeply affected—it's often extremely private and personal sections of their lives. It's really amazing. It does validate the whole thing for you. You know, you go through periods where you think "What the hell am I doing this for, and who's listening?" and then you only need one or two of those, and you go "Okay, well, right there that makes it—that's worth it right there." So it's very important to hear those stories, I think.

Humans understand our experiences through stories. Timmins's tale is a classic example of a story in which he, the protagonist, has a profound response to music. This leads him to a quest to make music.[13] The difficult path is threatened over and over by the Dragon of Doubt, but fans intervene, keeping the dragon at bay by recounting their own profound responses to his music. Timmins's point—and all good stories have one[14]—is the importance of fan storytelling.

We need other people to recognize us in order to become ourselves.[15] When audiences validate musicians' work, artists may feel the sense of affirming recognition that helps them become the person they want to be. Since what is recognized through music is often private and inarticulable, this recognition can create a particularly personal sense of connection. There is no greater validation for most musicians than seeing that their music made a difference for others. People need to feel needed. Rawlins writes: "In moments of extreme self-doubt we may believe that our actual presence on the earth makes no difference to anyone. These are times when we particularly need confirmation of our singular value from fellow persons. Feeling acknowledged and cared for by people in our world may call us back to ourselves through meaningful connections with others."[16] To the extent that musicians have invested their work with their selves, seeing it acknowledged, cared for, accepted, and given meaning affirms their very humanity. Rawlins puts narrative practices, especially the stories we tell about turning points and significant moments in our lives, at the center of friendship.[17] Storytelling between friends brings the self into the other's story and the other into the story of the self. Storytelling sustains and directs how we understand our past self and how we transcend that self moving forward. For musicians and audiences alike, the personal nature of fans' stories can blur boundaries between friendship and distant relations, as well as between close relationships and therapeutic ones.

Music's Social Work

Musicians find validation in hearing that their stories touched and helped others. Two particular kinds of stories were most meaningful to them—that their music had served as a sort of emotional therapy for others and that their music had facilitated others in building their own relationships. They also took special pleasure in the relationships they were able to build themselves as their music took them to people and places around the world.

Feeling

Composition and improvisation can help musicians process and step outside their own feelings and moods. Their performances, whether live or recorded, can help audiences do the same. Since ancient Greece, commentators have described music as a resource to shape feelings, moderate moods, motivate, and help us cope with difficulty.[18] Culture shapes the emotional meanings that music conveys and how it does so.[19] Across cultures, music serves this therapeutic function, taking us deep inside ourselves even as it transports us outside of ourselves.[20] Music offers "a special kind of 'feelingful' activity and engagement."[21] It adds "another dimension to the human capacity to feel, a dimension not available except through music. Music is an essential way to expand, deepen, and vivify the feelings humans are able to experience. It is among the most powerful means humans possess to fulfill their need for an abundantly feelingful life."[22] Music's power to produce feeling forms the basis of its power as an entertainment medium, but it is also seen as threatening in some cultures. Islam, for instance, often forbids the use of music for purposes other than religion. In the Middle East and North Africa, the regions most likely to censor music, its affective resonance may be seen as a political challenge to government.[23]

I find Nacho Vegas's songs exceptionally evocative, despite—or perhaps because of—my embarrassing incompetence in Spanish. I've spent countless hours feeling my heart crack a little when his voice cracks a little, feeling my anger rise when he yells. When I asked him to compare language to music, he described them as opposites, echoing Tomlinson's discussion of how early-human gesture calls split into symbolic and nonsymbolic paths. "When you talk to a friend, you think in a logical way," he said, choosing his words carefully, "but there is another way of communicating to people, a way that has nothing to do with logic, with your reason. These are the confusing things that you have to put in songs. You make a song, you don't understand anything, but at least you got it and you can see it from outside and you say, 'there is a better life of sensitivity that is hard to explain.'"

Feelings we cannot articulate can be isolating. By evoking and communicating them, music helps overcome that isolation,[24] offering the gift of connection in the face of the inexpressible. When musicians see

Figure 1.4. Nacho Vegas, L'Auditori, Barcelona, January 2009. © Quique, and made available under a CC BY 2.0 license. https://www.flickr.com/photos/quiquelopez/3251554200.

that their music helps others manage and celebrate their feelings, they know that their work matters and so too, by extension, do they.

Recognizing a song's feelings as your own requires cultural familiarity with musical genres and also a degree of self-identification.[25] Musical preferences "encode the power of your origins."[26] Music can thus serve as a locus of identity that provides a sense of belonging. This can be particularly powerful for oppressed populations. Music, argues Mark Anthony Neal, has been crucial to "the construction of community within the African-American experience."[27] In the racially segregated United States into the 1960s, the "Chitlin Circuit" of venues that allowed black musicians to perform, most famously New York's Apollo Theater, "was invaluable for the creation of common aesthetic and cultural sensibilities among the African American diaspora."[28]

The Cure have been striking in their ability to serve as figureheads for a subculture that stretches far beyond them. Their keyboard player, Roger O'Donnell, describes why: "It's about them feeling that we understood it, and perhaps we went through it when we were their age, and that we've helped them. [They feel like] nobody else in the world understands what they're going through, apart from the Cure and the Cure's music. Time and time again people would come up to me and say, 'I would've killed myself if it wasn't for the music of the Cure and that understanding.' We don't need to be going through what they're going through. But I think we could understand it. We had an understanding for them."

O'Donnell attributes much of this to songwriter Robert Smith's lyrics, but the same words set to up-tempo disco beats would hardly convey the necessary sense of darkness. Saving people from suicide is surely one of the most valuable things a human can do. Songs like R.E.M.'s "Everybody Hurts," seem designed to give solace in times of darkness, and they do. But providing meaningful emotional help needn't be so critical. It may just mean cheering people up for an evening. "At the most we're just here 40 minutes to make songs, at least to entertain—if they're in a shitty mood, get them in a better mood," the American singer-songwriter Jill Sobule offers. "At least we can do that. We just provide a social service. Maybe we're therapists or the garbage collector."

Zoë Keating talks about the emails she gets, "like I played this piece when my father was dying or I played this piece when my son was born." The stories that stand out, for her and for the others, were those about providing comfort in difficult times. Keating recounts two that most moved her. One was from a scientist who wrote from a research expedition. "There was a storm. They were inside for six weeks. They couldn't go outside. And they lay down in their bunks listening to my album." The other came from a soldier stationed in Iraq: "He said he and his mates, his buddies, they liked to listen to my music while they were driving their tank across the desert in Iraq. And I was just imagining what that must be like. And I often think I make music for big open spaces, like that's the perfect way to listen to music. And I was thinking that gosh, I hope that that makes it so that if they see somebody running across their field of view maybe my music would make it so they don't shoot."

Musicians took particular joy in feeling they had soothed people who were suffering from illnesses. "I mean you get all sorts of bleeding heart situations where some girl has cerebral palsy and her mom wants tickets to the show and then you meet her," one musician told me. Another illustrated his point with a story about a chronically ill teenage fan with whom he'd been corresponding. She got her grandfather to bring her across state lines to see his band.

> It was like some kind of crazy pilgrimage for her. She was so happy to see the band. I got a million letters from her, about how much she liked us, and how "I wish I could come see you play" and stuff, and she was just a sweet, sweet girl. And it would realize apparently one of her life's dreams by seeing us. And I felt so good about it. It was so nice to have this. At that point we had probably been corresponding for a couple of years, and finally getting a chance to see her at a show and meet her and talk to her was really really really nice.

The great Miles Davis spent most of his autobiography ignoring audiences, mentioning them only briefly as women who became lovers and supported him financially or crowds and critics at whom he was proudly unwilling to smile: "I didn't look at myself as an entertainer like [Dizzy Gillespie and Louie Armstrong] did. I wasn't going to do it just so that some non-playing, racist, white motherfucker could write some nice things about me. Naw, I wasn't going to sell out my principles for them. I wanted to be accepted as a good musician and that didn't call for no grinning."[29]

But then, toward the end of his career and of the book, when he returned to the stage after a long absence, skeptical of his abilities, he found redemption in the approval of "this little crippled black guy who had cerebral palsy sitting down front in a wheelchair." Davis

> was playing this blues, and he was sitting right in front of the stage. I played it to him because I knew that *he* knew what the blues were. Halfway through my solo, I looked into this guy's eyes, and he was crying. He reached up with his withered arm, which was trembling, and with his shaking hand he touched my trumpet as though he was blessing it—and me. Man I almost lost it right then and there, almost broke down myself and cried. . . . It was almost like he was telling me everything was all right and that my playing was as beautiful and strong as ever. I need that, needed it right at that moment to go on.[30]

What's telling about these stories is not the effect the artists had on those they perceived as ill or disabled, but the effect that their sense of having helped had on themselves. Disability serves as a "narrative prosthesis," a "crutch upon which literary narratives lean."[31] In such narratives, including the ones I've just recounted, disability is seen as unwanted, "what we flee in the past and hope to defeat in the future."[32] By casting themselves as able to subvert others' disability, if only temporarily, musicians can see themselves as transforming the unwanted into the desired. That the people of whom they speak may not see themselves as flawed, nor experience concerts any differently than their more able-bodied peers, is overlooked.

The story musicians most often told was about learning they had helped someone through grief. All cultures use music to deal with death, though which musical qualities lend themselves to processing death are not universal.[33] The musicians might hear death stories in person, but usually they came through emails or private messages on social media platforms like Facebook. Steve Lawson, who makes ambient solo-bass music "for people who don't like ambient music," received an email that said, in its entirety, "My father just died. All I can do is listen to you." After putting the sender's name into Google, checking the Last. fm profile in the search results that tracked all of his recent listening activity and thus determining that he had indeed been playing his work on repeat, Lawson responded that he was humbled, and asked if there was anything more he could do. David Lowery, the frontman for both Cracker and Camper Van Beethoven, who generally prefers to keep his audience at a formal distance, told me about getting a private message on Facebook from a fan he knew mostly from political arguments they'd had on his fan page. The message said that his mother was dying. Her last wish was to hear Lowery's song "Take Me Down to the Infirmary." Lowery was "stunned." It had never occurred to him "that our music could penetrate that far into someone's emotional life."

"Probably the most rewarding" experience for Greta Morgan "is actually really kind of a sad one." There were two brothers who were really big fans. They "shared the music with their family and that kind of thing. And they both died in a car accident last summer." Morgan heard that their father, who worked for a national radio broadcaster, had used one of her band's songs repeatedly in an on-air remembrance. Her own

Figure 1.5. Greta Morgan, The Pike Room, Pontiac, Michigan. © Dan Cox, and made available under a CC BY-ND 2.0 license. https://www.flickr.com/photos/dancox_/5452577069.

father heard it and told her. She looked up the parents and sent a consolation note, telling them that the boys, who were handsome, charitable, charming, and great students, seemed incredible. A few months later, the mother began writing back. They struck up a correspondence. The parents created a foundation to benefit the charities for which the sons had worked. Morgan's band played an event to honor the foundation, raising almost four thousand dollars, "which for a new band is a lot of money to be able to raise." It was "a very sad but a very rewarding experience of seeing how even sending one note or playing one charity event can really brighten these people's day or a few months, even though they're going through this extreme kind of loss."

More than a decade after its release, Stephen Mason told me that people still tweet about how Jars of Clay's "Valley Song," with the lyric "When death, like a gypsy, comes to steal what I love, I will still look to the Heavens," is helping them cope with loss. When they meet, fans tell them "that song gave me language for something that I didn't have words for." "What I think poetry does at its best," Mason reflects, "is it gives new words to feelings and maybe helps develop a new context to understand feelings. So that's why we love what we do. That's a large part of it."

There's an affective cycle with music. Musicians give shape to inchoate feelings through song. Those songs help others live with their own emotions. They show musicians their own feelings, and this can create feelings of compassion, gratitude, humility, and self-worth in the musicians, validating the significance of their work and giving them incentives to continue. At the same time, musicians aren't therapists, and they don't have the explicit boundaries and professional codes of ethics that bound and guide their relationships with their audiences as they share these intimate moments. It can get too close for comfort. As we will see in chapter 6, a few people move from the sense of shared emotion to the illusion of close relationship.

It may also be that once musicians have been able to step outside their feelings through song, the cycles of audience response keep pulling them back to the pain. Morgan wrote a song to help her deal with a close friend's suicide. She never talked about the song's origin, or even that it was about suicide, but some of the images were clear enough that people who had lost someone to suicide "sensed that was what the song was about." At shows, fans would approach her to talk about losing an uncle or a close friend to suicide. "They want to have this really intense conversation with me and connect on it." From her perspective, it had taken a long time to deal with her grief. She'd written the song, she'd put it out there, and she was done. She appreciated her audience's openness and confidence but didn't want to deal with the "waves of emotion" these conversations aroused.

Relationship

Christopher Small argues that the way music arouses emotion lets us explore relationships experientially. "The act of musicking establishes in the place where it is happening a set of relationships," he writes, "and it is in those relationships that the meaning of the act lies."[34] He posits that music is not so much about relationships "which actually exist in our lives as about those that we desire to exist and long to experience: relationships among people, as well as those between people and the rest of the cosmos, and also perhaps with ourselves and with our bodies and even with the supernatural, if our conceptual world has room for the supernatural."[35] Yet music often does foster relationships that actually exist. For some musicians, this may be the reason to make music. "The whole point of being an artist," writes Amanda Palmer, is "to connected to people. To make a family. A family you were with all the time, like it or not."[36] Music brings people together as cultures, as subcultures, and as individuals, connecting "the 'we' and the 'I' without subordinating one to the other."[37]

Much has been made of music's ability to foster subcultural distinction.[38] The performing arts are "fulcrums of identity, allowing people to intimately feel themselves part of the community through the realization of shared cultural knowledge and style and through the very act of participating together in performance."[39] Music helps people feel a sense of belonging with others in a transnational subculture, in local contexts, and in dyadic relationships. Finding meaning in music is "a continual process of drawing social boundaries between those who are 'like us' and those who are not."[40] For many, music provides solidarity in the face of public cultures that do not feel like home. Fans of the Cure were "the weird ones at school," as O'Donnell put it. "You wore black clothes and you had black hair. You were pretty depressed, and you were on the margins." The Cure gave the fans "something to make them feel not so alone" and around which they could build a subculture of people who felt marginalized. One need only look at the commonalities among fandoms around the boy bands of the day over time (think of One Direction's "Directioneers" or Justin Bieber's "Beliebers", fandoms around the Beatles, or my own 1970s preteen fan experiences described in chapter 3) to see that they have much more to do with the pleasures and lessons girls experience in building community with one another through common practices that set them apart from other demographic groups than with the specific young men around whom those practices take form.

Transnational fandoms may take distinctive local forms as people use music to speak to their concrete conditions. Emma Baulch describes this in the context of death metal fandom in Bali, where metal fans adopted "the universal death metal aesthetic" and began performing metal publicly and locally as a means of positioning themselves against the tourism dominating their region.[41] They viewed this genre, in contrast to the more popular and tourist-friendly genre of reggae, as a "spirited expression of the soul which, in their view, conflicted with tourism's demands."[42] Similarly, in rural Texas, where Aaron Fox spent years playing and studying in honky-tonks, "Real Country" was a genre, an identity

Figure 1.6. Billy Bragg at SXSW, 2008. © Rolando Tanglao, and made available under a CC BY 2.0 license. https://www.flickr.com/photos/roland/2332529078.

and a shared social experience, even though, as Peterson shows, the genre of "country" was manufactured in part by urban businessmen far from Texas or other parts of the American rural south.[43] "Speaking and singing artfully, improvisationally, and with minimal reference to exchange value have remained essential to the social construction of history, identity, and sociability" in the region despite difficult times and the profusion of mass-mediated culture in everyday life.[44]

The British political indie-folk singer Billy Bragg is particularly passionate about the sense of solidarity among his audience members. People often tell him live performances of his song "I Keep Faith" made them cry. When he plays it, he introduces the song by talking about his faith in the audience's ability to change the world. "I'm just a guy," he tells them: "I just play guitar. I'm gone tomorrow, you're still here. It's your job to change the world. Look at this room full of people. They all want to change the world too. All I can do is bring you together and make you feel like you're not alone, and you have to go out and do it. Believe in those people standing ten yards behind you in the dark, that you've never met. Now if push comes to shove they'll stand beside you for the things that you care about." On one level, he tells me, the lyrics are about his wife, something their son is eager to remind him. But it's also about his politics and his beliefs about social order. "It's about trusting strangers," he says, "the fundamental underpinning of socialism and solidarity."

Bragg has a community of fans who hang out in his web forum. "They're really good people," he tells me. "I've known some literally for my entire career. I've watched them go from a drunk climbing on stage to dance with me to being married with children." These audience members may not even like his music anymore, but going to his gigs together is integral to their relationships. "I spoke to one of them the other day," he says, "and she's absolutely clear she's not listened to an album I made in the last ten years." He doesn't worry about that. "It doesn't bother me, the fact that I provide them with a social framework." He tears up telling me about the death of a man on his forum who was the longtime partner of the group's most prolific member. "We're not just talking about fans," he sighs. "This is something else. These are friends." Musicians' power to foster this kind of social solidarity among their fans raises issues of how to position themselves vis-à-vis fans and the communities they build. We will return to this in chapter 4.

Music also brings people together as pairs and helps support their ongoing relationships. Many of the artists I spoke with glowed as they talked about learning how their music had helped strengthen relationships. Timmons reflected on a "punked out or gothed out" young man who approached him after the show. "Me and my dad never got along. We couldn't agree on anything, we were always fighting," he told him. "The only thing that we ever, ever connected with was your music." The father had died six months earlier. Norwegian rock star Sivert Høyem offered a nearly identical experience, "Sometimes I get personal messages, people send me a message about how they were at a gig with their father and how they really connected through the music."

Two of Jill Sobule's fans, one in New York and the other in Salt Lake City, began writing to each other after realizing both were fans. Soon they were writing every day. They fell in love, but they had no money to meet. Sobule dreamed of running a Kickstarter campaign to fly them to see her and put them up in a fancy hotel. "You talk about things with fans," she says to me. "Any time you can be a matchmaker, that's the best. When you get fans that are saying 'I met someone through your music,' I mean, it's like making whoopee! That's when I feel like 'Wow, I'm creating a social service!'"

Musicians move in worlds where music is the basis of their own friendships with one another, with other people in music, and with their audience members in different locations. These relationships, developed through and around music, provide them with grounding in a transitory and unstable lifestyle. "One of the great things about music," the American indie artist Conner Oberst told music journalist Greg Kot, "is how

Figure 1.7. Jill Sobule and Steve Lawson at All2Gether Now, Berlin. Photo by Nancy Baym.

you discover it and share it. It's based on friendships. I think most of the people I care about in the world I somehow met through music. It's just such a powerful force. I think all art is meant to be communicated to other people and it's hard to put a price tag on things like that."[45] Vegas likewise celebrates music's ability to connect him to individuals everywhere he plays. "You know a lot of people in every place you play. And you always play music, and you always talk about music, and talking about music, it's something similar to talking about life. And you talk about music and then you talk about life. I made a bunch of friends that I know, just from playing someplace. You get your mind more open just by playing and knowing people and being in different places. It's one of the greatest things about being in music."

Touring musicians often speak of the value of meeting people from other countries. "Travel is one of the great parts of being a musician, forming those connections all over the world," said Richie Hawtin. Hawtin, an electronica artist who often performs behind a curtain with an LED light display that obscures his view of the audience, actively looks for them before shows to compensate for that distance. "Like if I'm playing Korea I might go on Twitter and ask 'where is everyone?' And someone will say 'they're eating salted squid next to the venue.' So I'll go there and try and meet some people." Originally from Canada and often associated with Detroit, Hawtin reflected on his years playing in Japan: "When I started way back playing in Japan my friends there—we didn't even speak the same language. But electronic music, because there's no vocals, it reaches people at a very emotional primal level. And we could build on that to become good friends. The music industry doesn't talk about it. They all think about sales. But if you talk to musicians they'll all tell you that's a really big part of it, when people from different cultures connect around music, that's really powerful."

The internet has broadened the geographic range within which artists can tour. An independent Swedish band, like the ethereal dream pop duo Club 8, may make a year's worth of income touring Asia or Brazil, where they have huge audiences if few record sales. A Scottish band like Mogwai, who did quite well in the United Kingdom, Europe, and the United States, may sell fewer records than they used to, but become popular in

Figure 1.8. Richie Hawtin performing as Plastikman. © Robert Emperley, and made available under a CC BY-SA 2.0 license. https://www.flickr.com/photos/emperley3/4732820841.

places like South America and Asia where they would never have had audiences before the internet. A Spaniard like Vegas may reach audiences in Spanish-speaking nations in the Americas he could not have found before without negotiating label deals for each country. The connections formed through touring can also come home. Steve Lawson has toured with huge acts but prefers playing house concerts. His favorite thing is "when people who we know off the internet go, 'Do you want to come and play in my house? I can pull together 25 friends and they're happy to pay 15 bucks each to hear you play.'" He and his wife Lobelia, also a musician, make many friends this way. Then they reciprocate, hosting house concerts for other musicians, or "they just come and stay for a holiday."

Music as Gift

Music is communication that does social work. Musicians work in the realms of commerce and sociality simultaneously, called on the one hand to be the focus of attention, selling their personas and wares, and, on the other, people communicating with other people, therapists, social service workers, and friends. Music, when it works, circulates. Its energy moves from artists to audience, among audiences, and back from audience to artists. Mason, whose band won Grammy awards and sold millions of records, describes it as life-giving: "Artists are alive when they create. And people that consume art are alive when they receive it, and they pass it on and they share it. And that's the antithesis of the music industry that we came out of."

Lewis Hyde's influential book *The Gift* argues that music, like all art, circulates in two economies simultaneously, one social and the other economic.[46] *The Gift* has become a touchstone for those seeking to reclaim the social value of art from an ever more mercenary market framing, as well as for fan-funding advocates such as Amanda Palmer who, in her own book *The Art of Asking*, cites *The Gift* heavily to explain how she got fans to give her more than a million dollars on Kickstarter when she had asked for only $100,000.[47] The bifurcation of messy realities into two distinct economies is simplistic. Economic and intimate activity "often sustain each other,"[48] even if the former is seen (erroneously, Zelizer argues) as a threat to the latter. "In all social settings, intimate and impersonal alike," says Zelizer, "social ties and economic transactions mingle, as human beings perform relational work by matching their personal ties and economic activity."[49] Nonetheless, the economic/social distinction is analytically useful.

As abstract ideal types, economic and social exchanges differ in a number of ways.[50] In the gift economy, art circulates as a present, moving from artist to friend, friend to friend, or child to parent. The basis of exchange is trust. What is owed and when it is due are unspecified, as we trust that presents will make their way to us in due time. The exchange creates a sense of connection and obligation. The same thing has different values depending on who gives it to you. In the market economy, art circulates as a product sold from producers to consumers. Economic exchanges are based on legal principles. There are clear terms of exchange with explicit time frames for payment. The transaction is impersonal, leaving no sense of gratitude or obligation. What's exchanged could come from anyone else and have the same value.

Social and economic exchanges are dialectical, indivisible yet defining each other by their contrasts and synergies. Once money became a way to mediate music, music's social value could no longer be understood apart from its economic value. Even music that happens entirely outside of commercial spheres, say singing around a campfire or at a party, becomes understood partly in terms of its noncommercial quality. When music circulates within commercial spheres, the market frame can lessen its social value. When money mediates interactions, it is harder to see the social processes they create and embody.[51] Without the resonance of gift giving, Hyde posits, "there is no art."[52]

Musicians find their validation in the social consequences of their work for their audiences and themselves, but they often work within a commercial context that treats their work not as a gift, but as a product. Today, that commercial environment is unstable and confusing. The kinds of exchange that are in play are interwoven in ways that are new and continuously changing. It's unclear which offerings will be reciprocated with money. The new strategy of reaching out to audiences with relational labor, trying to build relationships that feel close in hopes of evoking the communal bonds that make money an appropriate way to repay the gift of music, in many ways honors music's ancient origins. The value of musical work has always resided in communication and connection. Any efforts to make music economically profitable must be built on this premise.

2

Music as Commodity

Gary Waleik played guitar, sang, and wrote songs with the Boston-based band Big Dipper. Signed to a prestigious independent label in the late 1980s, they put out two records before being "upstreamed" to Sony. Their major label debut sold poorly. Sony dropped them. The band broke up. They found other careers in radio, in finance, in teaching. The bass player became a vintner. Nearly twenty years later they reunited to record a new album. In contrast to their first records, when the next steps seemed obvious, this time they didn't know what they were supposed to do. Should they sign to a label? Release it themselves? Digital only? Vinyl?

And what about Facebook and Twitter and all those other social media the younger musicians they knew insisted they needed? Waleik shakes his head: "You could see the progress from MySpace to Facebook to Twitter. Everyone just loses their minds at the latest thing, and says 'No, this is how you do it.' And there's never any sort of consensus. I mean as corrupt and horrible as the old record industry was, at least it was a barely stable way to get the word out about music. I'm glad to see the record industry go, because it was so corrupt and awful and evil. But I kind of miss it in a way, you know?" The path in the 1980s had been difficult, and ultimately had not sustained them, but at least it made sense.

Most musicians never earned livings through the recording industry, but for those who did, or who aspired to, the years since the recording industry's 1999 crash have been confusing. In 1999, U.S. music sales peaked at $14.6 billion U.S. dollars. By 2010, sales had fallen by more than 40 percent,[1] reaching a low of $6.3 billion in 2009, before beginning to rise as digital music markets became well established. In response to dropping sales, the labels laid off nearly a quarter of their staff and slashed artist rosters. Although digital and (unexpectedly) vinyl revenues are now increasing, labels still struggle with the "unstable and out-of-control logic of their business."[2] For musicians who might once have turned to record labels to help guide their path, the new terrain is ambiguous and constantly changing. Once-settled distinctions are gone. At every step in music's value chain, from inception to audience experience, inexpensive digital platforms continue to undo "the hard categories which characterized the old, industrialized model of music-making and consumption."[3] Record labels are less likely than ever to provide musicians with upfront financing, manufacturing, distribution, and publicity. Increasingly on their own, musicians are pushed toward social media in hopes that if they can just *connect* with their audiences, they might get by. This perceived need to be more social has created new anxiety. As Tim Anderson put it, "it was one thing to have no model to follow, it is another to have no goal."[4]

Today's upheaval seems remarkable, and it is, but it is far from the first time new technologies have upended the profession of music. Sensibilities about order and relationships have shifted before. Twentieth-century recording industries did a remarkable job of creating the sense that theirs was the natural order, but in fact they were a historical fluke resulting from a particular moment in which technologies favored highly centralized and industrialized systems of music production and distribution. As technologies change, dialectic dynamics that undergird artist-audience relationships change too. Technologies reshape the contextual pressures on the relationships and, in so doing, reshape the relationships themselves.

In the last chapter we saw how music, from its prehistoric origins, has circulated as a gift that helps people have more "feelingful" and socially connected lives. Throughout history, new technologies have altered the extent to which music is social or commercial, immaterial or material, participatory or owned, decentralized or centralized. Every technological advance has brought new experiences of music and given rise to new social relationships. "Foremost among these changes," writes Albrecht, "has been the unending drive towards commodification and the accompanying reduction of popular participation in the experience of music."[5] Today's musicians strive for participatory communal experiences based on emotion and social connection but are caught in market realities that define their relationship with audiences as producers making goods or providing services to customers. Their turn to social media as a solution to contemporary conditions is new, but in many ways echoes music's pre- and early-commodified past. To understand it, we need both to denaturalize the immediate context of the recording industry that came before and show the continuities with what has long been at stake. This chapter traces how technological changes have altered the dynamic tensions of musicians' environment, continuously pushing them toward new ways of getting by as music makers and, in so doing, toward different ways of relating to their audiences.

Inventing Musicians and Audiences

Until relatively recently in human existence, music was a participatory practice rather than something working musicians did for audiences at leisure. We don't know just when that began to change. Art from ancient Egypt and Rome is rife with images of people playing musical instruments for royalty, so certainly by then some people were making livings providing soundtracks for others. There were wandering minstrels. Yet well into the eighteenth century, musical creativity was generally understood as belonging to a communal tradition or the divine, rather than to a musician who might be worthy of admiration or adoration.[6] Until around 1800, music in the West was practiced primarily "either as a private amateur pastime, made among friends and family, or as an elaborate public ritual, either in street parades or at church services."[7] In these contexts, the concept of "audience" would have made little sense. That of "fan" did not exist. Participants in those private and public events may have loved music, "but its embeddedness in social functions made more likely that one loved that which the music enabled."[8]

The "heroic discourse of individual genius"[9] that is often applied to musicians took centuries to develop. Musicologists locate early seeds of these transformations in the late twelfth century with the invention of musical notation.[10] Notation represented sound as ink on paper, separating music from its playing and fixing an intangible experience in material, lasting form. Furthermore, paper could be signed, making it possible to affix enduring individual identities to compositions. While indigenous cultures such as Native Americans of the Northwest coast had strong rules about which families had rights to perform certain songs, the signing of notation laid the groundwork for the idea, eventually inscribed in law, that music comes from the minds of specific individuals and is hence "intellectual" property. The invention of the printing press enabled the reproduction of sheet music, making music not just a property but a commodity that could be bought and sold on the open market. "Even the strolling bards of antiquity depended upon the kindness of strangers to help them along their way," writes Robert Albrecht, but with printing, for the first time music became "a tangible, non-personal product that could be mass produced, mass distributed, and even mass marketed."[11]

The professionalization of musicians started in earnest in the 1600s when the first public performances were staged, beginning with a 1637 opera in Vienna.[12] Shortly thereafter, similar events were produced in England, but with a twist. Those attending had to purchase a new invention: the "ticket." Formal settings like concert halls were created just for musical events. Just a hundred years later, paying to hear music had become normal for those elites who could afford a night in the concert hall.[13] Many came to think of music as a thing you might listen to as much if not more than an experience you might create.[14]

The European leisure class of the period had plenty of time to learn to make music themselves. Many were excellent and enjoyed playing for one another in their homes. But to take money for it would have been beneath them. To be paid for performance was to demonstrate that you had lower social standing than those who listened.[15] For much of the early history of professional musicianship, musicians who took money were seen and treated as hired help. Pity the early-seventeenth-century professional violinist dramatized in Rose Tremain's novel *Music and Silence*, living and performing, as musicians really did, in the basement of Copenhagen's Rosenborg Castle, the sound carried from their musty, illness-inducing environs through the hidden pipes of the world's first indoor sound system up to King Christian IV and his surprised and delighted guests in the marble ballroom floors above.[16] No one stayed after the ball to get autographs. "A good 'professional' musician in those days was thus a servant, essentially an asset of the better sort, perhaps comparable to a head gardener or a racehorse."[17] Many great classical works were commissioned for specific occasions "as one might order a new coat or wig," created by craftspeople plying a trade rather than artists exercising genius.[18]

By the 1800s, there were established careers to be made performing public music. The new class of professionals had an incentive to limit their numbers and drew tight boundaries around those who counted as "musicians." Positioning themselves as seasoned experts in contrast to hobbyists enabled a subset of music makers to corner the market on public performance by the early 1820s.[19] American musicians unionized to help one another find work, creating the American Federation of Musicians (AFM) by the 1840s. This union worked well for those allowed to join, as it controlled who had the right to play in urban venues throughout the country and helped place its members in those jobs. For those the AFM did not consider "musicians," the consolidation of musicianship into a unionized profession was deeply exclusionary. Those in the newly invented category of "amateurs" were ineligible for membership. People who played what came to be known as "country music" couldn't join until the AFM fell under legal and social scrutiny for suing to recoup lost wages of Cincinnati union musicians when the (ineligible) Grand Ole Opry performed there in 1949.[20] African Americans were not allowed to join the AFM, and so created their own union.[21] Women were also excluded. Until 1979 even singers were omitted,[22] further marginalizing women, for whom public singing remains more accepted than playing most instruments (consider the novelty of a female drummer). Getting all these people out of public music performance had the benefit of ensuring access to those gigs for the privileged elite who remained, and hence to whatever income they might bring, but it also changed the work of music. It was no longer enough to please one patron; you had to have an effect on listeners that they were willing to buy.[23] You were not just selling music, you were selling feelings. For those outside this system, the centralization of power made it even more essential that musicians connected with communities of listeners that could sustain them.

Industrialization

By the start of the twentieth century, music was big business.[24] Throughout the Western world, industrialization had separated work from play. The leisure market had expanded. Audiences were plentiful. People had money to spend. New transportation technologies made it easier than ever to get out and about to experience public entertainment.

Professional musicians were everywhere, providing soundtracks for concerts, dances, and films, for shopping and dining. Employers hired musicians to create soothing and inspiring soundtracks on shop floors and in office buildings. In 1870, a mere sixteen thousand Americans listed their occupation as professional musician or music teacher. Fifty years later, ninety-two thousand did. In his detailed history of the AFM, James P. Kraft characterizes the music industry at the turn of the century as "diffused," "labor-intensive," and "artisanal."[25] Every moment that called for music still called for the presence of musicians.

Against this backdrop, one new technology posed a danger. The player piano had the horrifying potential to make music without anyone there to strike the keys. For the first time, a live musician was replaced by an object. By disseminating music without musicians, piano rolls obscured the human work and social relationships behind their creation. Music was thus transformed into a perfect example of the tangible, purchasable, seemingly labor-free "fetish object" of which Marx wrote. Indeed, this was the point.[26]

Player pianos posed a problem. But, in the decades after Thomas Edison first recorded "Mary Had a Little Lamb" onto foil cylinders in 1877, recording became a crisis. Film theaters had been one of musicians' primary sources of employment. Every movie house employed an in-house orchestra to provide the films' soundtracks. By 1934, just seven years after the first feature film with sound, *The Jazz Singer*, was released, "about twenty thousand theater musicians—perhaps a quarter of the nation's professional instrumentalists and half of those who were fully employed—had lost their jobs."[27] Furthermore, radio stations, which had hired live bands to perform in studio and provided a source of revenue for those locked out of the AFM, became increasingly connected, meaning that radio stations all over the country could get by with only one band. The crisis for music professionals was further compounded by the Great Depression, in which even record sales, which hit seventy-five million dollars in 1929, fell to six million dollars by 1933.[28]

As commercialized sound recording recovered, the value of musicians' skills—and their unions' collective bargaining power—diminished. The public then, as now, was loathe to understand musicians as laborers, thinking of them as "playing" music rather than working. A union representative from New York warned in 1937 that "the abuse and misuse

of mechanical reproductions of music constitute a threat which may an-
nihilate the profession."[29] Adding insult to injury, the musicians playing
on these new recordings were often more talented than local musicians.
Imagine the plight of the local tenor, suddenly having to compete with
Enrico Caruso, the first recording star, who released nearly three hundred records for Victor Records between 1902 and 1920. Imagine the
bliss of the opera lover suddenly able to hear so much glorious music
at home.

Recordings furthered the distinctions between professional musicians and everyone else. In many, though not all, genres, music went
from "a communal activity of music-making and concert attendance
to an industrial mass product that is consumed privately," creating "a
strict dichotomy between music performers and music consumers."[30]
The opportunity to buy a mass-produced Victrola Talking Machine or
to turn on the radio at home and listen to recordings of the world's best
changed how "most people thought about music and integrated it into
their lives."[31] Music making shifted even further toward music listening,
as records made it possible for people to hear so many skilled musicians for the first time. With new standards for what constituted "good"
music, adults grew more inhibited, afraid to sing or play before others.[32]
Participatory music increasingly gave way to performative music.

Some see the industrialization and commodification of music and
accompanying reduction of participation in music making as a crime
against humanity. In 1929 the American composer Gregory Mason de-
cried that industrial ideologies were degrading musical culture, "shack-
ling it to the logic of the market" and stripping it "of its potential as
a means of transcendent human expression."[33] "Our powers of making music for ourselves have been hijacked and the majority of people
robbed of the musicality that is theirs by right of birth, while a few stars,
and their handlers, grow rich and famous through selling us what we
have been led to believe we lack," cried Small.[34] Albrecht agreed, writing that "music making, which since Paleolithic times has been a cor-
nerstone and building block of sociality, has largely been replaced by
music consuming."[35] The ethnomusicologist Charles Keil went further,
warning that music "is our last and best source of participatory consciousness."[36] Clearly staking an extreme position, Keil insists that music
should never be recorded, let alone monetized: "Once you have come to

the conclusion that music is in its very essence communal, spiritual, the opposite of private property and at its best a totally shared experience, like love, a number of strong and clear positions on 'the music industry' can be stated: There shouldn't be a music industry. Music shouldn't be written or mechanically reproduced and mass-mediated. Music should exist live, for the moment, in present time, and its makers should be rewarded with happiness and barterlike reciprocities."[37] This position resonates with many of the points in the last chapter, but as the next chapter will show, it doesn't do justice to audiences, who developed new kinds of participatory practices through music fandom. Nor does the idea that recording and mass mediation has diminished humanity do justice to the power of recorded music to offer transcendent experience.

The more the mass industrialization of music lessened the likelihood that a listener and a musician might ever be in the same place, let alone meet, the more listeners were sold an image of musicians as personalities with whom they had a personal, if one-sided, connection.[38] Thomas Edison may once have said that he cared "nothing for the reputation of the artists, singers, or instrumentalists," as it was not his company's "intention to feature artists or sell the records by using the artist's name,"[39] but Victor Records took a different approach. Beginning around 1916, Victor began using snapshot-style photos of performers such as Caruso at home to add "a new, more 'personal' dimension to performers' public identities."[40] Magazines like *Life* published photo spreads of Caruso as a family man, marketing his personality and lifestyle. Like the new public figure of the movie star, the recording artist became "a symbolic figure offered for our consumption, contemplation and identification,"[41] helping to set the stage for the intimacy they are expected to foster on social media today.

The remote connections audiences came to feel through recordings were further fostered by improvements in music technologies and by the media. Recordings let people immerse themselves in the same sounds over and over again. Advances in microphones gave a new "advantage to the younger, small-voiced performers who learned how to work close to the microphone to get the desired feelings."[42] Singers like Frank Sinatra were able to transform microphones' metal and wires "into the perfumed ear of a woman who could now be whispered to rather than bellowed at."[43] As a result, "countless anonymous listeners could cultivate relationships with performers that approximated real intimacy, knowing the rhythms of another human being's breath, registering the grain of another's voice in one's own body, and perhaps experiencing genuine feelings of exaltation or ecstasy."[44] Coming from the phonograph as disembodied voices, the performers who felt so near could also feel otherworldly. The transcendent spiritual feelings music has always evoked were easy to transfer from deity to performer. Even as musicians became people with whom audiences could identify, they became people to be admired and even worshipped. This sense of knowing celebrities we've never met has often been considered "parasocial"[45] and (usually erroneously) delusional because it is not mutual. Nonetheless, it is both real and powerful.[46]

Musicians of the mid-twentieth century were concerned with matters more practical than the dehumanizing conditions of industrial ideologies. Some people were becoming stars in this new industry, but in these growing economies of scale, "more and more musicians worried about their jobs and careers."[47] In 1942, unionized musicians went on a recording strike, hoping to save their profession. In announcing the "recording ban," the wily and persuasive president of the AFM, James Petrillo, insisted musicians would not be forced to "play at their own funeral."[48] It worked about as well as the recording industry's later efforts to save itself from networked computing by suing peer-to-peer file sharers. The ban lasted two years. Musicians got little sympathy from audiences who then, as now, were more concerned about their own easy access to music they liked than with the protection of musicians as a laboring class. Nor did they get support from the U.S. Congress, which held hearings to determine whether the ban harmed the war effort.

Not all musicians were opposed to recording. For those locked out of old routes, new technologies offer new avenues toward careers. Recording offered a way forward for those excluded from AFM membership and the opportunities it offered. Early labels that released only music performed by black people, and marketed only to black audiences, may have been racist (for instance, in the 1920s all secular black music was categorized as "blues"),[49] but they got the music heard both within and outside of black communities. Technological advances and growth led to "an intense commodification of Indigenous African-American music forms"[50] that "often served to distribute the popular narratives of

African-Americans beyond the limits of their insular communities."[51] Nonetheless, recording remained a difficult career path, and only elite black musicians made it.

By the time the dust settled on the AFM's recording ban, recording had won. Professional musicianship changed from a career in which many, though never all who aspired, could make a respectable living through live performance into one in which an elite few did extremely well, a few more created middle-class lives, and most were unable to make ends meet. The musicians most able to adapt were talented, yes, but they were also the ones who lived in cities that became recording centers and were able to pick up and leave their families and homes to perform. Career musicians became expected "to work long, late hours and travel far distances for jobs, away from their family and loved ones."[52] For audiences, there had never been more music available. For musicians, there had never been so few opportunities to play for pay or so much need for relational sacrifice. Kraft describes the first half of the twentieth century as devastating for working musicians. He voices pessimism about what this historical encounter with new technology portends for workers in other fields, worrying that these musicians' experience "suggests that the benefits of new technology will be distributed unevenly, and more or less according to power relationships between the major groups affected by technology."[53]

The Major Labels

In the new "centralized," "capital-intensive," and "highly-mechanized"[54] industry of the second half of the twentieth century, only a handful of major players had the economic capital necessary to fund the production, distribution, and marketing of recorded music. These recording companies came to be synonymous with "the music industry," and in particular the major rather than independent labels, in public discourse. Jonathan Sterne argues that this definition buys into the tactics of the recording industry by ignoring other important music industries such as instruments, concert halls, software, and computing.[55] That record labels were able to corner the definition of "music industry" speaks to how much cultural sway they have held. Their power has been based on music as intellectual property rather than shared experience, technology that contains and limits that intellectual property to material forms, and the prohibitive expense of transforming intellectual property into physical objects, marketing it and distributing it to retail outlets. Most musicians worked and continue to work outside the major labels, but these labels' influence continues to set many terms of the regulatory and cultural grounds on which everyone works.

Intellectual property markets are inherently speculative. It is impossible to know in advance what will sell.[56] Labels need to recoup their costs, which requires making good guesses about what audiences will like. The handful of record labels that dominated the early twentieth century, companies like Edison, RCA/Victor, Columbia, EMI, and CBS, found their solution in the star system pioneered in the sheet music businesses of New York's Tin Pan Alley.[57] In this star system, staff songwriters churned out songs while those who employed them banked on the occasional big hit, much as today's major labels hope for a Taylor Swift or Beyoncé to justify the expense of the many acts whose names you don't recognize. The star system ensured that those with perceived potential to sell on a mass scale were those most likely to get financed, and that most would be discarded shortly thereafter when they did not sell as well as the labels wanted. As of the early 2000s, 80 percent of artists on major labels did not sell enough to earn royalties beyond their advances.[58] Record companies thus produce much more music than they end up promoting. They focus their marketing efforts on "a small number of superstar artists, thus further increasing the divide between the artist and the consumer [and] between the superstars and the smaller-scale merely local performer/artists, who may succeed in recording, but could never hope for wide distribution."[59]

Music produced within industry is designed to sell and make money.[60] Recording industry logic assumes that anyone seeking a career in music seeks stardom. As an A&R person at a major label put it at a conference I attended (articulating Roger O'Donnell's fear), "you either want to be Jay-Z or you're a hobbyist." He was wrong about aspirations, but it is true that the industry in which he works offers little place for musicians seeking sustainable careers between hobbies and celebrity. Whether early or late in their career, the "scene-based" artists with whom I spoke rarely sought fame or fortune, even those who had achieved it. Some, like Kristin Hersh, had been with major labels and no longer were. Many were releasing their work through independent labels or direct-to-fan through platforms like Bandcamp. They aspired to a predictable income that would allow them to feed their family, afford a home, and focus on their art. They sought a dedicated audience that would stick with them and grow over time. They were happy to diversify, so long as it was into other areas that interested them. They wanted to perform only where they could hold their heads high. They wanted to take an occasional vacation without feeling guilty. "I can't imagine becoming a musician and thinking you're going to make money," Hersh laughed. "We felt lucky when we were working! That's what the money was for, just to work."

Not surprisingly, given that they see most musicians as disposable risks, record labels have a bad reputation. When the British Phonograph Industry (BPI) launched its "Home Taping Is Killing Music" campaign in the early 1980s, picturing a cassette tape with a skull and crossbones, mockeries ran rampant. A popular bumper sticker used the image but read, "home taping is killing the music industry and it's about time." The punk band Dead Kennedys released a cassette in 1981 with one side featuring the EP, "In God We Trust, Inc." The other side read "HOME TAPING IS KILLING RECORD INDUSTRY PROFITS! WE LEFT THIS SIDE BLANK SO YOU CAN HELP." Public Enemy's Chuck D once described major labels as "the biggest pirates."[61] "Any artist who has been on a major label knows that the last thing they're concerned about is the musician making a living," Michael Timmins told me, explaining why Cowboy Junkies left RCA to create their own label. "The only thing I know for sure," said Nacho Vegas, "is if some new band or new singer asked me for advice—I don't like to give advice to anyone—but the only thing I'd say is 'Don't ever sign a contract.'"

There is no question that record companies have exploited many musicians. As music journalist Greg Kot describes, labels "instituted payola, routinely manipulated shady contracts to take away publishing from songwriters, and engaged in questionable accounting practices to deny royalties from record sales to the vast majority of its artists."[62] Many of these shady practices continue. A 2015 report on fairness and transparency from the Rethink Music initiative found that little of the fifteen billion dollars of 2014's global recorded music revenue for sound recordings went to musicians as ongoing revenue. Labels have had little incentive to pay out royalties. Their accounting is famously opaque, making it easy for labels and publishers to keep recurring revenues after costs have been recouped. One might wonder how much the figure Stahl mentions, of "80 percent" of records that didn't earn back advances, is inflated by underhanded book keeping.[63] Labels' failure to pay musicians is further compounded by disorganized and dispersed rights databases. Artists have no way to know how their music is used or purchased, and are hence unable to seek compensation they may deserve. Many musicians understand that the advance is the only money they will see from recordings, even if they sell well.

All this being said, labels nonetheless provide a crucial infrastructure for building professional careers in recorded music. Love them or hate them, without their investments and capacities, we would not have much of the music that soundtracks modern life. Labels may never have supported as many artists as wanted the support, but they took and continue to take large financial risks on those they sign. For those in whom they did invest, labels also took care of a great deal of the work. Adequate advances and support staff allow artists to be full-time music makers. Labels can provide teams of specialists who guide the music from development to production, distribute the music and fulfill orders, manage licensing, sort out international distribution, oversee promotion, get the music on the radio, take care of booking at times, finance tours, and so on. As labels sign fewer artists, fewer get access to those advances they might never have earned back or get help with any of this work. It is no wonder that most of the musicians I interviewed, even those who had left major label deals, believed labels were still needed, especially for those who did aspire to stardom.

The recording industry worked its centralized magic to great effect right up until 1999 when, in a move that foreshadowed the global economic crisis, sales began to crash. This decline has been well documented in books like Kot's *Ripped*, Patrik Wikström's *The Music Industry*, Aram Sinnreich's *The Piracy Crusade*, and Stephen Witt's *How Music Got Free*. The standard, inadequate explanation that each of these books critiques goes something like this: When "pirates" began ripping and circulating mp3s online, outside the purview of authorized markets, people stopped buying records. Napster and other peer-to-peer file trading systems decimated sales. Labels and music publishers dropped the ball, losing valuable time as they tried to stop file sharing instead of developing new digital markets.

This story accurately assesses the losses but is incomplete at best in assessing the causes. The worst of unauthorized online file sharing, it turns out, began in the industry's own pressing plants.[64] Academic research into the connection between file sharing and sales is inconclusive at best, calling into doubt an easy cause-effect relationship between the two and at times finding that downloaders may also be the recording industry's best-paying customers.[65] Furthermore, many factors beyond file sharing must shoulder blame for the changing climate for music sales. There was a global financial crisis. Local music scenes collapsed. People had less disposable income and more choices for how to spend what entertainment budget remained. New forms of entertainment like streaming on-demand video and gaming (the latter of which, importantly but rarely discussed, commissions and licenses a great deal of music) garnered the attention of the idle. Finally, despite their protests, the major labels remain extremely lucrative, grossing fifteen billion dollars in the United States in 2015.[66] As with the rest of the economy, one might ask whether the problem lies in the distribution rather than the presence of revenue. The International Federation of the Phonograph Industry (IFPI) complains that despite the first growth in music revenues in fifteen years, "the revenues, vital in funding future investment, are not being fairly returned to rights holders."[67]

The Shift to Digital

Personal computing, especially networked computing, has transformed music production, distribution, and consumption, eroding the technological and capital boundaries that separate professionals and amateurs and creating new opportunities. With far less investment than studio time with a producer and recording engineers would cost, aspiring and accomplished musicians alike can create complicated music using powerful software like Ableton Live on home computers. Home recordings can sound professional. You don't even need other musicians. "All you've got to have now is an idea," UB40's Brian Travers waxes enthusiastically: "You don't even have to have a band or a guitar. You can have it all in an application. I think we're going to hear some incredible musicians.

We're going to hear the likes of Beethovens and Chopins and Mozarts again, because you no longer need to get all these other egomaniacs to play instruments and play the parts you want them to play, which they won't do, and they insist on playing their own bits. We're going to start seeing the rise of the solo composer again." Musicians can use the same computers on which they compose and record to make what they create available for listening or for sale through cloud and streaming platforms, social networks, or other websites, either on their own or with the help of inexpensive third-party services. They can sell downloads directly to their audience. In the abstract, if not always in practice, there's no more need for packing, physical shipments, or retail distribution.[68]

The result of pervasive recording is "a cultural economy of ubiquity," as Spotify's musician-in-residence D. A. Wallach put it. Mogwai's Stuart Braithwaite marvels that "every single piece of music practically ever, you can find in five minutes and listen to and buy if you want to. It used to be, if you heard a song on the radio you had to go around to every record shop and maybe have to ask them to order one in to hear it again. If you said that to a sixteen-year-old kid now they'd think you were talking about the stone age!" No longer bound to objects or locations, music is nowhere and everywhere. It is encoded in bits that hide on our phones, in our computers, our cars, our pockets, in the air.

With music and every other form of entertainment and distraction available all the time and everywhere, it's considerably more difficult to get anyone to pay attention. Audiences, once easily reached through a manageable number of media outlets (if you were lucky enough to break through their gates), are now fragmented across a dizzying array of media for discovering, discussing, listening to, and purchasing music.[69] Artists can set up websites and profiles, post their music, tweet, update, share snapshots on photo-sharing sites, make videos, and do any number of other things to speak directly to their fans. Just as recording offered a way for those excluded from live performances by the AFM to find careers, scene-based musicians excluded from the recording industries may be able to parlay the skills they developed on their own into what hip-hop promoter Steven Wiz calls the "digital hustle." But without major financial investments in publicity or an audience already gathered, it is extremely challenging to get audiences to notice. And with any song available anytime, anywhere, it is hard to get people to pay for what they can find for free.

Like musicians of the early twentieth century, suddenly faced with recording, people seeking to commodify their music must figure out new ways to turn their labor into income. There are more opportunities, but there is more work to be done and little money to pay people to do it. "You have to look at it like a full-time job," the manager Ariel Rivas insists, "not just a one-hour performance job, in a club. When you leave the show, the rest of the day you need to work like you have a full-time job. The artist's state of mind needs to be very concentrated and focused on developing his career. He needs to dedicate time. Every day."

Pulling off a professional career making music demands an array of nonmusical interests and skills in business, technology, and, most of all, relationship building, that many musicians and other long-time actors in the music industries neither have nor want. Just as the early years of recorded music shifted to favor some musicians over others for reasons that were as much about location, race, sex, mobility, and marketability as they were about talent, passion, or work ethic, these new technological contexts favor people with some sets of nonmusical skills, not others. Musicians must be "omniprofessional" entrepreneurs able to perform a wide range of jobs themselves.[70]

"The flipside to this integration of new and social media into the production process," writes Jeremy Wade Morris, "is a greater burden on artists to take control of aspects of their career that they previously delegated to labels, managers, or other ancillary staff."[71] The artists with the best odds are creative about business as well as music and are willing to take risks. They are the ones who know how to hustle. "All of the artists on my roster have had managers before," the manager Emily White told me, but those managers were not open to artists' ideas, often shooting them down. In contrast, "when they come to me with ideas, my response is, 'Hell yes, let's try this, let's figure it out. It's an experiment, and if it doesn't work, we won't do it again, or we'll tweak it and try a different strategy.'" An approach like this is "exciting for somebody like me and the younger artists," but she concedes, "it's frustrating for people too, who just want to make their music." Pearl Jam's Eddie Vedder is hardly the only artist who would describe himself as able to "work on a bridge

part of a song for three weeks," but unable "to imagine listening to anything about the business ideas of what we do for more than an hour
without taking a hammer to my head."[72]

It's also helpful to have technical skills. Those who want to make their
own music need literacy in production software. They need to understand a vast array of potential distribution channels and make decisions
about how best to get their music out there. They need to know how
to create and manage websites and social media platforms. Honeychild
Coleman's experience with MySpace is not unusual: "when I first joined,
I made my artist page first, but then I couldn't figure out how to get back
in it to update it, and then I lost everything. So then a couple years went
by, and I made another page, and then I realized, 'Oh, that artist page is
still there, and I need to update it. And it's old, and people are going to
both.'"

When we spoke she was in the process of trying to move her musical
identity from her personal Facebook page to her Facebook fan page.
"This is another job. I don't have time for this. It's so much work, it's incredible." "If I have fifteen minutes," asks American jazz singer and guitarist Kate Schutt, "am I going to read some fucking, excuse my French,
but fucking small print about Facebook, you know, who can view this
and that and try and figure it out in my brain or would I rather practice
my guitar and become a better musician? I would rather practice my
guitar and become a better musician." Schutt is very engaged with her
audiences, but prefers postal mail. She's had an ongoing "game" called
"Mail Me 1 Thing" in which she invites audiences to mail her one thing
and in return she will send them one back. Her "Postcard Project" invites people to send her a postcard, which she too will reciprocate in
time. But from Schutt's point of view, the sense of needing to use social media comes from fear rather than thoughtfulness: "The collapse of
the music industry has sort of caused this knee-jerk reaction in a lot of
musicians. It's like, 'Oh my God, I got to Twitter!' 'Oh my God, I got to
Facebook!' And they think all these things. 'I got to be on twenty-seven
sites, I got to have my music on every single site.' But nobody stops to
think, 'do I really need to do that?'" She raises good questions.

There is nothing intrinsic to business or technical skills that requires
they be wielded by the musicians themselves. But only musicians can do
the relationship building they need to sustain their careers, even if only

to build a relationship with someone they can hire to build relationships on their behalf. Zoë Keating explains that "it's really all about relationships: I have relationships in all of these different areas that allow me to have this career. I'm sort of good at making those relationships and making those connections and making things happen. If you're not very good at that, you need to have a manager who can manage those relationships for you or who has the relationships on their own. And if you want to become, I think, a big artist who's doing a more pop sphere, you need a team of people who has all of those." In my interviews, musicians described working relationships with (among others) other musicians, managers, publicists, sales teams, engineers, producers, crew, contact people, booking agents, publishers, distributors, lawyers, promoters, and journalists. Often equally important in doing the work that needed doing were friends, spouses, nannies, and parents.

More important than ever before are fans. Both musicians and labels now value social capital over record sales, capital "that allowed them to better license themselves, sell merchandise, bring crowds to concerts, and, perhaps, sell records and downloads."[73] To get this capital, "artists and acts have had to experiment with opening themselves and their work online so that users could make them topics around which connections could be formed. The proposition to the fan is that an act's online presence, the work, and the activities can be used as a source through which community can be formed and explored."[74] If fans can be reached, they can be essential allies in providing publicity and, as chapter 4 will show, they may also take on tasks like website design and maintenance and tour planning that artists might otherwise have to pay for or go without. To cultivate the relationships needed in a creative career, musicians need "considerable personal and organisational resources."[75]

Social media are crucial to this new work of relationship building, even if individuals need not use many of the available platforms. Rivas explains that even those with major label contracts need to be extroverts who build their social networks and keep in touch with their audiences:

> You need to work like you don't have anybody other than you. If you forget that and say, "Oh, I signed with a record label, they do everything," that's not true. The record label can't invest millions, and millions, and millions. If you don't move from your house, and you don't stay in touch

with your friends, and you don't want to do the interviews, or you don't want to be in your social network to develop it, it's very difficult. If I knew a new artist had the opportunity to sign with a record label, I'd say, "Don't forget that you need to be in touch with your niche, with your fans, with the people." And if you don't have the opportunity to sign, just do the same.

The internet and social media are often posited as a solution, but many of the musicians I spoke with weren't sure that the social connections they were being urged to build, rewarding as they may be in their own right, actually lead to increased revenue. Michael Timmins puts a great deal of effort into the Cowboy Junkies website, but "whether it's equated with making money, I don't know. It's hard to say. I mean, money comes in, but if I was to add up the hours, how much am I making per hour? I don't know. But it's definitely worth it for the communication side of it."

The singer-songwriter Erin McKeown sees herself as having two different careers, one online, where the questions are "how do you communicate with those fans? and what do you do for them? and how do you cultivate that interaction?" and a second in the concert venue, where the questions are "do you give a good live show and when are you coming to this city?" Artists with more followers, more likes, and other evidence that they can rally attention may have an easier time getting opportunities like gigs and recording contracts. I've spoken with managers who tell me that artists they work with get considerably more engagement and ensuing revenue when they post to social media themselves than when they let the management team do it. But there have been no economic studies to examine whether building and maintaining relationships with audiences through social media really results in making more money for most, let alone all, artists. The success of artists like Adele, who eschews social media entirely, and the low sales and revenue that have accrued to countless musicians who do use social media regularly, suggest that, at best, the connection between relational labor done through social media and income is complicated.

David Lowery, of Camper Van Beethoven and Cracker, reminisces that when his bands began, either they were getting publicity or they weren't. "Now that you can get publicity in a social media way, there's always work to do." When I spoke with Braithwaite, Mogwai were in the process of "hiring a company to manage our online presence, because the sheer workload is getting to be overwhelming. Things like collecting email addresses and managing the list are too labour intensive." On top of the call to come up with fresh content and to monitor messages sent to you across platforms, there are friend requests to be approved, spam to be deleted, hackers to be vanquished, terms of service updates to be read, new sites that maybe you are supposed to use. Like housework, there is always more to be done and more you could have done. The feminist labor scholars Soile Veijola and Eeva Jokinen argue that since the 1970s, more work has come to resemble domestic work in that it requires "practical management of boundless and endless, never-finished, mostly immaterial tasks and chores" that intermingle and overlap in time and space.[76] The social relationships of new work "have started to resemble affective and communicative relations usually connected with home." As one musician described it, keeping up with the daily social media demands of his job is "like doing dishes."

New Music Worlds

In his classic *Art Worlds*, sociologist Howard Becker shows how many roles are implicated in the creation of art, ranging from the person considered the artist to those who make the paintbrushes to those who curate collections.[77] His point was that the idea of "artist" as a lone genius is absurd. One cannot create "art" without a web of interconnected people, each serving an essential role that makes it possible and shapes its meanings. Now, as has happened before, upended by technological change, previously distinct roles in musical art worlds have broken down. Artists can, at least in the abstract, fulfill any role themselves. But to do it all, let alone do it all well, pushes the boundaries of human capabilities.

The support structures that have shaped and constrained musicians' professional careers have shifted throughout history as technologies have reshaped music's possibilities. Conditions have been more hospitable for some kinds of musicians at different times. With each technological innovation—sheet music, printing, the player piano, recording, the internet—music's form, flow, and ability to be contained and owned have been changed. So too have musicians' relationship with audiences.

Musicians have gone from community members to hired help to expert professionals to inaccessible objects of identification and adoration and now back to something both distant and close.

The next chapter will show how, during the late nineteenth and twentieth centuries, when musicians were pushed away from audiences through mass mediation, audiences went on to build participatory cultures of their own around music, creating networks and practices that are now ideally suited to help musicians, if—and this is a big "if"— artists can get fans to feel connected and mobilize that sense of connection effectively. We can see this new call for musicians to connect with audiences as a return to a time before recording and broadcast technologies took so many musicians out of local contexts and away from their audiences. We can see it as an extension of historic marginalized music scenes, such as black communities' Chitlin Circuit, the Jewish Borscht Belt, and salsa musicians' Cuchifrito Circuit.[78] But this is also a new phase in the history of music, one in which boundaries between community and star, creator and fan, professional and amateur, public and private, and home and work demand to be redrawn.

PART II

Participation

3

Audiences

There weren't a lot of people online in the early 1990s. Mark Kelly, keyboard player for the English band Marillion, early internet adopter and self-titled "co-inventor of crowdfunding," was an exception. One night after a concert someone handed him a stack of papers—printouts from an email list of Marillion fans. Kelly went home, cranked up his modem, and subscribed. What he found surprised him. The list, founded by a Dutch fan, had about a thousand fans. And though the band's primary market was the United Kingdom, the list was multinational. Most subscribers were in the United States. Marillion had never even toured the United States.

Kelly spent the first couple of years reading without posting, watching the discussion in secret. But the internet is the internet, and finally, someone said something so wrong that Kelly couldn't stop himself from jumping in to correct him. His cover was blown.

Immediately North Americans asked why they didn't tour in America.

"We don't have a record deal in the States," he told them, "and every time we toured in the past it's always been with money from the record company."

"Oh, well," a Canadian fan wrote, "why don't we raise the money for you to come and tour?" Others quickly agreed that this was a good plan.

"Well I think you're a bit crazy," Kelly told them. This was, after all, nearly two decades before Kickstarter popularized crowdfunding. "But if you want to do it. I mean, obviously we can't have anything to do with it, but if you guys want to go ahead and organize it. We're not taking the money."

Kelly told them they needed about $50,000 to make it happen. Someone set up an escrow account. Within a few weeks they had raised $20,000. Before long it reached $60,000. It seemed so improbable, Kelly hadn't even told the rest of the band.

Marillion did the tour in 1997. The fans who had fronted the money also bought tickets. Being fan-funded generated publicity. "Each gig

Figure 3.1. Mark Kelly. ©
lrheath, and made available
under a CC BY-SA 3.0
license. https://commons.
wikimedia.org/wiki/
File:Markkelly2009.jpg.

that we were playing, there'd be a little local newspaper that would run
the story about the tour fund and how the American fans had raised
the money for us to tour." It was exciting, a moment of transition, and
a master class in "the power of the internet, and how rabid fans can
change things, make things happen."

In many ways, the industrial production of music worked well for
music listeners. They gained more access to high-quality music of different types, in different forms, at the varied and often private times
they chose to hear it than at any point in history. At the same time, the
shift to industrialized, centralized music production disempowered the
people who became audiences, reducing them to "consumers" in which
their "only power is that of consumers in general, to buy or not to buy."[1]
"Audience" is itself a "fictional construct" used to abstractly pull together
distinct individuals having varied concrete experiences.[2] Audience
members speak with many voices,[3] use music and other cultural materials in many ways, and have different levels of attachment to the objects
of their attention. Industrial market logic views these people as atom-
ized, perhaps with demographic characteristics by which they can be

grouped and counted, but rarely as immersed in relationships with one another.[4] But what really happened when people were carved off from what had historically been social co-participation in musical rituals was not that audiences became isolated. It was that listeners turned—as they always had—to one another.

Where musicologists see mass media as thwarting audiences' capacity for participation, audience researchers have spent decades documenting and analyzing how productive and creative audiences became in their wake. Just as industrialization and digital media changed the work of being a musician, they changed experiences and opportunities for audiences. While musicians dealt with the challenges of building and maintaining careers in the face of the new realities of their field, audiences developed new histories of participating with one another on their own terms. Now, even as musicians struggle to find their ways in an internet-mediated music world, audiences flourish. The internet has pushed their "hitherto marginal (and marginalized) tendencies into the very mainstream of media use."[5] No sooner did the first nodes of what became the internet make their first connection than fans began using it to build stable and persistent group infrastructures for their fandom. They wove fan practices into the internet's core, helping to shape contemporary media and shifting the balance of power between audiences and professionals. Practices hidden in private spaces for decades became visible and accessible, amplifying their impact.

What Jay Rosen famously called "the people formerly known as the audience" can no longer be treated only as abstract numbers in a spreadsheet.[6] "We need to radically rethink how media audiences are positioned in our new media ecosystems," Tim Anderson argues.[7] What used to be an audience is now "an altogether new actor that is explicitly positioned as an essential part of the design and architecture behind the production, distribution, and exhibition of information that circulates throughout new media ecosystems." Audiences distribute and exhibit others' works. They also make their own creative works—remixes, stories, covers, art, videos, designs—that can at times become more popular than official works. They create museum-worthy archives of musical information on websites and wikis. They write blogs. They share information (both accurate and wrong), recordings, and photographs. They create spaces and networks where they build and share supportive resources, identities, relationships, and practices. They are the ones who spread the word, who watch the gates of popular culture, and who set the norms for how it will transpire. They are the ones who "make things happen."

With few exceptions, it took musicians years to realize that networked media could be used to communicate with fans. When musicians now come to the internet to "connect," as they are often told to do, they find people who are already immersed in communities of their own around popular culture and, for many like those with whom I spoke, around them. The last pair of chapters looked at music, tracing musicians' paths as music became a commercial product while still serving its timeless social functions of managing feelings and relationships. This chapter turns to fans, asking how they spent the twentieth century, and how it is that they find themselves now in such an unprecedented position to set the terms for interactions around music, including those between themselves and musicians. I focus on fans, especially fans who are active and vocal online, because they are the most visible and influential of audiences, but they are by no means the only audiences musicians encounter online. Most listeners are not "fans," and most fans are pretty low-key in their fandom, more apt to lurk than perform. Those that do perform may not be fans. In the chapters to come, we see musicians deal with "anti-fans" actively invested in disliking them,[8] casual fans, and entirely different sorts of audiences such as family, friends, potential collaborators, business people, and random antagonists.

Understanding Fandom

The kind of fandom musicians encounter online developed over the course of the nineteenth and twentieth centuries, beginning even before mass communication technologies.[9] When opera companies and other performers began doing national tours in the 1850s, they created a novel opportunity for young people to center their musical experiences around public, commercial events such as concerts and theatrical performances. Niccolò Paganini and Franz Liszt are said to have had early fandoms (as did poets such as Lord Byron), but certainly the most spectacular early music fandom formed around the "Swedish songbird" Jenny Lind. P. T. Barnum, the man who set the standard for marketers everywhere, gave her that descriptor and then brought her to the

United States for a legendary mid-nineteenth-century tour. Barnum was masterful at creating "a sense of anticipation and desire through his use of publicity."[10] Adoring throngs waited outside theater doors, went to the wharf to watch her boat arrive, stood outside her hotel room, and lined the streets hoping to catch a glimpse of her carriage. Lind's tour dominated everyday conversations, much to the consternation of non-fans. A Boston satirist complained in the weeks leading up to her 1850 appearance that wherever he went, "all the cry was, Jenny Lind and Barnum, Barnum and Jenny Lind!" Even his friend, a seemingly responsible adult, was "so full of madness and music that he rushed through the streets with the fearful velocity of an escaped locomotive," he too calling out their names.[11]

What Is a "Fan"?

The definition of "fan" remains unsettled,[12] but fan scholars and fans alike generally agree that what differentiates "fans" from other listeners is the level of feeling invested in the object of their fandom and the kinds of practices in which they engage. Fans feel for feeling's own sake. They make meanings beyond what seems to be on offer. They build identities and experiences, and make artistic creations of their own to share with others.[13] A person can be an individual fan, feeling an "idealized connection with a star, strong feelings of memory and nostalgia," and engaging in activities like "collecting to develop a sense of self."[14] But, more often, individual experiences are embedded in social contexts where other people with shared attachments socialize around the object of their affections. Much of the pleasure of fandom comes from being connected to other fans.[15] In their diaries, Bostonians of the 1800s described being part of the crowds at concerts as part of the pleasure of attendance.[16] A compelling argument can be made that what fans love is less the object of their fandom than the attachments to (and differentiations from) one another that those affections afford. Carrie Brownstein of legendary Riot Grrrl band Sleater-Kinney (and later cult television show *Portlandia*), begins her autobiography, *Hunger Makes Me a Modern Girl*, like this: "My story starts with me as a fan. And to be a fan is to know that loving trumps being beloved. All the affection I poured into bands, into films, into actors and musicians, was about me and my friends."[17]

The term "fan" wasn't used until the late 1800s, when a journalist abbreviated "fanatic" to describe baseball spectators. By the 1930s, it was a "widely accepted American colloquialism, used in reference to sports, film, theater, and even politics."[18] In the intervening years, many fans had organized themselves into clubs. From the start, these groups were both productive and self-reflexive. They created their own media, exchanging letters and publishing and circulating newsletters.[19] They also built archives to document and preserve their communities.[20] Among the most well known were the elite male-dominated science fiction and Sherlock Holmes literary fandoms. Others focused on dance, sports, and, of course, music.[21]

Throughout the twentieth century, as mass media developed, fan groups grew increasingly common and complex. As travel got cheaper and communication technologies tightened connections between nations, fans began making pilgrimages to significant sites and to meet one another, particularly after World War II.[22] Fans appropriated new technologies as they developed to make their own creative works, often before other groups.[23] Among the new media these "audiences" used in their productions were "photographic setups, telephones, film cameras, tape recorders, mimeograph machines, home movie cameras, industrial staplers, and other innovations."[24]

Television fandoms that developed in the second half of the twentieth century took fan creativity to new heights. They also had different gender dynamics. Women, "excluded from the male-only club science fiction fandom had largely become," found in television fandom a way to "develop their skills and hone their talents."[25] By the time distant computers made their first connections in 1969, fans, especially women, were "remixing television footage to create their own fanvids, writing and editing their own zines, creating elaborate costumes, singing original folk songs, and painting images, all inspired by their favorite television series."[26]

Just as musicians have tried hard to be good capitalists (as we saw in the second chapter), while not wanting their work reduced to capitalist values (as we saw in the first), fans too are caught in the tensions between the social values music offers and the capitalist environment in which it is produced and circulates. In many ways, fans operate and are defined by their unwillingness to adhere to the norms of capitalism.

Not content to merely purchase and use, fans insist on feeling and relationship. Where commercial markets call for anonymity and limited, ephemeral involvement, fans form deep attachments. Fans "creatively imbue their participation in musical life with a lasting personal connection and depth of culture."[27] They "organize themselves and make and distribute their own creative transformations of the media they love."[28] They act more like communities or publics than like audiences,[29] focused on their connections to one another and the group rather than to what is so blandly called "content."

Yet even as they push back against it, fans embrace their consumerism. This began in many ways with Barnum, who gave "a commodity focus to the artist/fan relationship, allowing the experience of fandom to be prolonged and intensified through personal investment in a set of fetishized objects" peripheral to the music.[30] Lind fans could buy Jenny Lind dolls, gloves, scarves, and handkerchiefs.[31] I sleep in a "Jenny Lind" bed, a nineteenth-century American furniture style so popular it was the cheapest decent antique bedframe I could afford on a graduate student stipend. From early on, fandom has thus fostered collecting. Many become completists, buying every version of every release they can. Fans also create new economic value; the feeling and meaning they invest can make even items with no inherent value, like an autograph, expensive.[32] Fans in contemporary capitalism deploy "both media texts and brand messages as carriers of cultural meaning and as resources for everyday life" even as companies profit from their practices.[33] "Economic imperatives and 'authenticity' are thus expressed and experienced simultaneously."[34]

Fans are often aware of the tensions their dialectical status as (anti) capitalists creates between themselves and media producers. They see how "industry attempts to incorporate the tastes of the fans, and the fans to 'excorporate' the products of the industry."[35] They know that corporate interests are always essential to, yet working against, their own. Their modes of participation "may benefit, run counter to, or be entirely irrelevant to the interests of producers and marketers, whether such activities are authorized or not."[36] Bound together in fandoms, audience members engage in "a collective strategy, a communal effort to form interpretive communities" that challenges the power of popular media.[37] As we will return to in the next chapter, for artists and others in the music industries, the ability of fans to interpret, create, and distribute media among themselves is a mixed blessing, depending on what they are doing and on each artist's individual willingness to cede control. The inevitable friction between those who create mass media and the fans who remake it[38] becomes increasingly palpable when those who own intellectual property routinely co-opt fans and their practices for the added value they bring to their products, while simultaneously demanding that fans should "not divert from principles of capitalist exchange and recognize industries' legal ownership of the object of fandom."[39]

An Exemplary Fandom

The Norwegian death-punk band Turbonegro has a fandom that demonstrates both how bands provide grounds for participatory communal experiences that transcend them and how inseparable those communal experiences are from commercial markets. Cocky and ironic, Turbonegro are aggressively not radio friendly. Their look suggests flamboyant sailors. Their album and single titles are often raunchy or absurd ("Ass Cobra," "I Got Erection," "Fuck the World (F.T.W.)," "Hot for Nietzsche"). Without radio to promote them, they need their fans. Just as KISS had their army, Turbonegro relies on their "navy," Turbojugend (German for "Turboyouth," a name riffing on Hitler Youth, reflecting the same dubiously appropriate jokes of the band's song titles).

Clad in matching denim jackets embroidered with a sailor hat, and often sporting white sailor hats like the band's, these fans provide both word of mouth and an instantly recognizable visual brand. Their denim jacket, lovingly called the Kutte, is a symbol of the fans' transnational unity and local identity. Made by Levis, then outfitted with specialized embroidering, the jacket is sold through a central hub in New Jersey via the fan club's website. "Noncommittal" fans can pay $100 for a version with an embroidered Turbonegro logo and cap. Serious fans join one of the 2,300 worldwide chapters (or start their own) and pay $135 for their local chapter's version, available only by application. These Kutte say "Turbojugend" instead of "Turbonegro" and identify the local chapter to which its wearer belongs. Turbonegro's bass player, Happy Tom, describes the Kutte's significance like this: "You see another person wearing the jacket and basically it's like meeting somebody you've known for

Figure 3.2. Turbojugend at a Turbonegro show in the Netherlands, 2016. © Francis Bijl, and made available under a CC BY 2.0 license. https://www.flickr.com/photos/frenkieb/218971074.

a while. All these people it's like they're made out of the same ilk. I think a lot of the guys in the band are from that same ilk."

As "ilks," fan communities have strong ideas about what constitutes appropriate fan behavior and are not shy about policing one another for adherence online or off.[40] There are power struggles. Groups of fans oust one another.[41] Turbojugend, for example, have rules, many rules, most of which are tongue in cheek, and many of which concern the Kutte. Having, let alone wearing, a jacket from a chapter that isn't yours is a borderline criminal offense. Local identity is to be respected. But adorning your Kutte with patches and pins from other chapters represents a willingness to travel to meet with distant brethren and thus appropriately displays commitment to the community of the whole. Wearing the Kutte is required on certain holidays. July 27, Happy Tom's birthday, is compulsory. The Kutte is expected attire at concerts, wherever you may be publicly recognized, and at fan club meetings, whether local, regional, or the annual international Turbojugend convention at a beer hall in Hamburg. Through the music, the Kutte, the chapter structure, the gatherings, and the internet, Turbojugend foster an opposition to mainstream music consumption, much like the Jimmy Buffet fans John Mihelich and John Papineau describe as "oppositional in a broader cultural sense, keeping alive a particular version of an alternative world."[42] In the case of the "Margaritaville" ideal of Buffet fans, their alternative vision fosters "a more general cultural premise, a traditional sense, of leisure, rest, and celebration." Turbojugend celebrate beer rather than margaritas, but they too use the fandom to establish "an alternative basis for obtaining meaning, in contrast to the basis offered through market capitalism or materialism."

For all the humor, Turbojugend, a fan club whose very name references fascism, leads the "rules" section of its site with a "manifesto" that's quite serious: "By joining our association we expect that you do not tolerate fascist or racist behavior in your Turbojugend chapter and you won't tolerate members with such tendencies. Our utmost concern is to have fun together. But it is also evident for us that everyone wearing a Turbojugend jacket is aware about this serious topic. You represent a community and should not ruin our image by thinking a jacket gives you a free ride to act stupid or run amok." Wearing a jacket is a moral commitment about the kinds of relationships true fans are expected to build with one another. They expand on this in the "Turbojugend values" that follow: "Turbojugend has always been and will always be something like a family. It's got to do with family values, with friendship, with loyalty, with respect. Treat your brothers and sisters like brothers and sisters. And keep an eye on each other—it's the old thing: United we stand, divided we fall."

Much like Billy Bragg's fan who no longer liked his music but still went to his concerts because that's what she and her friends do, the camaraderie among Turbojugend is more important than their appreciation of the band. Happy Tom is flattered to have such a loyal following, but he knows that nearly everyone voted against the band when Turbojugend did a survey asking whether, if forced, members would choose them or the fan club. "So it's just bigger than the band is. It's like the German guy said"—he fakes a German accent—"You have created the Frankenstein monster, and now it's out of your control."

Commercial markets are integral to Turbojugend's participatory community. Fans buy Turbonegro music, tickets, hats, and jackets. They buy Kuttes, which don't make much money for Turbonegro directly, but helped associate them with denim to the point where Levis launched a Nordic advertising campaign featuring the band. In a nod to their antiestablishment stance, the website rules command them never to wash the Kutte ("Kuttenwaschverbot" it yells in bold font), yet they endorse Proctor and Gamble's Febreeze air freshener as an acceptable alternative and provide a link to the brand's website in case their other suggestion, going for a swim while wearing the Kutte, doesn't solve the problem.

The Author as Young Fangirl

Turbojugend exemplify the idea of music fandoms as organized groups that cohere around a particular band or artist. We can also understand fandom as a context for and means of self-discovery, affirmation, and friendship that moves from object to object as identities and circumstances change across the lifespan. I was no Turbojugend, but my own youth as a music fan illustrates some of these other key dynamics of fandom and some of the significant differences between fandom before and after the internet, which we'll return to at the chapter's end. I grew up in an American college town, firmly positioned in the middle class, with spare money, time, and the freedom to indulge in fandom that brought. One of the most significant gifts of my childhood was a small white AM transistor radio my best friend bought for my birthday in 1974. I lay awake nights listening to WLS, Chicago's Top 40 radio station. My friend and I discussed the songs endlessly. We knew nothing about who made the music, but knew they must be alluring. And probably sexy. Whatever that meant. Soon we were caught up in preteen girl culture, subscribing to *Tiger Beat* magazine and projecting our emerging sexual and romantic identities onto the heartthrobs seductively pictured in the magazines' centerfolds. We never questioned that our bedrooms should be covered with pictures of Shaun Cassidy and Andy Gibb (she preferred Leif Garrett). Nor did it occur to us that, like the girls before us who turned the Beatles into sex objects, we were upsetting gender rules about who was supposed to pursue whom.[43] I started hanging out at the local independent record store in Campustown, a neighborhood in

Champaign-Urbana, Illinois, where I lived, talking to the guys behind the counter. I wanted to know everything I could about the music I liked, and I didn't want to miss any music I thought I should know.

I lacked the language to call it "sexism" or "ageism" at the time, but the more I read music criticism and interviews with musicians, the more it stung to hear how blithely they used the trope of "thirteen-year-old girls" as prima facie evidence that whatever music we liked was bad. They still do and it still stings, though at last thirteen-year-old girls have an idol willing to sing their praises in Harry Styles. "Who's to say that young girls who like pop music—short for popular, right?—have worse musical taste than a 30-year-old hipster guy?" Styles told a *Rolling Stone* reporter who asked if he worried about proving his credibility to older audiences. "That's not up to you to say. Music is something that's always changing. There's no goal posts. Young girls like the Beatles. You gonna tell me they're not serious? How can you say young girls don't get it? They're our future. Our future doctors, lawyers, mothers, presidents, they kind of keep the world going."[44]

The age stigma disappeared, at least until it returned in my forties. The gender stigma remains, although for a time working in a record store brought me some measure of legitimacy as a person who may actually know something about music. Never mind that the music industry has marketed musicians as sex symbols for years, that they so often perform songs about being desperately in love with "you," or that some musicians are, in fact, pretty hot, women who notice that a serious musician like "David Byrne is an anatomically correct male are misguided at best."[45] I learned quickly that "to admit, in mixed company, to having a crush on a rock star is to overstep the bounds of proper feminine behavior."[46] By the end of my teen years I understood the difference between having a crush on the musician I imagined versus the real human being, but I've never stopped having occasional crushes. How could I—*why* would I—when a musician's songs are designed to evoke such strong feelings of love and longing?

My development as a teenage fan was fueled by mass media and by other people. The music press—American magazines like *Creem, Trouser Press*, and *Rolling Stone* and British papers like *New Music Express* and *Melody Maker* became required reading. "College radio," especially Jon Ginoli's punk and new wave show *Going Underground* that aired late

Friday nights on WPGU, became essential listening. Most days I hung out after school with my closest friend, Jennie. We played records for each other, bonding over our love of the Buzzcocks and Split Enz and distinguishing ourselves from each other by whether we found the first Clash album or the first Generation X album more compelling. I have an autographed copy of that Clash album displayed at home, but at the time I sided with the latter for validating every angsty teenage feeling I had. Musicians still seemed far away and fabulous, but, in keeping with our adolescent quest for identity, music was now about finding ourselves, together. With the Sex Pistols, the Clash, and other British punk and new wave bands playing on the turntable and radio in my bedroom, I cut off my long hair (by myself, of course), dyed it unnatural colors, and pierced my ears with safety pins. My high school graduating class voted me "boldest" and "best hair." I owe both to music fandom.

Jennie and I bought bootlegs on vinyl at the other local record store, the one willing to risk the illegality (they were eventually busted, though they remain in business today, unlike the one where I hung out). It felt a little seedy. Where did they come from? Who was getting the money and was that really okay? But bootlegs helped us in our quest to piece together more of an artist's career and showed ourselves and each other our commitment. Eventually, Jennie and I found ways to start going along with our record store friends to see local bands and touring acts live. I still have the concert log I kept throughout the 1980s. I still have the ticket stubs and flyers.

Between the record store and the concerts, by our senior year of high school we had befriended much of the local music scene that Holly Kruse describes in her book *Site and Sound*.[47] There were parties and after-parties where the cool kids ten years older took us under wing and brought us up to speed on essential 1970s acts like David Bowie, Roxy Music, and Sparks. Before MTV launched, one local musician (still a professional drummer) and his wife dominated the party scene after they bought the crowd's first Betamax player. The videos they played for us late into the night, like Bowie's sexy, gender-bending "Boys Keep Swinging," left a powerful impression that shaped my emerging self-understanding and self-presentation. Local musicians became friends, but they never felt like equals. Not only were they older, there was a clear implicit hierarchy. Fans nearer to musicians were nearer to the top than other fans, but unless they were romantically partnered or working with them, they'd never be as cool. With no interest in performing (years of piano lessons had revealed deficits in both talent and caring), I decided I'd like to manage bands when I grew up.

When I got to the University of Wisconsin as an undergraduate in 1982, I sought out friends who shared and could expand my taste and who wanted to see live music with me. With my two best friends in those years, Helen and Lisa, I took advantage of free time, no job, and spare cash to road-trip across the Midwest, seeing our favorite bands any place we could drive to and from without missing too much school. Helen and I had met through a mutual friend, Jamie, who had lived there longer and was more immersed in the Madison music scene. I met Lisa when a friend set us up to drive together to Summerfest in Milwaukee where Sparks, whom I loved, and R.E.M., whom she loved, were playing the same night. I had seen R.E.M. at a bar in Madison a few months earlier, and met their guitarist at a party after the show. My roommate was playing them on repeat. They got under my skin. By fall of 1983 all three of us—Lisa, Helen and me—were in love with R.E.M.

At the time R.E.M., who didn't even dress up to perform, seemed so different from the other bands around. Where others were all angles and image, R.E.M. were soft and ambiguous. Was "R.E.M." a reference to dreaming or not? Was it one syllable or three? The music was murky and layered. You couldn't understand a word. They seemed to do everything a band shouldn't do and they were beating the system anyhow. The lesson I took, at the formative age of eighteen, was that any artifice I'd spent the last several years refining wasn't necessary. I felt like my real self was surfacing.

We saw R.E.M. dozens of times, seeking the precious peak moments when something clicked during the concert and it became spiritually transcendent. I thought about my life in segments divided by R.E.M. albums and tours. They put us on the guest list as we followed them around the Midwest. We met bands they toured with, their crews, their friends, their business representatives. We felt at the center of an exciting, affirming, and creative participatory culture that touched us at every level, showing us ourselves and binding us to others. Yet the experience also alienated me from the industry in which I'd imagined I might work. In Denise Sullivan's oral history of the band, *Talk About the Passion*, there's a brief segment where R.E.M.'s first label representative mentions

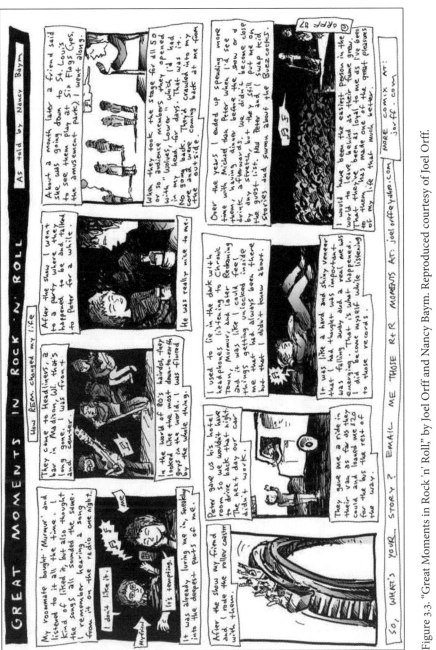

Figure 3.3. "Great Moments in Rock 'n' Roll," by Joel Orff and Nancy Baym. Reproduced courtesy of Joel Orff.

us.[48] "In the Midwest there were three girls, one black and two white, and they were everywhere," he was quoted as saying. He listed the kinds of the places we'd appear before concluding, "I think they slept with some of those girls, but they handled it really well." I decided that a field where that was even a question, let alone the default assumption, wasn't for me. All praise to the women who persisted nevertheless.

The local scenes of my high school years gave way to a network of local scenes, connected through touring bands and the people who moved along with them. My fellow fans, these musicians, people they worked with, and I traded resources in webs of gift exchange guided by friendship, obligation, and prestige alongside money, maintaining social ties, and building community as we did.[49] We offered our homes to touring musicians and their crews and stayed at other fans' places when we traveled. We told one another our stories. We played music for one another and traded music recommendations. In high school I'd bought bootlegs, but once in R.E.M. fandom someone gave me a live recording on cassette and introduced me to tape trading networks. Refined early on by Grateful Dead fans, these networks forbid monetary exchange. As Condry notes in an article about Japanese hip-hop fans, music fans feel a moral obligation to share music they love with one another.[50] To sell would be to violate that basic value.

My big break as a trader came when a member of the North Carolina band the dB's, who'd taken a liking to me, told me to write to his friend and tell him he'd sent me. I did and received the gift of what was then the most exclusive R.E.M. live recording of them all, their first performance, at the 40 Watt Club in Athens, Georgia. As my quest for live recordings expanded, Helen and I began showing up at local venues with a boom box and a large microphone to make our own recordings, always asking permission, and always getting it except from the one band that seemed too drugged to notice us asking. I spent hours typing up my tape list (first on a typewriter and later a KayPro PC with a dot-matrix printer), and literally cutting and pasting it over a collage I'd made from photocopies of old gears and watch works.

I parlayed my meager initial selection into an extensive collection of difficult-to-acquire live recordings. It garnered me tremendous personal pleasure. I listened to them endlessly. It also garnered me a lot of cool within my local and national music communities. As I worked my way

Figures 3.4 and 3.5. Tape trading, 1986. Photos by Nancy Baym.

from adolescence into my graduate school years, I continued to climb in the "social hierarchy where fans share a common interest while also competing over fan knowledge, access to the object of fandom, and status."[51] I'd acquired qualities of an elite fan.[52] I'd seen hundreds of live concerts. I had deep expertise. I had immaculately complete collections of official releases, and my collection of live recordings was the envy of my peers. I had an impressive collection of posters and other ephemera (I still do). Most of all, I'd gotten to know musicians personally.

Having access to these musicians, especially R.E.M.'s charismatic and enigmatic front man, Michael Stipe, showed me aspects of fandom that had been less apparent and, in retrospect, planted seeds that became this book. I saw whole restaurants or coffee shops fall silent and turn toward him when he walked into the room. Most kept their distance, but I watched fan after fan approach him everywhere he went, focused on their own excitement, eager for a moment they could take away and keep. It seemed exhausting. I heard him use the phrase "psychic vampires," and saw him make instant judgments about whether the stranger in front of him might consume too much of his energy. I'm sure he enjoyed my company, but I saw also that my public female companionship before and after shows sometimes served as useful protection.

The friendships I had with musicians also complicated my relationships with other fans. I didn't like turning a connection with a real person like Stipe into a chit in a competition I couldn't decline. If I mentioned that I knew R.E.M., I was boasting. If I didn't and people found out anyway, they told me I was arrogant. There were awkward encounters. A fan in a concert-hall bathroom, curious how I got the laminated all-access backstage pass Stipe had loaned me, accused me of lying when I told her the truth. So did a co-worker. A fan outside a venue, having seen me with Stipe, approached me, shaking, and asked breathlessly, "what ARE you to him?" I saw the absurdity of the power fans can grant people who don't deserve it. When musicians and audiences really do connect, I learned, sometimes fans get pretty weird.

How Music Fans Came to Rule the Internet

If, in the 1980s, I'd known half as much about computing as I knew about R.E.M. and their ilk, I'd have seen that even as I was co-creating these participatory fandoms through travel, cassettes, pen, paper, envelope, and typewriter, other fans were augmenting their music fandoms through the new, nascent computer networks that evolved into the internet we know today. Computer-mediated communication networks first emerged at the start of the 1970s, more than a decade before personal computers were available for home purchase. These early networks included ARPAnet, the U.S. government-sponsored network that became the backbone of the internet; other early geographically dispersed computer networks such as PLATO at the University of Illinois; and a host of local systems accessible on public computer terminals, internal networks, and dial-up Bulletin Board Systems. These early proto-internets were quite different from the world of ubiquitous access so many of us now carry in our pockets. They were text-based, and, in the case of the growing internet, which was funded by the U.S. National Science Foundation until 1994, a commerce-free zone. National and international commercial dial-up services, including America Online, Genie, Prodigy, and CompuServe did not connect with the noncommercial internet until 1994.

From the start, there was an unusual synergy between fans, including music fans, and the developing world of networked computing. Wherever there was networked computing, there were music fan communities leading the way, long before the masses, most musicians, or those in the music industries caught on.[33] My elementary school classroom in the mid-1970s was outfitted with an early computer networked called PLATO. PLATO ran a system called "Group Notes" where people shared "public notes files for subjects like books, movies, religion, music, and science fiction."[54] The first public computer-based bulletin board, Community Memory, launched in 1973, put music fans at the center of the community whose memory it sought. Its first, and for a time only, terminal was located in a record store, Leopold's Records in Berkeley, California. The terminal sat beside a traditional bulletin board where musicians and others posted "cards, flyers, and papers promoting performances, classified ads, efforts to organize, and general humor and philosophies."[55] Community Memory's users left one another electronic messages about these same topics. A directory of the music postings was printed weekly and left by the terminal for people to skim. The system's popularity soon spread to other communities in the Bay Area, providing "groups of people who had never used computers with new levels of access to technology and information-sharing" and a new way to discuss a wide range of topics.[56]

The Bay Area was also the home of the Grateful Dead, who were themselves interested in both technology and the fandom emerging around them. Among their local fans were computer scientists at key sites of the internet's development, such as the University of California–Berkeley and Stanford. Some of the first email mailing lists, launched soon after email was invented and available only to those working in the computer science labs where the technology was under development, were for music fans. Paul Martin of the Stanford Artificial Intelligence Lab began dead.dis@SAIL, for Dead fans in their lab.[57] A fan himself, Martin and another at SAIL also collaborated to create a giant electronic repository of Grateful Dead lyrics, a collection that eventually made its way to the Dead lyricist John Perry Barlow, who was reportedly so impressed he jumped headlong into digital culture, where he remained an influential presence.[58]

Throughout the 1970s and into the 1980s, people also launched hundreds, perhaps thousands, of local dial-in computer bulletin board systems (BBSs), reached through modems connected to telephone wires. Some were devoted to or named after the Grateful Dead, among them the Mars Hotel BBS in Roachdale, Indiana, and Terrapin Station in Darien, Connecticut.[59] The most influential BBS was the WELL, based (of course) in the Bay Area and frequented by the likes of Barlow and Howard Rheingold. In his history of BBSs, Kevin Driscoll describes the WELL's founders as consciously designing "a community-oriented system" by pulling together locals who were already connected, including "a large population of tech-savvy Grateful Dead fans." It was their income that supported the more "experimental, niche areas of The WELL." Known now for its centrality to early cyberculture, in Driscoll's telling, the WELL was "primarily an interest-driven BBS for fans of the Grateful Dead that occasionally featured salon-style conferences hosted by well-known thinkers on the transformative potential of social computing. But by the 1980s, followers of the Dead were no longer the countercultural vanguard they once might have been, and a Deadhead BBS was hardly headline material." One of the WELL's luminaries, Howard Rheingold, describes in his early classic *The Virtual Community* how the

Deadheads brought their affective investment in Dead fandom to the WELL.[60] They bought the technology and spent the time to learn the system's software "solely in order to trade audiotapes or argue about the meaning of lyrics."[61] Not all the Dead fans circulated outside the WELL's Dead forums, but those who did "ended up having strong influence on the WELL at large." The WELL hosted seven Dead forums, including one for tapes, one for tickets, and one for tours. There were also two private Dead mailing lists. Other public conferences that likely attracted fans had names like the Beatles, Jazz, MIDI, Radio, Songwriters, Zines/Fanzine Scene, Music, Audio-videophilia, and CDs.[62]

As ARPAnet grew into the internet, spreading to universities, government, and research sites throughout the 1980s and 1990s, music fans continued to create groups devoted to "every style of music and to most major (and many not-so-major) artists."[63] Some of these, like the (since renamed) Springsteen mailing list Backstreets Digest became crucial communal sites for debating song meanings, following an artist's location and activities, discussing how to get tickets, sharing concert reviews and set lists, and maintaining a sense of community, especially for the fans who didn't have other fans they could befriend locally.[64] Among the artists with fan-created mailing lists popular in my scene in the late 1980s and early 1990s were Kate Bush, Jazz Butcher, Robyn Hitchcock, Tori Amos, the record label 4AD, the "tweenet announcement" list that came out of that 4AD list, and an ambient music list. There were hundreds, if not thousands of others. The list I followed most closely was murmurs, for fans of R.E.M.

Against the grain of the liberatory rhetoric of equality surrounding the internet at that time, early online fandoms were eager to replicate dynamics of offline fandoms, creating hierarchies, boundaries, and norms for acceptable in-group behaviors. As fan mailing lists, such as Phish.net for Phish fans, grew, fights developed between new and old members. It's hard to maintain a sense of participatory unity when there are tens of thousands of people posting.[65] Similar dynamics around tolerable and intolerable behaviors played out across this early internet as fan groups, ever more accessible and visible, worked to "monitor the boundaries of a specific form of subcultural performance" on USENET forums such as alt.gothic.culture and alt.gothic.music.[66] The R.E.M. mailing list dealt with this by disbanding and becoming one of the hundreds of music-oriented USENET newsgroups, which anyone could read or post to through a "newsreader" rather than having to subscribe and receive messages in your inbox.[67] Once moved from mailing list to USENET, the quality of conversation on murmurs quickly deteriorated into endless queries as to whether or not Michael Stipe was gay, each launching a long thread chiding the poster for posing a question the group had long ago decided was off-limits. In response, a small group of fans from the original list created a secret invitation-only mailing list.

In 1994 these decentralized, text-based forums were joined by the new hypertextual World Wide Web. At the time, only 14 percent of Americans used the internet.[68] Mostly male, affluent, and well educated, that 14 percent, along with the smaller numbers of internet users outside the United States, included a lot of music fans. They immediately started creating websites. The Goth fandoms about which Whitaker wrote created websites like www.darkwave.org.uk, to lay out rules of etiquette such as whether or not it was appropriate to discuss feelings about Marilyn Manson (no) or what exactly distinguished Darkwave from Nu-Metal (you tell me). One of the most successful of the early fan sites eventually led to the demise of the secret R.E.M. mailing list. Ethan Kaplan, then sixteen years old, built Murmurs.com, a site Lucy Bennett has discussed in depth.[69] Just as my own R.E.M. fandom began to wane, Murmurs.com became the central place for R.E.M. fans to congregate. In contrast, the band's website, like almost all official websites of the time, was pathetic. The industry and musicians had taken very little notice of what fans were doing online.[70] While they ignored the internet, fans gained the power to overtake official online efforts. R.E.M.'s label, Warner Brothers, hired Kaplan and put him in charge of creating web presences for all their artists.

While audiences were building persistent and interconnected communities that attracted more attention than official sites, musicians and industry representatives viewed the internet primarily as a means of promotion rather than audience connection. In 1994, around when Kelly outed himself on the Marillion fan list and just before Kaplan launched Murmurs.com, the *New York Times* declared the internet "the biggest promotional tool for the music industry since the invention of the press release," reporting that "nearly every major record label and many independent ones have staked out space on line, where they supply fans with information (and dispel rumors) about bands and offer pop musicians for live chat sessions."[71] The comparison to a press release was apt. Just as Marillion found that their story of a fan-funded tour generated news in local papers everyplace they played, with some notable exceptions, mainstream artists and their representatives understood the value of the internet at that time in terms of its ability to generate publicity in more traditional media. "With only a fraction of the world's record buyers plugged into the Internet," the *New York Times* article continued, "what can be more valuable for a band is the publicity that comes with breaking new ground."[72]

Some bands sought big media coups with online firsts. In 1994, both Aerosmith and David Bowie claimed to release the first songs online.[73] But they didn't. "A service called the Internet Underground Music Archive had already made some 75 songs available only on the Internet."[74] More ambitious were the Rolling Stones, who broadcast a performance at the Cotton Bowl in Dallas in November 1994 live on the internet, "becoming the first major rock band to do so on that network of millions of computers."[75] The Stones too got scooped. An amateur band who just happened to work at Xerox PARC, one of the premiere computer science labs of its time, knew more about computer networks. The Stones's "moment in the limelight was tarnished by a little-known band called Severe Tire Damage. Knowing that the channel carrying the Stones was open to anyone, and wanting to take advantage of the worldwide audience the Stones would attract, the group broadcast an impromptu performance from the Xerox PARC offices in Palo Alto, Calif., directly before and after the Stones concert."[76]

Widely lauded digital innovators like Prince released an entire album, *Crystal Ball*, online with liner notes in the form of web pages in 1997. A year later Bowie launched Bowienet, a website that also offered its subscribers internet service and an email address.[77] People like Prince and Bowie were certainly early innovators. But, for the first time since mass media put them in positions of power, they were following the fans.

The Author as Old Fangirl

One of the most memorable gifts of my midlife was when my husband gave me the first iPod in 2001. About the same size as my childhood transistor radio, and also white, it reawoke the music fandom that had lain dormant as I built my career and family in a new city without connections to the local music scene. With gigabytes of space to fill, I began ripping every CD I had. Eventually, I got bored listening only to music I already knew. I went hunting for new music to love. When I was younger, I'd been immersed in social worlds where people I saw in daily life would play or tell me about new music and where it was easy to see shows and discover new music that way. Now there was no record store down the street where they knew my taste. There were no Jennies, Lisas, or Helens. If I wanted to see a show, I needed to find a babysitter and stay up way past my bedtime. Fortunately, there was Parasol Records, an independent store and small family of tiny labels based in Urbana, Illinois, owned by Geoff, an old high school friend. Parasol had a web shop where you could stream or download songs they recommended. Sitting in my home in Kansas, I gorged, downloading and buying with a passion that I hadn't had in years.

One of the guys who worked at this record store was into independent music from Scandinavian countries. He'd tapped into a vein of music I'd never known that fit my sensibilities perfectly. For the first time since I'd worked in the record store I started discovering plentiful new bands to love. I devoured music by independent alternative bands from Sweden, Norway, and Denmark. They rarely had label deals in the United States, although sites like Parasol were helping to distribute them there. They almost never toured North America. My tumble into this fandom was abetted by a widely distributed network of fans of Scandinavian music. As I've described elsewhere,[78] these fans, both inside and outside Nordic countries, wrote mp3 blogs highlighting music they liked, posted videos, ran music news sites, created archives, and otherwise made it possible for people thousands of miles away like me to find them. Among the most important of these sites was It's a Trap!, run by Avi Roig, a fan (and computing professional) in Olympia, Washington. For ten years Roig posted daily tidbits of news, interviews, and links to mp3s. With some help from random other volunteers (like me), he also published record reviews. A blogger in Chicago ran SwedesPlease, where he posted brief articles about bands or songs with a link to an mp3 so we could hear (and own) it for ourselves. A blogger in Paris ran (still does as of this writing) AbsolutNoise, which, like SwedesPlease, posted daily recommendations of Swedish bands. Hello!Surprise! was a web archive con-

Figure 3.6. Sivert Høyem. Photo by and copyright Per Ole Hagen, used courtesy of the photographer.

structed by a fan that cataloged more than four hundred Swedish bands, each with a description and links to any mp3s known to be available.

In 2005, I clicked on a Parasol stream and first heard Madrugada, a Norwegian band with a Portuguese name who sang in English. I fell in love from the first note. I loved them as much as I'd loved R.E.M. In my office, I look up to see a gift from a Norwegian Ph.D. student, a framed photograph her father took of their singer Sivert Høyem, looking suspiciously holy as a spotlight radiates white light from behind his bald head. Madrugada had released five albums in Norway and other parts of Europe by the time I found them, but only their first was available in the United States. They had never toured in America. Challenge accepted.[79]

The internet was generous or, more accurately, the Madrugada fans I found there were. I made daily visits to a website run by Reidar Eik, a Norwegian fan living in Germany. One of the site's pages was a collaboratively constructed discography of everything they had ever recorded, no matter how obscure. I checked it regularly as I amassed my collection. Another offered a chronology of every show they had ever played, including whether there were any known recordings. There was a forum where fans talked, mostly about their live shows, posted links to interviews, and where they shared links to uploads of concert recordings. In the forum I met a fan in Paris, Cédric, who took pity on an American, cut off from all other Madrugada fans, and sent me, snail mail, a CD-ROM with more than twenty live recordings he had collected. I scoured the torrent sites, eventually finding every song they had recorded in the studio and nearly every live recording fans had circulated.

It had taken me years of making the right connections to get into 1980s tape trading networks, let alone build my collection. I was able to build a huge Madrugada collection in a few short months. No status required. As a fan, I reveled in my newfound ability to use peer-to-peer networks to amass these recordings, even as I mourned the material experience and status implications we old fans had lost to this more egalitarian means of distributing information and recordings. Fans' gift culture was different online. Once posted, the resources shared were available to everyone.[80] The internet had altered the flows of our subcultural capital, bringing "anyone with a few hours up to speed" on things that only a dedicated fan would once have taken the time to learn.[81] It had also taken any powers musicians and the recording industry had to control the circulation of the materials they produce.

Most of the sites that fostered my music fandom in the first decade of the 2000s are already gone, lost to the effort it took unpaid amateurs to continue producing them and the shift away from mp3 sharing to streaming services like Spotify. The growth of social networks, organized around individuals rather than topics, further diffused the intensity of these online fandoms, absorbing them and recasting them as items like any other in a feed alongside status updates, selfies, shared news articles, and quizzes to determine which 1980s rockstar you are. Interaction around music has increasingly shifted to official profiles and social networks, where audiences expect musicians themselves to participate.

The Madrugada board is gone. Høyem's Facebook page is buzzing, but not with the participatory culture of sharing information and recordings that fans had built on the fan site. Certainly intense music fandoms persist on social networks and in dedicated fan forums, but like the careers of so many musicians they are precarious, vulnerable to competing work demands and shifting technologies.

Encountering Participatory Audiences

The long path of industrialization and commodification that pulled musicians from participatory culture and away from audiences brought those audiences together. Mass-mediated pop culture became raw materials for fans to build their own social worlds. Instead of losing participatory consciousness, fans remade it, appropriating what could have been taken from them to do so. By 2008, more than five million bands, even those that had broken up, were "friending" fans on MySpace.[82] They were late to the show. Music fans had been making friends with other fans on the internet longer than many of those musicians had been alive, recreating and amplifying the participatory skills and practices they had honed over more than a century and setting the stage for today's more participatory environment. Musicians, even when they were online, were rarely participants in these fan communities, except sometimes as fans of other bands. Those who went online looking not just to gain publicity but to build meaningful connections with their audiences before the 2002 launch of MySpace were exceptions. When it came time to "connect," participatory audiences had long since set the terms for how online music culture was going to work.

Fans will buy, though not all of them, but among themselves they insist on gift culture, with its ambivalent relationship to commerce, its preference for the free flow of information and intellectual property, and its celebration of fans' "vernacular creativity."[83] Fans relate to and understand one another in part as communities, with all of their internal norms and hierarchy. They expect music and its discussion to be a ubiquitous, always available, a component of their daily lives. Online, fandom became an everyday practice. Fans cultivated "a kind of fluctuating, quotidian rhythm" that was "not so much spectacular but banal."[84] Musicians, once the powerful, elusive rock stars who dropped from the sky every four years and let you listen to their album if you were lucky, land now in a realm where the audience is deep in relations with one another and their own participatory practices of meaning making. For artists, fans' online gift cultures raise dialectic tensions between participatory desires for communication and connection and personal, economic, and artistic desires to control their work and image. As we see in the next chapter, any position a musician assumes toward fans' participatory practices sends relational messages about the appropriate distances, roles, and boundaries between them.

4

Participatory Boundaries

Throwing Muses were college radio darlings in the 1980s. They had recording contracts with the prestigious British label 4AD and Sire, a Warner Brothers subsidiary, in the United States. But by the end of the decade their leader, Kristin Hersh, knew her relationship with the industry wasn't sustainable. Warner Brothers viewed her as a mantelpiece artist, using her credibility with other artists to sign bands they expected to sell better and were willing to actually promote. She didn't want to be part of a machine she saw as pushing bad music for the lowest common denominator. Money was getting tight. But her real problem was that the industry was messing with her "religion." Once they'd signed with Warner Brothers,

> it was someone else's job to find fans. It was someone else's job to advertise for shows to get people there. It was someone else's job to deal with radio and press. We spent many years not having any idea who we were playing music for. You go out on stage and you can't see anything but lights and then you're allowed to hide in the dressing room and then on the tour bus. We found record signings incredibly moving because we would finally meet these people who were effectively the point. They were also what made it possible for us to practice our religion. And then we'd be hustled away and have no more contact with them.

Billy O'Connell, Throwing Muses' manager, decided there must be a way to reconnect. In 1991, he found it. America Online (AOL) was still a dial-up service not yet linked to the rest of the internet, and there Throwing Muses fans had created a discussion "folder" called ThrowingMusic. They'd built their own connections through Hersh's work.

O'Connell jumped right in. "I was there every day, I put in a lot of time answering questions so people got answers straight from the horse's mouth."

"Hey it's Billy O," he told them. "I'm the Muses' manager and I'd be happy to answer any questions."

The fans were delighted. They ended up "having a total love fest. I developed all these relationships. I got to know hundreds of them."

A few years later, when Hersh's first solo album came out, O'Connell realized that if something were to happen to AOL, or if they were to change their terms of service or even their design, they could lose those connections once again. He decided to persuade the fans to move to a domain the band owned. Trusting that he understood and appreciated the subculture they had established, the fans agreed. Launched in 1994, eight years before MySpace, and even earlier than BowieNet, ThrowingMusic.com, named after the fans' already-existing community, anticipated the rise of social networks that would follow. You entered the site through "The Place." O'Connell explains: "It was a destination page where a fan could create a profile, own their own page, post their own posts, receive email, friend other pages. The Place got to be very popular. We started to build strong community, with the intention of owning these relationships, not having them live outside our realm, our influence, our property. So we pushed along that way getting to know people, literally hundreds."

Not long after, when Hersh and Warner Brothers finally parted ways, she and O'Connell took the entrepreneurial leap. ThrowingMusic was already built. The fans were already there. Everything was in place to sell CDs and vinyl directly to the audience. They formed their own label.

It didn't work. Direct sales weren't enough to cover studio time. Throwing Muses broke up. Hersh continued on her own. Again O'Connell, who had fallen in love with mp3s, thought there had to be opportunity in emerging technology. "There's gotta be a way to have fun and make money with mp3s. We have all these relationships, people so bonded and close." The thought kept him up nights.

In a moment of epiphany, lying in the dark desert, he finally devised a strategy. "Works in Progress" would be a page on the website with new exclusive content posted monthly. To access it, fans would have to subscribe.

"I said to the fans at ThrowingMusic, 'we're doing this thing, we're going to offer you mp3s of bedroom demos, unreleased songs, demos, outtakes, things like that, are you interested?'"

The fans said "yes!"

O'Connell asked, "is $15 fair? At end of year you'd have a CD, 12 tracks."

They said "yeah!'"

After some more negotiations, Works in Progress premiered in 1998. Each month they posted a new song with the story behind it, revealing aspects of Hersh and her work that she hadn't shared before.

The specifics of the business model have changed over the years, as have the exact subscribers at any given moment, but the "Strange Angels" (or "Strangels") as Hersh calls them, have funded her career ever since. As of this writing, she offers tiered subscriptions ranging from thirty dollars a quarter for guaranteed spots on guest lists and exclusive downloads, to five thousand dollars for studio visits and executive producer status. She has subscribers from twelve countries on five continents, subscribing at each level she offers.[1] Subscription revenues cover her recording costs, allowing Throwing Muses to record again. "Every time I want to go to work I have to have enough money and they've made that possible. There was a huge question mark just hovering in front of musicians' faces for so long, 'Will I be able to make the next record?' And the answer is usually, 'Eh, probably not.' And now I know that I can make the next record." "Essentially," she summarizes, "the point is that we do this together and the recording industry got in the way. So now we're doing it together again."

In the last chapter we saw how, once marginalized from music production by the industrialized music industry with which Hersh struggled, passionate audiences got busy connecting to one another. They built fan communities, first through off-line clubs, then through an ever-wider array of interconnected online sites. These fan communities are consumerist, and their purchasing provides both revenues that keep musicians going and affective investments that give some of the things musicians have to offer, like autographs or handwritten lyric sheets, their value. At the same time, the norms that organize fans' behavior toward one another operate largely outside of commerce, privileging identity, relationship, internal hierarchy, fan productivity, fan creativity, and the free trading and sharing of resources. The dialectic nature of fans as communities and markets poses challenges for artists who depend on them for income. To the extent audiences are markets, it makes sense for musicians to approach them from positions of power with an eye toward control, asking how they can influence and manage audiences to maximize their revenue. To the extent audiences are communities, it's not clear how to cede power and take a more participatory stance when you are the center around whom their participation revolves. This chapter identifies strategies of relational labor that musicians use to find balances that work for them and, sometimes, their audiences.

Hersh and O'Connell's approach to the ThrowingMusic fan community is a remarkable example of creatively balancing competing tensions to foster her music's potential to build her own and her audiences' relationships, values, and meanings. Hersh and O'Connell accept that they work in a business. O'Connell teaches music industry courses at Loyola University in New Orleans. He uses the phrase "monetizing passion," hating the way it sounds, but finding it articulates their philosophy of seeing "profit as a byproduct, not the point of doing the right things—providing value, a great experience, fun." "When you sell toothpaste," Hersh writes, "you should be selling a goo that helps prevent cavities. And when you sell music you should be selling sound that enriches the listener's inner life."[2]

Happy Tom, who described his band Turbonegro's fan club as a Frankenstein's monster they created but cannot control, warns against treating audiences as markets rather than communities:

> When you approach it as I'm the star and I'm going to sell you my product, you're really selling yourself short in terms of what kinds of engagement you can have and what kind of value too. If you treat it like marketing, people perceive that you're trying to sell them something. I think a lot of artists got trapped because it's all about my new single, my new product. And then they think, "oh, this is a neat community." But, I mean, do you want to be part of a community which is all about sales? I think a lot of people kind of mix that up. They think we need a community. It's a big buzzword. Well, treat it like a community. Treat it like something you're part of, not a sales channel. It's not a TV shop. . . . I think that's something we should cherish like a little baby bird.

Sometimes being part of that community means being in a position of power at the center of attention. When Happy Tom is at Turbonegro

Figures 4.1 and 4.2. Happy Tom. Two posts from his Instagram picturing him with a tattooed fan. Tattoo by Lars Vegas Christoffersen. Photoshop by Ole Andreas Drønen. Both images used courtesy of Tom Seltzer.

fans' worldwide conventions, people want to get photographs with him. He's "kind of in an ivory tower" on "the pedestal" of the stage. He enjoys it. But the fans don't idolize him for long. "The fans just piss on the tower. So after a while, I just go down and have a beer. We just hang out like everybody else." For him, it's "the best of both worlds."

The philosopher Martin Buber argues that people need both the participatory experience of approaching one another with an I-You stance, open to whatever emerges in the space between them, and the I-It stance, which sees others as objects we can use to better control our own paths.[3] Both ends are ideals. In practice, we move between them, juxtaposing wondrous moments of participatory engagement and flow with more calculating approaches that to help us to step back, make sense, and decide how to act. Musicians, rarely, if ever, balance the dialectic between participation and control by choosing one extreme or the other. Music is too inherently participatory and connective to make feasible a full commitment to control. For those seeking to earn money from audiences, it is bad business to focus only on participation. Love may be converted into the revenue to fund a career. Hersh did it. But it takes strategic control to make it work.

In practice, strategies of control and participation are interwoven in complex ways. Artists often cede some control within a framework that they control, or they seek to impose control in frameworks where they feel disempowered. There are three dominant controlling strategies right now: territorializing to locate fans' participatory practices on sites musicians own and can monetize, invoking the law to protect intellectual property against participatory practices, and datafying audiences and their communal practices in order to act strategically on knowledge gleaned from analytics. These strategies require resources and skills that are not available to less entrepreneurial, less networked, and less well-supported musicians. When artists orient toward participation, they use one or both of two main strategies. They may decenter themselves, stepping back to accept—and in the case of intellectual property, grant—autonomy. They may also collaborate with audience members, positioning them not as passive consumers but as active co-participants in a shared enterprise. Musicians pick and choose from both controlling and participatory strategies in different combinations and with different weights, as they try to set the boundaries of participation in their relationships with audiences.

Strategies of Control

Territorialize

When musicians territorialize, they seek to control the sites where audiences engage in their fan practices and possibly the practices themselves.

Official websites and, to a lesser extent, mailing lists are the primary means of territorializing. Marillion may have learned early that the internet could be used for fan funding, but they were slow to realize the importance of territory. Like many bands, they had to acquire the domain name marillion.com from a fan who had already registered it and created a fan board. Throwing Muses, exemplars of participation that they are, also engage in controlling practices. They territorialized their fans by pitching ThrowingMusic.com as a chance to enhance and preserve their practices in a place that would be protected. They took the fans' very name, ThrowingMusic, as their own.

Hersh's manager spoke of moving them from AOL to a website the band owned as a means of "owning these relationships, not having them live outside our realm, our influence, our property." Similarly, Zoë Keating, who as we have seen is more than willing to offer much of her private self to her audience through social media, speaks of getting all her fans to sign on to her mailing list "because I always want to own my fan base." The language of ownership is a response to the platforms. At this historical juncture, one needn't really question whether O'Connell was right that it was better for the band to own the community than for AOL to own it. As people increasingly let Facebook, Twitter, Instagram, Snapchat, and a host of other platforms host their fan communities, more might follow his lead. At the same time, to think of fans as a thing you "own" is hardly a participatory stance.

In his analysis of musicians' official websites, Paul Théberge showed how they position audience members as consumers to be monetized and undermine the social practices that bind fans together, even as they provide fans with resources they want.[4] Official fan clubs of the early twentieth century were often run by fans, and often under the auspices of celebrities or, more likely, their staff. These clubs, with their newsletters and mailings, afforded a rare opportunity for musicians to engage their audiences outside of live events or mass mediation. They provided a way for fans to feel a sense of belonging to a larger fandom. Now, official websites serve this function, but when fans can so easily form communities on their own online, seeking to contain their engagement to sites you own sends power signals it did not before.

Official sites are promotional resources for bands. They are also revenue sources. Most sell merchandise. Many offer direct access either to other fans or the musicians. Some artists use their official websites to organize fans into street teams who can help with local promotion. Lloyd Cole first gained his audience with a major label contract in the 1980s with his band the Commotions. He now has a long-standing group of "Young Idealists" organized through his site. Many acts sell preferential access to concert tickets and events like meet and greets before and after the show. Some bands also offer tiered pricing models. While this grants audiences more access to artists and one another than ever before, they also orient the status markers of fan communities even further toward money. The opportunities may be framed as connections, but "there is nevertheless a tendency on many club sites to equate fan commitment with dollars spent."[5] Hersh's subscription model, for example, offers different tiers of subscription at different rates. The most expensive option includes greater access to her. The Dave Mathews Band instituted a program giving long-term members of their websites better seats, as did Nine Inch Nails, who offered two levels of membership with better rewards at a higher cost.[6] This privileging of fans with money can rub some artists the wrong way. Marillion, seeking a more egalitarian model, has stuck to presales where everyone pays the same price for the forthcoming record they are funding and is entered into a raffle for the kinds of prizes high-tier fan funding might purchase for others.

Well-intended official sites can undermine fan community by providing resources that fans would have traded to build community and status in their internal gift cultures. D. A. Wallach of Chester French—the first band on Facebook (they were Harvard students when and where the site first launched)—for instance, thought that the ideal official website (which he saw few artists, including himself, as attaining) should be "an extension of the fan experience," but also "the absolute best place for you to go to get anything you need related to us. To find out any information about us, to see any pictures you want. It should be [that] anything related to us should not be accessible in better form anywhere else." Sensible as this is, when artists are the ones to post things like set lists or other information, they move fans' resources for building participatory relationships back under the bands' control.[7]

Artists may territorialize fans' creative practices as well, sponsoring or hosting select creative works by their audiences. As early as 1992, Madonna, always ahead of the curve, teamed with MTV to let fans submit videos for her song "True Blue." The network broadcast the best for twenty-four hours.[8] In 2008, Coldplay held a contest for fans to produce a video for their song "Lost," posting the winning entries on their website. While such contests validate fans' creativity and productive capacities, it also ensures that intellectual property is managed on artists' own terms. That the winners in contests like these are often professional or aspiring freelancers hoping to secure work through the exposure of winning is an ironic twist; there are nesting dolls of exploitation and precarity in these tales.

Done well, fans can be quite happy about being territorialized. Housing fan practices on an official website that someone is committed to maintaining and managing (hopefully for pay) can provide the stability and longevity that let fan communities thrive. It can provide a bulwark against the rise and fall of different social media platforms and the precariousness of fan-driven sites and all the information and other resources they amass. As we will see, people can also foster participatory practices by setting some parts of their official sites, like the fan board, aside as a place for fans to do what they like. Yet creating an official site, using it to offer resources that then lose their social value within fan communities, and reshaping fan hierarchies through differential access based on wealth and willingness to be monetized, are inherently controlling actions and inevitably position audiences, at least in part, as markets to be managed.

Invoke Intellectual Property Rights

A considerably more aggressive way to seek power in relation to audience participation is to invoke the law, either as a lawsuit or the threat of one, to shut fans down. Many artists and even more labels and other rights holders use their intellectual property rights in efforts to keep the circulation of music, lyrics, images, and so on within boundaries they authorize. From a market perspective this makes perfect sense. Intellectual property is the core asset. Going after audiences for (mis)use of intellectual property reclaims power, wresting the ability to communicate as they wish away from audiences.

The most delightfully perplexing exemplar of this was Prince. No one could build that lasting and adoring a fan base were he not adept at cultivating a relationship fans found deeply meaningful. He was known for participatory gestures like inviting fans into his home for parties. Yet, few have been quicker to turn to the law to limit fan practices online and off. Prince was rightly lauded for the control he demanded over his intellectual property and masters recordings in fights with his record label, but that same control turned toward fan practices, whether by him or his label, carried the message that he was the one in that relationship who wields the power. In a famous example, in 2007 he and Universal Music Group ordered YouTube to take down a clip of Stephanie Lenz's baby dancing to his song "Let's Go Crazy." In turn, Lenz sued Prince and UMG for abusing takedown notices to squelch fair use.[9] Around the same time, he threatened three fan blogs—www.housequake.com, www.princefans.com, and www.prince.org (collectively referred to as "Prince Fans United")—with legal action to stop them from sharing images of him and anything linked to his likeness. Among the offending images were photographs fans had posted of his face, tattooed on their own bodies. Prince Fans United refused to take down the sites, claiming the request was unlawful.[10] Prince and Universal backed down quickly and the issue was settled out of court, but all three sites disappeared. Prince was also notorious for sending cease-and-desist and takedown notices to platforms where fans shared his work, including the Pirate Bay, Facebook, Twitter, and Instagram. In 2013, the Electronic Frontier Foundation (of which John Perry Barlow, Grateful Dead lyricist and early member of the WELL, was a co-founder and board member) awarded Prince its new "Lifetime Aggrievement Award" for "extraordinary abuses of the takedown process in the name of silencing speech," an award many disputed.[11]

Prince was a huge star with people who could pursue legal claims for him and had the money to pay for it. That was not the case for most musicians I interviewed, or others who work closer to the margins. Some would have done so but lacked the time, expertise, and money to keep up with unauthorized uses of their intellectual property. Their tales of trying to exert legal claims were often endless games of bureaucratic whack-a-mole with opaque intermediaries. I spoke on a panel with the jazz composer, conductor, and artist rights activist Maria Schneider. She doesn't see herself as going after her audiences, but she has testified before the U.S. Congress and elsewhere, arguing for policies to force platforms like YouTube to get her out of the Sisyphean task of requesting that her music be deleted item by item. David Lowery of Cracker and Camper Van Beethoven is also a vocal advocate for artists' rights. He has often spoken out against platforms such as Google for earning income by embedding advertisements in search results for unauthorized downloads and YouTube (owned by Google) for hosting them. By 2015 he had turned much of his attention to Spotify, against which he filed and later settled a class-action lawsuit, alleging that they knowingly allowed streaming of songs to which they had not secured rights. Like territorializing as a means of protecting both artist and fans from platforms that may come and go, pursuing legal and policy action against platforms seems to be a power move against platforms rather than audiences. Yet it is audiences who are posting, looking for, and streaming those links artists seek to take down, and so any move against them is inevitably a move against the audience. It may be justified, but it is nonetheless a means of empowering one's self at the audience's expense.

Datafy

A third strategy for controlling audiences is to reduce them to data so they can be analyzed until they are predictable. Artists datafy audiences to inform their decision making and reduce risk.[12] James R. Beniger argues that the industrial age unleashed many technological and social forces that challenged the human ability to control what it created.[13] In response, people began to amass and exploit information on unprecedented scales, in what he called the "control revolution." Media industries have long datafied audiences by counting them, historically with production numbers, sales counts, or measures of exposure.[14] Press and periodical runs were the first form of quantified audience measurement.[15] Since the 1970s, counting and related forms of measurement have become less intuitive and more systematic.[16] In music industries, audiences have traditionally been measured through sales and, to a lesser extent, radio exposure. Until the 1990s, *Billboard Magazine*'s charts, based on telephone surveys of record store personnel, were the industry standard. Big data came to the industry in 1991, when Mike Shalett and Mike Fine developed Soundscan (now part of Nielsen) to measure music audiences by tracking over-the-counter sales through bar codes.[17]

Among the musicians discussed here, datafication takes many forms. Two of the most important are counting fans and mining their practices to assess their engagement and affective investments. As with using the law to stop fan practices, datafying audiences takes resources and skills that many artists may not have, even when individual platforms provide analytics they could use.

Musicians have long datafied by collecting fan addresses. The Grateful Dead, not surprisingly, were pioneers in this as well. In 1971, four years after the release of their first album, they included an insert in their live *Skull and Roses* album asking people to send their name and address so they could keep them informed. They also hired a fan and gave him the duty of manning a booth at their concerts signing fans up to their mailing list. In the spring 1972 issue of the newsletter they sent to these fans, they expressed the hope that they could establish a communication system for all, but lamented that money had stopped them from realizing this inclusive vision. Within six months of putting the insert in the album, they had information on ten thousand fans. By 1976, they could sort sixty-three thousand fans by zip code and name. They further took control by establishing their own ticketing agency, and used this to build social bonds among the fans. Knowing who their fans were, how many shows they went to, and being the ones who sold and could hence choose where fans would be seated, the Dead were able to seat the most passionate fans up front, ensuring they would become familiar to one another and tightening the community on which they ultimately relied.[18] By the mid-1990s, when they finally converted their mailing list to email, they had five hundred thousand subscribers.[19]

Mailing lists require the conversion of fans into entries in a database that can then be managed and even estimated in terms of economic value. The fan management platform Topspin (which has since shut down) analyzed five years of "marketing and transactional data that has taken place across a sample set of over 29,000 artists who have used the Topspin platform to reach more than 57 million fans collectively." They found that fans acquired through one of their campaigns (such as exchanging an email address to download a free song) were worth a "lifetime average value" of $3.78, although some artists realized more value and others less.[20] Most of the artists with whom I spoke rarely used the number of entries in the database as a means of demonstrating their economic value. For them, the size metrics such databases yielded were by-products of their desire to reach audiences directly.

The advent of the internet and digital media, with all of their traces of previously ephemeral practices left by audiences, further amplified the trend toward datafication. Visible metrics of audience practices, things like counts of friends, followers, likes, replies, and retweets, make it easier than ever to think of audience members and practices as numbers. More sophisticated customer (aka fan) relations management (CRM) software now allows technoliterate musicians to do far more than count and sort by zip code. Wallach used Salesforce to develop software for managing their fans and quickly started modifying it for use by other artists. The platform allowed them to generate user reports, transform subscribers into segments, and target them using geography, demography, or any other "data points that we have on them." Keating, like Wallach, is at ease with code. In an effort to understand and more effectively communicate with her audiences, she exported her audience information from different platforms and compared them. She found only five hundred overlapping fans between her two Facebook pages (the personal and the fan), a different set of people altogether on MySpace, and a third group on her mailing list. This helped her understand the differences between the audiences and the need "to talk to them differently."

These datafication strategies work by quantifying data fans provide on the artists' profiles or sites they control. Today, artists and those working with them must monitor far more than their own territories if they are to make sense of their audiences. Both manual eavesdropping and more sophisticated tools like sentiment mining and machine learning can be used to analyze who audiences are and what they are saying across the internet. Wallach kept an eye on communication about the band using a variety of tools including Google Alerts, RSS feeds from Twitter, IceRocket ("kind of like a social search engine"), and links people sent him in email messages, trying to "cast my net as wide as possible." Ariel Rivas, who manages a roster of acts from Central and South America, talks about his and his team's daily rituals of mining and managing data to help focus publicity, plan tours and ticket prices, and identify and build relationships with fan leaders to reach his artists' audiences. Rivas uses every tool he can: TweetDeck, which he describes as "incredible," "like having three or four million reporters connected and sending data to you," Facebook demographics, and Google Analytics. When we spoke he was also using Topspin. He described his work with Rubén Blades:

> We're monitoring what happens on all the social networks and on Twit-ter, and we know that we have a huge amount of fans in Venezuela. We know that, because we have a lot of hits from Venezuela. Or we have a lot of fans in Colombia, and we can do more publicity or we can sell our shows at a higher price in that country. . . . So, now we have a lot of tools to know what exactly is happening in each market. In the old days, they didn't have that ability to know what happened in each market. You just had to call the radio stations.

Datafication can be powerful but, like the law, can remain out of reach for artists working on their own or with fewer resources. Historically, musi-cians have rarely had access to their own sales figures, and though they can certainly see the size of their live audiences when they perform, know how many people subscribe to their mailing list or fan club, or view the numbers of likes their messages and accounts garner, it can be difficult (or uninteresting) for them to develop the computational skills to maintain audience databases or the critical analytic skills to best interpret the kinds of numbers that digital metrics and data analytics provide.[21] Mark Kelly, who, as we will see below, exploited Marillion's large fan mailing list to finance much of their career, knew the importance of collecting names and addresses, but did a poor job of maintaining them. "Unfortunately, when people left we would just destroy their details, we never kept it all. So there's probably thousands and thousands of people who went through the fan club, we have no idea who they were because we weren't so clued up about the sort of things that you should be doing." Many musicians I spoke with had lost their audience data at least once. When platforms, fan management systems, and the tools used to make sense of audience activities online routinely change or go under, musicians move from one to another, often losing their datafication work as they do.

Wallach is well educated, interested in business, and excited about technology. Keating worked in computing before turning full time to music. But most musicians, like most people, are poorly equipped to access, move, manage, or interpret the data it takes to track and mea-sure their own audiences. Without support to help them, musicians may feel overwhelmed rather than empowered by the relentless flow of data. Mike Timmins, of Cowboy Junkies, sees the flow of metrics. He's "sure there's a way of figuring them out and looking at that stuff." But he doesn't feel he's got the resources: "God, who knows how to do that? And who has—and that's more time. That's more time involved. I think if you had a team of guys working on your website, which I'm sure some of the bigger bands do and their labels should but they probably don't, yeah, all that stuff could be figured out. I mean, it's always there. All those metrics and all those tools are there to do that stuff, but, God, I can't even be.... It's hard enough to just do a blog, never mind do all that stuff."

These strategies—territorializing, invoking intellectual property rights, and datafying—are routinely deployed to transform the unwieldy and unpredictable lived experiences of human beings in their audiences into discrete phenomena that can be understood from a distance and manipulated. Even as they objectify and undermine, they can also enhance fans' experiences as individuals and as communities. But perfect control is an unattainable ideal, hampered by labels that may keep data hidden from artists (see chapter 2); expense; the challenges of managing, analyzing, and meaningfully interpreting data; and, as I turn to now, the simultaneous competing desire to approach audiences not as objects to be used but as communities meant for participation.

Strategies of Participation

Music, as a social practice, is inherently participatory. This pull toward participation in a business that requires control can cause frictions for commercial artists. UB40, for example, had an official fan club early on but stopped because they found it embarrassing. Growing up in a working-class city amid strong worker solidarity movements, having a fan club felt too much like a power trip. "We all find it a bit disingenuous, you know, I mean, a little weird," Brian Travers told me:

> But remember we're like raving socialists. We love nothing more than going on marches against, you know, right wing, they were called the National Front then in Britain, the British National Party, the BNP. So having a fan club, it just felt a little bit too Duran Duran. Nice guys, and I don't mean that, but you know, it's having that commercial mind. I mean,

we put a website up. We have a bulletin board, you know, a forum, and we try to play the game a little. But I do prefer just talking to people, you know what I mean? Do you know?

Egalitarian, participatory socialists that they want to be, they still feel the need to "try to play the game a little." The only way musicians can avoid controlling strategies is to opt out of capitalism. The rest, like Travers, have to find ways to insert participation into a media industry structure that has left a legacy of centralized control and market thinking. The two main ways of doing this are to accept fans' autonomy and, as Hersh did, incorporate them into your business plans as collaborators as well as customers.

Accept Autonomy

The controlling strategies of territorializing and invoking intellectual property rights seek to manage where audiences practice their fandom and which practices they are allowed to do there. When artists accept audience autonomy, they leave fans to their own devices to do their own things, either providing a home for, ignoring, or explicitly supporting them as they do. Throwing Muses may have territorialized, but when they moved fans to ThrowingMusic.com, they designed the site to give each fan a profile page of their own and a forum to allow them to continue their discussion on the same terms they had on AOL. Official websites like this often make space to foster "a sense of belonging" alongside a space for direct marketing.[22] Artists cede power by giving fans a space and letting them use it as they like, yet just as a Facebook fan page belongs ultimately to Facebook rather than the artist, an official website belongs ultimately to the artist rather than the fans. This can be a source of conflict. Billy Bragg has an active and long-lasting fan forum on his official site. "It's real autonomous," he says. "Sometimes they get pissed off with me and they criticize me or I do stuff that they don't particularly like for whatever reason." Sometimes their arguments with him are political, but sometimes they have to do with changes that have been made to the forum they see as theirs.

A more participatory way to accept autonomy is to accept that fans create their own places for discussion, either on their own sites or through social network platforms, and either encourage them to do so or leave them alone. The fan site I relied on when I fell in love with Sivert Høyem's band, Madrugada, was created by a fan (see chapter 3). Madrugada and their management knew about the site and, feeling (correctly, alas) that they "sucked at the internet," they decided it was better to leave them alone. Though there were rumors that some people who worked with the band were present on the board sometimes, if the musicians ever came by, they hid it well.

Mogwai likewise let a fan-run site serve in place of an official fan forum. They knew the person who ran it, and looked at it to see what people were saying, but left its management in the fan's hands. "I don't think we would have the time to moderate that. Although they do a good job, so maybe we could just get them to do it for us," Stuart Braithwaite mused. "But I think it's better that they should have their thing because I think if it was our own board, I don't know, you kind of feel tempted to kind of have no one say anything negative and I think that kind of wouldn't really be fair." A few artists, such as Franz Ferdinand, actively encourage fans to create their own spaces. Their official website links out to more than fifty fan sites around the internet on websites and social media platforms including Facebook, Tumblr, Instagram, Twitter, and YouTube. Artists may not necessarily approve of what happens on these sites, but when they have chosen to accept autonomy, they let it be. One musician I spoke with complained about the fans' internal hierarchy, which seemed to exclude new fans:

> That whole thing kind of freaked me out a little bit, because it seemed like they really claimed the band for themselves. "A fan since 1999" or something. You didn't have a right to take part, and it all had to be done in this very kind of correct tone. They had their own kind of way of writing messages to each other and stuff. I liked to think that that wasn't what our fans were like. To be honest, I didn't really—I didn't like that much, that whole thing, and the way they tried to reduce it to just very detailed nerdy things. It turned into a club.

Another expressed distress at watching fans bully and compete with one other on Twitter, wanting to intervene, but knowing it was likely to cause more trouble than resolution.

Musicians may also take participatory stances toward uses of their intellectual property by encouraging their audiences to share and create new things with them and their music. Again, the Grateful Dead led the way, nurturing the tape trading networks their fans were creating by establishing taping sections at concerts and encouraging fans to share their recordings. The artists I spoke with had mixed feelings about letting their audiences share recordings of either their albums or concerts, but, with exceptions like the artists' rights advocates I described earlier, they generally saw the free circulation of music as having long passed the point of no return. Some who had opposed it made their peace. The Australian DJ Deepchild, who lives and works in Germany, described how his feelings toward this had changed. "I used to feel really very defensive about that notion and now I almost feel the opposite. I'm happy for people to take my music for free whenever they want." Some were just resigned to a fate they found unfortunate but no longer worth fighting.

Artists also have mixed feelings on people sharing concert recordings. It is common to suppress this from the start. Some put up signs requesting that the show not be photographed or even use third-party companies to render mobile phones unusable for the duration of a show. Others, like the drummer of a prominent indie band I spoke with, "don't care about any of that" and "think that's fine."

I shared with him what Nacho Vegas had told me about his trouble balancing his desire to control his music with politics that support audience power. "The audience has got more power than you, so it's great but it's strange. You know when you play live, it's something that happens in that moment and you don't think it could be like in the web. So it's just strange. Sometimes I think 'I wish I never played this song' because now it's in the web and I don't like it the way I played. But I think I have to change my mind, because it's great that people have these phones. I don't know, it's strange for me."

The drummer laughed, "yeah, yeah, exactly. Well, practice more." You can't change it, he says, "you've just got to get your head around it and deal with it because it's not changing. It's not going to go back to where people don't post those things." I think of my son's reaction to signs at a Bryan Ferry concert explaining that cell phone pictures were forbidden: "Who is he to think he can exempt himself from the modern world?" Indeed, the minute Ferry took the stage, out came the cameras.

Martin Thörnkvist, who manages Swedish singer Moto Boy, had only enthusiasm for these fan practices. It is no coincidence that for a time he shared an office with a founder of the Pirate Bay. He looked for fan concert videos, downloading the best versions of each song and compiling them into a YouTube concert. We could say that Thörnkvist was being controlling, harvesting fan work for promotion, but we can just as honestly say that he not only left fans to do their own thing, he brought Moto Boy into their participatory realm by recirculating their work on his behalf.

Audiences also exploit intellectual property by transforming it into their own creative work, including videos, art, remixes, and fan fiction in which musicians are cast as protagonists in tales that may include fantasies of romantic and sexual relationships that do not exist. The artists I spoke with did not always like the results. Some thought fans' creative works were unimaginative; others thought it was not appropriate. One, who found fan fiction featuring her having sex with a friend of hers, found it downright creepy. "I have Google Analytics for my name," she told me. "I'll check once a week." The week before we talked, a piece of fan fiction had come up featuring her and a female friend in another band. It was "so disturbing."

> It was just this really, really disturbing sex scene between us. And then at the end, you know, all these kids can comment on it, and someone says like "Oh, that was very smart and very classy." And then another girl goes "Oh, what a great pair." And that kind of thing just really, really weirds me out. Like I haven't seen [my friend] yet since I read it, but I'm probably going to feel weird even when I see her, even though she's not involved in it at all. But it's just like one of those like weird, creepy obsessive kind of things.

Most tolerated these kinds of fan creativity, some wished their fans did more of it, and some celebrated what their fans made. For Kristin Hersh, witnessing (some of) her audience's creativity proved both surprising and profoundly rewarding: "I didn't know they'd be willing to come through with their own projects like remixes of my songs, time lapse paintings to my music, films, covers, all of that sharing they do, all that effort and all that involvement. It's one thing to be made someone's

Figure 4.3. Stephen Mason. © Ian Muttoo, and made available under a CC BY-SA 2.0 license. https://www.flickr.com/photos/imuttoo/441591562.

soundtrack for a while, that is truly the highest honor I could ever hope to achieve. And they go one step closer to making the music together by actually making the music together."

I also asked Stephen Mason what he thought about practices like fan art. "Oh, I think it's cool," he said without hesitation. Honestly, it's people getting involved and interested in finding ways to—in its own way, it's a response. It's a response. These days, it would be foolish to just say anything other than, 'I'm excited that people are engaging.'" Art, he added, "can continue to grow and develop into new things, all the time. All the time, depending on how people engage it."

Let Them Help

Musicians, especially smaller and independent ones without significant industry investment in their careers, can feel overwhelmed by the amount of work to be done and the omniprofessionalism their career now demands. Like Hersh before her Strange Angels, they can also have trouble finding the money for recording costs. Fan communities operate on principles of gift exchange, in which obligations are balanced through the giving and receiving of resources. Listeners often feel embedded in an exchange relationship in which they owe the artist a debt for what the music has meant in their lives.[23] Such fans can be happy to balance out their debt by working on musicians' behalf, whether that is through actual tasks or direct funding. Artists who use collaborative strategies based on this fan desire to help invite audience members to participate in the "art worlds" of musicking (described in chapter 2), where there are always roles to play and always work to be done.

Letting audiences participate has symbolic value in the relationship above and beyond any actual help they provide. After eight albums on a major label and three with an independent, Marillion did the math and realized that at the rates they were being paid, they had to record an album a year. They left their label. Remembering that fans had come up with the idea of directly financing their North American tour a few years earlier, Kelly saw a solution. "What about all these fans that gave us all this money a few years ago?" he asked. "Why don't we see if anybody would be interested in buying the album in advance of us making it, like a sort of preorder, advanced order?" He knew it would take a "leap of faith," a "trust" in the band—preorder was a novel idea at the time— but he also knew they had "fans that have been with us, some of them for 25 years or whatever, that given the opportunity they'd like to show their appreciation." The mailing list they had spent years building had twenty-three thousand subscribers. When they offered the presale, they got advance orders for thirteen thousand, enough to finance the album *Anoraknophobia*, released in 2001. They then took the finished product to their former label, EMI, who distributed it to retail outlets on terms far more comfortable to the band.

After doing this for a few more albums, Marillion had enough money saved to fund their own album production. They decided it was "cheeky" to keep going back to fans whose money they didn't actually need. "I think I was probably wrong at the time," Kelly reflects, "but I said, it feels a bit like when you go to a friend and ask for a bit of help. 'Can you lend me some money?' and they lend you some money. And then you go back again and you say, 'Oh well actually we need you to lend us some money again.'" They decided to self-fund the next record. Fans were angry and disappointed. "There was all that stuff which made them feel, one, financially they knew they were financing it and two, they were very much involved with the whole process as it was going along. So there was a sense of disappointment I think that we didn't do it. People felt that somehow it wasn't as special." The band returned to presales, not because they needed the money, but because it gave fans a sense of participating in "the whole process."

Pay-what-you-want models are another strategy that simultaneously acknowledges fans as customers, yet gives them room to transform their act of paying from transactional to participatory. The most famous example of this remains Radiohead's 2007 experiment, in which they offered people the opportunity to choose their own price (including nothing) for their surprise album *In Rainbows*. The average price paid was considerably less than the album later sold for in stores, but at an estimated $2.40 per download going directly to the band, they likely made more money than they would have from their previous label, EMI.[24] Entire labels have chosen to do this, like Conner Oberst's Saddle Creek label. "We appeal to common sense," Oberst said. "If you can afford something you like, you'll buy it because that benefits the person who created the thing you like."[25] Intermediary platforms may also offer the ability to overpay. Magnatune, with the motto "We are not evil," recommended that customers pay eight dollars for each album on their site (splitting the proceeds fifty-fifty with the rights holders) but let customers choose a price between five dollars and eighteen dollars. Regner and Barria found that only 14.5 percent of customers paid the minimum price.[26] Most paid the suggested price. On average, though, they paid $8.20. Regner and Barria's survey of customers found that the biggest reasons for paying more than the minimum were a desire to support the artist, a sense of guilt at paying less than the recommended, and a desire to restore reciprocity.

The solo bassist Steve Lawson makes his (plentiful) recordings available through the direct-sales intermediary Bandcamp, which allows him to set a price of free, yet gives fans the opportunity to pay as much as they like. He also uses the platform to sell limited-edition, specially designed USB sticks containing his entire collected works for twenty pounds. For some time now, Bandcamp sales have paid his rent. Bandcamp urges musicians using the site to leave the "let fans pay more if they want" option checked, advising them that "fans pay more than the minimum a whopping 40% of the time, driving up the average price paid by nearly 50% (in fact, every day, we see überfans paying $50, $100, $200 for albums priced far lower)."[27] By 2016, fans had paid artists nearly two hundred million dollars through Bandcamp, buying a record every three seconds.[28]

David Lowery has not pursued direct fan funding for music, but he used it for the blog posts he used to write about the stories behind his songs. Beside each article was a tip jar, which netted him around two hundred dollars, sometimes more, per post. If he were the "idealized economically rational person," he tells me, "I would actually not play Sunday through Wednesday and instead write my blog." Wikström argues that tip jars are unlikely to become the norm.[29] Indeed, after giving them a try, YouTube removed them as an official feature in late 2016. However, the potential of direct micropayments outside direct purchasing remains underexplored.

Artists may also encourage fans to participate in promotion and the many tasks of pulling off a career in music today. Fans are great marketers, ever willing to convert their "desire to express themselves through the music" into free publicity.[30] As Lowery put it:

> You actually enlist certain sort of self-appointed fans, basically to do much of the actual work that bands relied on record labels, and publicists, and other professionals to do. You sort of have this informal—like "get the news out on this," "tell your friends about this," "here's the link to buy tickets, pass it around." . . . That was a lot of the work of managers, publicists, record labels, et cetera, did in the past. And now you have this other kind of exchange going on where you're sort of enlisting people that could do work for you.

Rivas, whose artists have audiences in many countries but may not live in well-connected nations themselves, relies on such audience collaborations. Speaking of Cuban artist Silvio Rodriguez, he says: "They don't have these high-speed internet connections to start connecting every day and put posts. They post interviews, but I think they need the fans to be more creative and post information about them. A lot of information you find on the internet are fans' postings, no? And that's the important part of the fans, because the fans are working with you to maintain your life." Rivas also uses the data flows around his artists to identify influential audience members. When he saw that a Rubén Blades fan in Chile had created a Facebook fan page with a hundred thousand followers, he contacted the fan, thanked him for "the wonderful work," and asked him to "be part of us." His organization sent him "albums, tickets, and flowers," and kept him updated on news and events in hopes he would share that information with the fans he had organized.

Fans also provide technical and logistical support, from providing couches to sleep on to website management. Lloyd Cole described how his community has "been a great help" to him. After he shut down his MySpace page,

> I got an email, or notes through my website, from various people saying, "If you'd like, we'll run your MySpace page for you." So they do. I have a guy in Glasgow called Paul who runs my MySpace page, and he puts all my—anything I put on the website to do with concerts, he keeps it all up to date. He uploads the latest songs and things. I basically have a great MySpace page, and I don't do anything. He also actually helps me with Google Maps for the venues when the tours are announced. He puts all the venues on my Google Maps so that I can plan hotels and things.

"That's just a volunteer who just loves you and wants to give back?" I ask.

> Yeah, absolutely. Actually, I've got several volunteers who do various things. I've got this group called the Young Idealists, and they sell CDs for me at concerts and they put up posters in coffee shops and bars and things. And one of them actually is a JavaScript expert. I did nearly all of the coding at my website, but I couldn't make the music player work with Flash, and it turned out to be a JavaScript problem, and another Paul in Glasgow, whose regular gig is a philosophy professor and he's a part-time web designer, he fixed the JavaScript issues for me. So he's another person I'm greatly indebted to.

Singer-songwriter Jill Sobule told me she's "had a couple people that were like fanatic kind of and could be kind of a touch stalky or weird." But then, "I just put them to work and then they stop being weird. And

Figure 4.4. Lloyd Cole, 2012. © Anna Osbat, and made available under a CC BY 2.0 license. https://www.flickr.com/photos/annurca/7005651843.

now some, they're like free employees." "I'm kind of being humorous," she adds, "but it was just you had a feeling like this person was, you know, just passionate, but they're actually a sane kind of person that might have a skill that could help you in exchange for something." One fan designed her web page. Another road-managed her for a few shows. A third translated a song of hers into French for a concert in Paris.

Challenges of Participation

Much as they may seem to promote equality and participation, participatory strategies that rely on fans' sense of gift economics can be threatening to artists. They may think that accepting gifts turns them into beggars or blurs the professional and personal boundaries that should separate them from their audiences. Amanda Palmer describes the fear of seeking fan funding as a concern about "being seen as a burdensome member of the community instead of a productive one," echoing Kelly's concern about being "cheeky" by going back to the fans asking repeatedly for money.[31] Norwegian metal frontman Sindre Solem of Nekromantheon sees fan funding as "kind of begging." He told me: "I've seen some bands say, please preorder and pay now for the exclusive LP, and you will get like, a bonus hat or whatever, signed, and they need the preorders to actually pay for the pressing of the LP. I don't know what I think about that, actually. I wouldn't do it myself. I don't think it's classy." Inviting fans to participate can make you feel too indebted, too powerless relative to audiences. Gifts are often ambivalent.

Participatory strategies that invoke gift economics can also leave musicians with social obligations that would not be there were the transactions clearly bounded by market economics, with terms of exchange explicit. Gift exchanges bind people together socially and even intimately by creating the feeling that having received, you must now give.[32] The artist Sal Randolph argues that "the relational nature of the gift economy is both its strength and its constraint.[33] It both establishes relationship and requires relationship. The market economy works on the principle of even exchange. Every transaction is complete in itself, balanced, leaving the participants free of each other. But while the gift economy is free in terms of money, it is constrained by the qualities and requirements of human social relationships."

The sense of obligation recurs in all of the stories of collaboration artists tell. They will fund you, but you better keep them in the loop after you do. They will market for you, do technical support for you, translate for you, but they may feel you owe them a spot on the guest list, albums, flowers. You are, as Cole put it, "greatly indebted." When gifts are offered as contributions to the group, failing to show appropriate emotion or gratitude can be a kind of "antipayment" with the potential to create hostility.[34] Lowery finds that using fans as free promotional labor is "where it gets weird, because the fans sort of think of it as this friendship, and actually what you're doing is actually kind of not really manipulating them, but you've been using them to get your informa-

Figure 4.5. David Lowery (in straw hat) with Cracker and Camper Van Beethoven at the merchandise table. Photo by Clinton Steeds and made available under a CC BY 2.0 license. https://www.flickr.com/photos/cwsteeds/315621116.

tion, your art, you're using them to promote your band, basically. And sometimes fans think it's more friendship, and it's not, really. And so that's weird and awkward."

For some artists, the dialectic of walking this line between a job that is easier when fans participate and keeping those fans at a distance never stops being challenging. Lloyd Cole, for instance, describes his "incredibly active" fans as "something like a second family, not what I set out to have." When I ask what he set out to have, he answers, "an audience." The process of moving from audience to second family, a move away from control toward participation that feels much more intimate, took Cole "through various levels of uncomfortableness." The relational labor required to maintain it remains both necessary and delicate.

Lowery's solution to this conundrum is to "just kind of be a little more honest about relationships." He encourages fans to participate at the business level but leaves the social worlds of participation to the fans alone: "What I try to do instead of that is to encourage the personal relationship between everybody that are fans, and the fans that are helping you out, and essentially helping you promote your band or whatever like that. To encourage fans to develop friendships among themselves. It becomes a very tightknit strong community if it's done properly, but, do you know what I mean? And that's indeed a reward."

For fans, participating through funding or other assistance may feel exploitative, especially if the artists profit too much or turn on them, but it can also be a means of participating in an art world that matters in their lives. Free labor is not necessarily exploited labor, writes Tiziana Terranova in her foundational article on free digital labor; it is also "willingly conceded in exchange for the pleasures of communication and exchange."[35]

Participation also raises challenges for artistic integrity. For centuries, art has been associated with lone geniuses and "authentic and autonomous subjectivity."[36] In many genres, the "authenticity" audiences prize depends on a belief that the music was created free from market pressures, including listener preferences. Many artists, even the most participatory, thus draw the line at letting audiences participate in the creation of the actual music, a point even made by Amanda Palmer, who spends an entire book extolling the virtues of a participatory communal approach to audience. Some artists will actively invite audience participation in song or album-crafting but still draw a line at composition. Sydney Wayser, for instance, solicited input on which finished songs should go on the album and in what order. "They're the ones that I want to buy the record so I want them to like it. I'm going to take into account everyone's favorite songs and their opinions, but if one person gives me a track list and I really don't think it's the right way to go, I don't have to keep it. So at the end of the day I feel like I still have the creative power of attorney, it's still my project and I can kind of pick what I want."

Jazz singer/guitarist Kate Schutt went further than this when she invited her audience to send her love stories for an album she was writing. "It was a cool thing," she said. "I had incredible conversations with the people, with my fans that submitted things by email." She was shocked by the power of what they sent:

> people submitted the most honest, heart wrenching, beautiful, they were so—I don't even know how to describe it. They were so forthright and so willing to share some very deep, personal moments with me. I was

Figure 4.6. Kate Schutt. ©Kate Schutt and made available under a
CC BY-SA 4.0 license. https://commons.wikimedia.org/wiki/
File:Kate_Schutt_Guitar.jpg.

shocked, and I never thought I would get what I got. You know, beautiful sort of stream of consciousness elegies. The love story could be about anything. It could be about a place, a person, a street, a time period in your life, a person living or dead, famous, not famous, family not family, whatever. And so, I got beautiful first person stream of conscious elegies about somebody's dying grandmother to little scribbled notes about a street corner to, like I said, works of art to love affairs, you know, secret love affairs, to total erotic things that shocked my pants off, anonymously submitted soft porn, basically. I mean, you know, I was shocked. I was totally shocked. It was so cool.

But when it came to composition, could she "take a letter and mark that A and then take a song for the new album and mark that B and draw a straight line between them? No. We can't do that." But

was I in an ongoing conversation with myself and my fans about what makes a great song? Yes. Their letters were the reason I was doing that.

Now, I always have that going on in my head when I'm writing. I mean, I'm critical. I'm a critical reader and thinker about—and so do I always have that going on? Sure, I do. But I had a reason to do it, you know, every week. So do I think it made the songs on *The Telephone Game* what I consider to be my strongest songs yet and my most pers—that most sound like me, where I hit the target of what I'm trying to do more closely, you know, closer to the center? Yes.

Another musician told me that their "artistic vision has to remain independent of what the fans want. We'll listen, but it has to still remain independent." "You have to be true to what you want to do," said another. "You have to make your own music the way it comes out. And if there's an audience, very great. If there isn't, then it's too bad." "I think the only way to be honest with your audience," said Nacho Vegas, "is not giving power to your audience. When I make songs for a new album I try not to—I am in my home alone and I try not to think about this thing of some people saying you are good or you are not. It's my duty, you know, to make songs as if nobody will listen to them. I try to make something in this pure way and songs that come from you but songs that have nothing to do about what people think of it or your audience or something like that."

Straddling Unattainable Ideals

Musicians seeking to make money making music are caught in a relational dialectic between the unrealizable ideals of control and participation. No amount of territorializing, takedown notices, data, or sophisticated algorithms will ever overcome the essential unpredictability and risk of music careers, even when presented in dashboards with easy-to-read interfaces. Audiences are too unruly and empowered to be controlled. Managing and understanding them takes time and skills most people lack. Yet control remains a potent motivation. The fact that we cannot attain perfect control does not mean we can't do it at all. We can put people, things, and ourselves into order and make them subject to coordination. Indeed, we must. Artists, like all of us, need to be able to detach from and objectify others, making Yous into Its as they make sense of their audiences and strategically try to build, maintain, and earn money from them.

Participation too is fraught. It is desirable, yet cannot be fully realized within market systems that rely on the depersonalizing principles of economic exchange. Furthermore, when the ground shifts away from control toward participation, the relational principles on which artists and their audiences operate change too. Audience participation can leave artists who might otherwise welcome it feeling too needy, too intimate for comfort, or as if their artistic autonomy, and hence integrity, has been compromised. The lived experience of the participation/control dialectic is thus one of ambivalence. Every action inherently implicates both participation and control, and often in ways that sit beside one another uneasily. Hersh has found a balance that lets her flourish musically while enhancing her fans' attachments to one another and to her. She remains poor and her commitment to her subscribers leaves her little time off, but she got her religion back. Even when it's successful, balancing this dialectic and finding a power balance between artist and audience that works for both takes effort. The relational labor of managing ambivalence through facilitating, tolerating, enclosing, and limiting audience practices is never done.

PART III

Relationships

5

Platforms

In a *Guardian* profile,[1] Bruce Springsteen described meeting fans at book signings, estimating he'd signed seventeen thousand copies of his autobiography. He assured the reporter he'd enjoyed it: "You meet the fans—but you meet them one by one. And they have an opportunity: what's the one thing you always wanted to say over the 40 years of the relationship we've had? I actually found it quite moving. Always enjoyed that part. I used to love to drift around, bump into people, see what their lives were like, wander into their lives for a few moments then drift back out. It appealed to the transient nature of my personality. I liked the idea of being here and then being gone, this little spirit moving through the world."

Springsteen describes his relationship with his audience as moving and long-standing, but also transient and ephemeral. He is a "spirit," wandering into their lives, then drifting away. Recordings fostered deeply significant emotional attachments, yet always at a distance. To really connect, musicians in the past needed platforms like concerts, fan letters, and brief, often-ritualized, in-person encounters. Norwegian star Sivert Høyem describes himself as "one of the last analog musicians," having started his career at a time when you'd only meet your audience "after the gig or before the gig or in the t-shirt lines or record signing."

Today it's hard to even list all the sites where artists meet their audiences. They still come together at concerts and many other forms of in-person encounters. But musicians also meet audiences on fan sites, their own websites, their blogs. They maintain profiles on Facebook, Twitter, MySpace (less now), Tumblr, Instagram, YouTube, Bandcamp, SoundCloud, Indaba, Snapchat, Line, Twitch, you name it.[2] Some have apps or use bots that interact with fans through instant messaging platforms on their behalf. As the communication ecosystem has grown, new media generally complement concerts, book and record signings, and other modes of direct encounter rather than replace them. Each platform offers options and poses challenges.

"Affordances" are qualities of an object or interface that people perceive as creating possibilities for action, just as a button seems to invite pushing.[3] Whether built of code or wood, platforms make persuasive rhetorical arguments about the kinds of interactions that should take place upon them.[4] Far from neutral, relational affordances, such as those I describe in this chapter, shape interactions, relationships, and the work of maintaining connections. As Arlie Russell Hochschild writes of organizational institutions, the settings in which we interact "guide the way we see and what we are likely to feel spontaneously."[5] Settings shape what Erving Goffman calls the "participation frameworks" of everyday conversation, or the continuously shifting roles people take toward one another and the things they say in their interactions.[6] This chapter compares the three settings for audience encounters that artists mentioned most in our interviews. I compare two settings in the concert hall, the stage and the merchandise table, to online platforms to show how each social setting, online and off, provides relational affordances that influence who is there, who has power relative to whom, and how ritualized their interactions are.

Jennifer Lena reminds us that "it is extremely important to analyze the spaces in which music is experienced because spatial arrangements impact the form and nature of community engagement."[7] Among the arrangements she mentions are "the size of the venue, the amount of distance and interaction between musicians and audience members, and the volume of the music."[8] Christopher Small's classic *Musicking* shows how orchestral halls afford particular kinds of relational dynamics among those present, offering them a chance to announce their identities to themselves, one another, and anyone else who may observe. To attend, people must buy tickets, affirming "the separation of those who produce from those who consume and the impersonal relationship of a society whose dominant mode of relating is through the passing of money." Small argues that the concert hall raises questions that "concern relations of power" among those present, asking, "Who decides what is played and how it is played? Where does the authority of the person in charge come from? Who cedes it to him or her? Such questions involve not only the performers but also the audience and may extend beyond the walls of the concert hall."[9]

Ultimately, Small argues, the concert hall "dramatizes and makes visible certain types of relationships," bringing some people together and keeping others apart, giving some dominance while positioning others as subordinate, and facilitating "communication in one direction but not in the other."[10] To drive home his point, Small invites us to "imagine a performance in which the members of the orchestra sold the tickets themselves, arranged their own seating and moved the piano around and where everyone, audience as well as conductor, soloist and orchestra members, stayed afterward to clean up." The result would not necessarily be a better set of relationships, he argues, but it would reflect and support a social order that saw people as equals and encouraged them to know one another as individuals.[11]

We don't normally think of settings like concert halls as platforms in the same way we think of a site like Facebook as a platform, even if stages are the original, literal "platform."[12] Yet the concert hall, with its inner settings like the stage and the merchandise table, are every bit as influential in shaping the relationships between artists and their audiences as are online platforms. In comparison to the stage and the merchandise table, social media afford a new norm of everyday closeness, removing historic barriers between musicians and audiences, while offering little ritualized guidance for how to behave. While once musicians could show up at a concert hall, where audiences would come to them, social media encourage artists to go to the audiences, seeking them where they already are, doing what they are already doing, and engaging them in ongoing interactions. The relational dynamic shifts as audiences gain equal access to the floor, more topics are raised, and power becomes more evenly spread.

To say that platforms shape interactions and relationships is not to say that they determine them. There are many other influences. People perceive and make sense of affordances, and make choices about how to use platforms based on those perceptions.[13] For one musician, a platform like Facebook may feel natural and easy. For another, the uniformity of its template may feel anonymizing and mechanistic. Groups develop idiosyncratic and social norms about how to use platforms, from the symphonic audiences who expect assigned seating and silence when musicians are on stage[14] to the indie audience members who cluster densely, actively, noisily, even violently, in front of the stage.[15] Individual social media platforms develop their own emergent norms. Facebook may be a "nice" place, at least for male musicians, while YouTube comments are famously mean, and Twitter is known for enabling harassment. The norms of the world outside also shape what happens on any given platform. Platforms arise from and are permeated by existing social dynamics, but as people work out new norms for behavior within the limits they afford, they create new social dynamics that can extend beyond their boundaries. The widely used affordance of posting mobile phone photos on social media, for instance, has reshaped concerts into photography events at which audience members may seem as focused on their phones as on the stage.

Concert Halls

Before recording technologies, all music was "live." Now liveness, once taken for granted, carries meaning of its own. "The live," Philip Auslander writes, "was brought into being by the possibility of technological reproduction."[16] As music took technological forms that freed it from temporal and spatial limits, the time- and place-bound embodiment of "live" encounters became more ritualized and special.[17] "As people don't buy records as much as they used to," the Swedish independent label entrepreneur and musician Johan Angergård told me, "gigs seem to grow more important as a way of connecting to the bands in a bit more physical way. Only listening to mp3s on your computer without ever having seen the band, the artwork, read the lyrics, seen the pictures might be a bit to un-personal for many."

Concert events create bases and boundaries for relationships between artists and audiences before anyone shows up for the event. Audiences gain access through buying tickets, which, as Small describes it, frames the relationship as that between a producer and customers. Furthermore, at least some, and probably most, of the people who buy tickets are fans, or at least people willing to give musicians the benefit of the doubt for an evening. This too positions audience members as different from the performer, while positioning them as similar to one another. Time is important too. Concerts put temporal boundaries around the relationships they create. They are events in which musicians and audiences spend a few hours together, perhaps less, then part. Fans may follow bands on tour, and musicians and audience members may also be friends, but from the event's point of view, once the lights come up there is no further relational obligation, no promise of continuity. Concerts are designed to foster a powerful ephemeral sense of connection, not a foundation for ongoing person-to-person relationships between musicians and those in attendance. Within a venue, different spaces afford different relational possibilities. Two of these, the stage and the merchandise table, are central to musicians' relationships with their audiences and illustrate well how different platforms give rise to different relational possibilities.

The Stage

Stages, and the seating or standing room before them, tightly constrain the roles and behaviors available to those in attendance. Stages are built for "presentational" performances,[18] which cast performers as elites before a larger group of people in the collective role of audience. Before a show, in most concert venues, musicians are kept backstage and out of sight, taking advantage of an architectural affordance that not only offers little social contact between them and their audiences but, like the hall as a whole, "seems, in fact[,] designed expressly to keep them apart."[19] "We don't really meet people face-to-face anymore," Mogwai's Stuart Braithwaite said, "because the places we play all have dressing rooms behind the stage so we don't really get out among the people."

Once on stage, the architecture and other infrastructures and technologies of the event put musicians in charge of audiences who observe. "There is no bigger difference than being in the audience and looking up at the stage and being on the stage looking at the audience," a musician told Wendy Fonarow.[20] Only the musicians pick what comes next. Only they have the elevation, amplification, lighting, and infrastructural support to speak loudly and command all the attention. The space is designed so audiences face the stage, most explicitly when there are rows of seating affixed to the floor, but even when there is open space for standing or dancing. At larger shows the audience and stage are separated not just by architecture but by security personnel—what Brian Travers of UB40 described as "an electrified fence with crocodiles in front of the stage."

Musicians hold the floor—indeed they are obligated to do so—while audiences cede it. To earn this right, musicians are expected to perform in their "musical personas" lest they seem self-indulgent.[21] Performers are, after all, at work, while the audience is at play, further instantiating the division between them.[22] The musicians' job is to make music. They may engage in some between-song banter, although they can also get away with none, as Bob Dylan famously does, or with lines clichéd enough to rival athlete interviews: HELLO BOSTON! ARE YOU READY TO ROCK? HOW YOU ALL DOING TONIGHT? THIS ONE'S FOR THE LADIES! Though their communicative repertoires are limited, they're limited in ways that put the focus on the modes of communication they've chosen, including, most of all, music.

Those on stage often experience it as a seat of power, whether they think they are deserving or not. The Rolling Stones' Keith Richards explained the way his audiences react to them on stage as evidence that humans need demigods. "In lieu of finding out what that greater power is," he told Jenny Boyd, "people set up their own earthly version of it in order to express it. I stand on the stage and I'm thinking, what are you looking at me for? A damn old junkie hacking away at the guitar, what is this? This must be a primal need."[23] Frank Foster, who led Count Basie's Orchestra, described himself as "hypnotizing" the audience from the stage, looking at someone in the center of the auditorium. "I can't see their face clearly, but I look directly at them while I'm playing, and I am actually hypnotizing that person," he told Boyd, "I'm aware of some kind of movement, something is vibrating when I look directly at someone, and I imagine this to be some kind of power coming from or through me. It's concentrated on that one point where that individual is then it vibrates; it spreads from that one point, and it's somewhat the same as a pebble being dropped in a lake. It expands outwards. It expands through the auditorium and spreads to everyone out there."[24] Peter Frampton likewise told Boyd, "It starts to become a sort of emotional feedback. I become totally uninhibited onstage. People in the audience are reacting to my actions and my mood as well as the music. I know that I can control the feeling in the audience."[25]

The stage's affordance of focusing attention on the musicians fosters a power differential, but can also prompt a transcendent sense of togetherness. "I always felt connected to the audience," the Cure's Roger

O'Donnell swore; "it doesn't really matter to me if there's fifty people or fifty thousand." The experience of connection between "performers and listeners may be close, intimate, and even loving [as] the back-and-forth passing of energy from performers to listeners and back again can carry the musicking to a tremendous pitch of excitement that can approach and even cross the threshold of possession."[26] One of my favorite concert moments came at a Feelies show, a band whose concerts consistently bring me bliss. This night, during a lull between songs, a fan near me took advantage of the quiet to yell "You make people happy!" The band grinned as the crowd all laughed with self-recognition. We were focused, together, and we were, indeed, happy.

Audiences willingly cede the floor, in return for which they get not only the music, but also "the right to examine the speaker directly, with an openness that might be offensive in conversation."[27] Sexualized gaze, sometimes demanded, sometimes unwanted, is often a given. "Sexual/romantic appeal and fantasy are one of the great draws for music audiences," writes Turino. "While it is often considered impolite to stare at attractive members of the opposite sex, there is special license to do so when they are on stage."[28] Turino doesn't say it, but there is even more license to stare at members of your own sex when they are on stage. Writes Fonarow:

> The gig is one of the few Western spectacles in which female (rather than male) spectatorship is fetishized—overvalued and expressed. . . . By locating sexual desire in the female spectator, the rock performance inverts the traditional Western object of erotica from the female to the male. Here both men and women gaze upon men, and men are recognized to be the libidinal objects. Bono, the lead singer of the band U2, once said: "Being a rock 'n' roll star is like having a sex change. People treat you like a girl—they stare at you and follow you down the street."[29]

The concert is one event where both men and women can freely examine others' bodies.

Yet, even as the stage empowers musicians, its affordance of immediate visual and auditory audience feedback undermines the artists' dominance. The very frame of "performance" means that audiences have the right to evaluate how well you do.[30] There is a reason most of the few scholarly articles I could find about musicians' interaction with audiences focused on overcoming stage fright. The lights may be bright and performers may "use a variety of gaze strategies during performances to suggest that they do not see audience members,"[31] but generally musicians are keenly aware of individuals in the crowd. As one told Fonarow, "I could tell you everything you did during the show and you'd never know I was paying attention."[32] An audience's feedback is crucial to musicians' experience and to the relationships people construct during a show. "We're not in a band to make records," Wilco's Jeff Tweedy told Greg Kot. "We're in a band because we like to play together, and feel good about doing it, and have people respond to that in a way that is immediate and unfiltered."[33] Audiences may respond with adoration. Like Beatles fans, they may "sob uncontrollably while screaming 'I'm gonna die, I'm gonna die.'"[34] More likely, if they like you, they smile or clap, dance or sway. Some may hold signs. But audiences can also be antagonistic and disrespectful, challenging the authority inscribed by the setting. While some musicians feel empowered on stage, others interpret the dynamic differently, seeing power as located in audiences.

Live performances are sites where musicians can resolve the "anxieties about the significance and effect of their work," as discussed in the first chapter.[35] But live audiences can also stoke those anxieties, sometimes simultaneously. "The feeling I get when I'm playing to an audience," Buddy Guy told Boyd, "is 'Am I reaching you?' 'Am I getting to those people through communication with my music?' And I look out and I see a smile. Something tells me then, you've got it. But there are also days I don't get that smile. My message is not getting to you, so I've got to go back and figure how to get my message to you through my music—and that's what keeps me going with my music."[36]

The tension is exacerbated when you don't fit the mold audiences expect in your genre. David Grazian described the frustration white blues musicians felt performing before white audiences who aggressively "threaten their authenticity and self-respect."[37] Honeychild Coleman is a black woman whose bands play the predominantly white, male genres of punk and shoegaze. She's played festivals "where people were angry or annoyed or condescending because they didn't like the instrumentation of my band. They thought I was gonna get up here and go *shoo-bee-doobie-doo-woo-woo-woo*, and do an R&B song even though I'm

Figure 5.1. Honeychild Coleman. © istolethetv, and made available under a CC BY 2.0 license https://www.flickr.com/photos/istolethetv/2726296565.

wearing a RAF t-shirt and a leather skirt. But then nobody left. I was like, 'Yeah, they were holding their ears, but you notice nobody left.' So that's how I knew they were listening, and it just made me smile as soon as I saw it."

Despite the limited behavioral repertoires available to them while musicians are playing, like the happy Feelies fan, audiences have many ways of validating artists during a show. They yell between songs, they smile, they dance, they sing along, they stay. O'Donnell has his eye on the crowd and listens to them intently no matter how big the arena. "Whenever they're singing along, that's good," he told me, "and you can

Figure 5.2. Roger O'Donnell (right) of the Cure, in concert in Boise, Idaho, 2016. © Ken Wilcox, and made available under a CC BY-ND 2.0 license. https://www.flickr.com/photos/kenwilcox/27860225320.

tell if there's a couple and you play their special song and they turn to each other, those kind of things are nice. It's that sort of feedback from the audience that I think is really rewarding."

Audiences also engage in behaviors that challenge musicians' right to the floor, upsetting what they understand to be the tacit relational agreements guiding these encounters. O'Donnell complained of being distracted and annoyed when people move from their ticketed seats to new ones, particularly when security has to intervene. People who talk while they're playing bother him as well. "Save some money and save everyone a lot of pain, because it's just very disrespectful." Many venues derive most of their income from alcohol sales. This affords drunkenness, which can foster audience antagonism. For a time, people up front used to aim laser pointers at David Lowery's bands while he played. He began carrying his own so he could stop the performance on the spot and point back. In larger venues, audiences may throw bottles, something Casey Rain, whose Desi band, Swami, has been "bottled," described as "pretty funny but at the same time kind of upsetting."

For some, especially women, drunk audiences can be frightening. Kristin Hersh described the disappointment of finding that audiences for her noisy band 50FootWave attracted "this kind of frat boy element" that "get[s] really drunk." They "don't know the difference between smart music and loud music and those guys can be difficult for me. And so my [male] bass player now scouts out exits as soon as we get on stage so that I don't have to go through the crowd if there's a thuggy element. . . . It's just hard for me to deal with people like that. I should take karate or something."

Which audience members engage in which behaviors is influenced by the layout of most unseated venues. As Wendy Fonarow insightfully describes in her ethnography of British indie audiences, in unseated venues audiences self-organize into three zones.[38] Zone 1 is closest to the stage. These spots cost more, either in money or sweat equity and possible physical harm. The people there are demonstrating their interest by being where they are and are the audience segment most likely to be most enthusiastically engaged with the show. Fans who have seen multiple shows are probably up front, so there may be familiar faces for those on stage to look out upon. Increasingly, though, Zone 1 is filled not with enthusiastic faces, but with phones. Just as it can send messages of disengagement when among friends, looking at screens instead of stages can alienate performers. "Now photographers at shows click and then look at the screen and they miss everything that happens on the stage," Lowery's Camper Van Beethoven bandmate Jonathan Segal sighs; "that's completely weird addictive behavior." As we saw in the last chapter, in addition to the problems posed by the presence of the phones themselves, the fact that everyone in the crowd can then post their photos and videos online invites nonpresent participants into the occasion, often without musicians' consent and sometimes against their express wishes.

In Zone 2, around the borders of Zone 1, are people who are older, have seen more shows, or are just less interested. Their response is physically muted, although they may be contemplating the performance deeply. While people in Zone 1 are generally enthusiasts, it can be harder for musicians to assess where they stand relative to those in Zone 2. I was at a sold-out show in a club that holds a thousand people where there is both a main floor and a balcony level wrapping around the side walls and back of the venue. The crowd up front swelled with people close together dancing, clapping, and singing along. I stood in the side

Figure 5.3. Brian Travers. © Patrick Gaudin, and made available under a CC BY 2.0 license https://www.flickr.com/photos/voyages-provence/19978051399.

balcony so I wouldn't have to look at the middle of someone's back and would be free from pushing and jostling. That was not how the band's young frontman interpreted it. "I'm going to need more from you," he pleaded. "Even you important people up there," he said, gesturing toward our part of the venue, "You're intimidating. You're so nonchalant that you're at a concert."

It took Brian Travers twenty years of touring not to see what this frontman did. "There can be twenty thousand, thirty thousand people going crazy and dancing, and I'd see the one guy or the one girl who's doing this" he told me, crossing his arms. "And that's the only person I could see. And I would be looking at them all night, thinking 'oh what have we done wrong' and pointing the saxophone at them and trying to talk to them." Travers' epiphany came when he was in the audience at a Smiths show. He was listening intently to Johnny Marr's guitar playing when he looked down at his own body and realized he was that one guy. "I don't think I've jumped up and down at a gig since I was about seventeen or eighteen. I always stand there and go 'Wow, listen to him. Listen to her, isn't she good.' So even with all that experience, you know, we must have done, two thousand, three thousand gigs in twenty years. Even then, I didn't see it."

People who lose interest often wander to the back of the venue to Zone 3. This zone is filled with music professionals who don't have to pay to get in and are keen to distinguish themselves from those in Zones 1 and 2. These audience members don't need the affordance of the concert to build a relationship with the musicians, either because they don't care, or because they have "privileged access to the ultimate status markers, the performers themselves," before or after the concert.[39]

The relational power balance that stages seem to afford are thus not as simple as their architecture suggests. Within inflexible roles and tightly constrained behavioral repertoires, audiences have many ways to challenge musicians' apparent supremacy. Travers cautions his peers against misunderstanding the encounter:

You're there for them. They're not there for you. You're there for them. This gets confused, I think, and people lose the essence of what their gig's about. And the music suffers as a result, and the performance suffers. You've got to listen to the audience, and listening to them is looking at them in the eye, looking square at them. Music is the communication between the musician and a member of the audience and, more importantly, the member of the audience and the musician. What comes back, not just what you're putting out. It's what they're happy for you to play. That's another kind of complicated part of the relationship. It's not just giving them what they want. It's them letting you give them what they want. They give you permission to be what you're going to be onstage, because they don't have to clap. They don't have to clap. The audience gives you permission to be what you are onstage. You might think you're in control. That's not the case at all. You walk onstage and hopefully communicate with them, touch down with them and surrender basically, and then put them in charge. Because they are in charge, not you. And if you forget, the second you forget that, they can tell you're not listening to them. And you think the audience is there to listen to you. No. You're onstage to listen to them and to play to them, and that's the job.

Like Travers, musicians may reject the relational power dynamic the concert setting seems to afford through interpretation. Others may go so far as to avoid stages entirely. Electronic Dance Music performances, which (at least until recently) "relentlessly" seek moments of shared collective experience, often place DJs on the floor amid the dancers.[40] "I love music with people up front," the DJ Deepchild told me, "but I like the music that I do because it does feel more like people are dancing for each other rather than the person up front." Steve Lawson, the ambient solo bass player, plays primarily small house concerts, which "feels far more productive to me as a human being than me standing on a stage with a bunch of lights shining around playing to a bunch of people I can't even see who are all kind of varying degrees of enjoying it or worrying about something."

Musicians may also reject or play with the stage's implicit relational dynamics through media. Electronica artist Richie Hawtin delights in designing new technologies to disrupt the stage's power balance. For one tour he and his friends developed an iPhone app called Synk. During the concert, the app allowed him to instantaneously unlock the phones of everyone there who had it installed. Surprised audience members started seeing words moving around on their mobile screens. As they touched those words, moving them around and zooming in and out, they gradually realized their actions were affecting the sound around them. "At that moment," Hawtin said triumphantly, "I stop being the performer, they're performing."

The Merchandise Table

In small venues, immediately after a performance, artists often go to a table, usually toward the front of the venue, where exiting audiences will pass. An array of merchandise like CDs, t-shirts, posters, and stickers is displayed on top of the tables and often on a wall behind. People traveling with the artists or working for the venue sit behind the tables to manage sales while audiences line up to buy. From the stage, Jill Sobule pressures audiences to stop by and spend some money with humor. "I always end my last song with, 'I'll be out in the lobby selling my ware' and 'I have four children with no healthcare,' you know, I just make up something. It's always been that way. I always feel like a traveling salesman." Musicians like Sobule often stand behind or near the table to sign what audiences have bought and, sometimes with annoyance and sometimes with pleasure, pose for fan selfies.

The merchandise table offers very different relational affordances than the stage. It is the one institutionalized platform in the concert hall where the separation of artists and audience is breached.[41] Where the concert was about one-way communication from the stage outward, the merchandise table is about one-to-one interaction. The audience is no longer one large group with a few standout faces or irritants, but a series of individuals like those at Springsteen's book signings, each with as much access to the floor as the musician and the chance to finally tell them in person what they've always wanted to say. When audience members wait in line and interact personally, they become stand-ins for the crowd as a whole, translating "the feelings of excitement and connection that the audience has during the performance back to the performers."[42]

Interactions at the table, like those during the concert, are often highly ritualized ("Will you sign this?" "Sure, what's your name?" "Nancy." "Here you go"). Fans often touch the performer, more so than they would have before a show, which Fonarow takes as a sign that musicians have accomplished "the illusion of the effacement of barriers between audience and performer" during the concert.[43] Musicians sign autographs, pose for pictures, hug fans, listen to their stories. For British folk-punk singer Billy Bragg, these conversations can last longer than the shows. "It can get a bit crazy sometimes. But you get a look in their eyes, you get to feel up close and personal, what it means to them, how they feel about me and my music. I wouldn't miss it for the world. That's the most important bit to me, of all the communication I have with people who like my music. It's that after-show connection."

I ask him if the after-show connection is more important than the performance itself. "On stage it's a different thing," he responds, "you're in control and you're taking them with you. You're looking out for them and you're picking up on them." He continued:

> But once you're down from the stage, you're on their level and look them in the eye in that small individual connection. Then you're in their control. When you're on stage, they're in your control. You're in charge.

You're setting the agenda and you're deciding what is going to happen next. When you're the one doing the t-shirts, each one of them decides what's going to happen next. You don't know what's going to happen next, you're responding to them, rather than them responding to you; it's a reversal. And that's when I start to pick stuff up and learn stuff and find stuff out and make mental notes. That's quite important.

Standing on the same floor both literally and conversationally, with no special lighting or amplification, musicians are brought down to their audiences' size.

Jon Ginoli, of the celebratory gay punk band Pansy Division (and the formative college radio show of my adolescence discussed in chapter 3), also appreciated this leveling, for reasons both activist and carnal. "Our music has always been about trying to break down boundaries and break down barriers so I wanted to do that personally as well," he told me. "I want to hear other peoples' stories. Especially people who were much younger than me who, were it not for my band, I really wouldn't have much contact with. So to be able to see what the next generation is going through, what their issues and crises are. And also, and I have to say this, it would be sometimes fun to meet people who I might sleep with."

These same affordances that Bragg and Ginoli appreciate—being on the same level, looking one another in the eye, touching, and telling personal stories—are hard for musicians who feel most comfortable communicating through music. Some may not feel the closeness their show has instilled in some members of their audience. They may not want to be touched. They may not yearn to hear stories, particularly when they become repetitive. "It's always like 'oh, what were you thinking when you did this?'" said one drummer, "or 'my cousin's boyfriend's stepmom's roommate's lover saw you guys here and you give a stick to him, don't you remember that?' And it's like 'no.'" Musicians may not feel like fending off sexual advances. "This sounds so stupid coming from the school of kind of punk rock that I grew up with," fun's touring bassist Nate Harold confesses, "but it gets annoying and overwhelming. I'm tired of taking pictures with people I don't know and having people make weird comments to you and signing shirts and stuff like that. Sometimes girls can be a little forward. That aspect of music has never appealed to me and it always weirds me out. That's usually when I make my exit."

Musicians may even feel trapped. Lloyd Cole is content with applause. "Knowing that the concert was extremely enjoyable for the people, does validate things for me," he says. But he knows that he will make more money if he goes out and interacts with his fans at the merchandise table. "Frankly, it's economics, and I try to be as courteous as I can in selling my CDs." He misses the early days of his career when you could

> maybe, if you were lucky, meet somebody in the street and get them to autograph a piece of paper when they were leaving a concert. But there was no way you could be standing next to somebody after a concert with them signing your CD and engaging them in conversation. Especially when you're drunk, which—that's the thing when I go out and sign CDs afterwards. Every now and again I get cornered by a drunk fan, and what can I do? I'm standing there and I'm just sort of nodding my head going, "Okay. This is how I make a living."

Being cornered by drunks is not the worst of it. In 2016, singer Christina Grimmie was murdered at the merchandise table at her gig in Orlando, Florida. "I get threats constantly—all female musicians do," the musician Grimes told the *Fader*. "People want to, like, rape and kill you. It's, like, part of the job. One time I was backstage at a show, and there was this random guy in my dressing room, and he just grabbed me and started making out with me, and I was like, Ah!, and pushed him off. Then he went, 'Ha! I kiss-raped you' and left. Shit like that happens quasi-frequently. When I play a show I have to have, like, three bodyguards in front of the stage, and then I have to have bodyguards on the side."[44] Hersh's suggestion that she learn a martial art is not hyperbole. The affordance of co-presence can be validating, but they can also be alienating, scary, and even lethal.

Social Media

Like concert halls, social media sites are built environments, designed to foster some social practices and discourage others. Unlike brick and mortar institutions, they are constantly changing, as are the devices through which we access them. At the time I spoke with them, the musicians I interviewed used a variety of sites, but there were three that everyone either used or felt compelled to account for not using: MySpace, Facebook, and Twitter. Today that list would likely include Instagram and Snapchat. By the time you read this, there will probably be others. MySpace, launched in 2002 with tight ties to the Los Angeles music scene, embedded music players in everyone's profiles, let musicians and fans "friend," post messages to profiles, and direct message one another. The impact for bands with established audiences was huge. "When MySpace became popular and people could write straight to a band," reflected Stuart Braithwaite of Mogwai,

> I think that was a point—I think a lot of people had never considered that you could just email a band. So when that first started we got a lot of correspondence through MySpace from people I don't think would have considered sending us an email. I mean I remember one guy, an American soldier guy in Iraq, sending an email about how he'd listen to our music to kind of try and you know escape from his dreadful day to day existence. And I can't see that guy having written us an email. So yeah that was definitely sort of a bump thing.

MySpace was like the merchandise table writ large, but without the merchandise. The site had fallen from favor by the time I started interviewing, but its influence on social networking sites and expectations of how professionals might use them cannot be understated. Facebook and Twitter were the platforms all the artists I spoke with thought of as most important.

The three sites share many features—there are profile pages for individuals and/or bands. Their network structure makes ongoing and visible links between musicians and individual audience members possible. They all label connections and responses, though they do so differently. Each platform offers multiple modes of interacting. All allow people to post updates, which are aggregated into personalized feeds for each user. All allow some form of one-to-one communication as well as both public and private interaction. All offer validated "official" accounts for musicians, although that does not always work as it should. All provide some visible metrics of popularity—how many "friends," how many "followers," how many "fans." However, in a crucial difference, MySpace's embedded music player let artists communicate primarily through their music if they chose. Facebook and Twitter, in contrast, encourage artists to interact through words, images, and videos, but make it hard to foreground the centrality of sound in their relationships with audiences.

Unbinding Participation

Concert halls limit and constrain the norms and forms of communication, as well as the relational dynamics among those there. Social media unbind them, opening an array of relational possibilities while imposing constraints of their own. Many social platforms explicitly label the connections they enable. On Twitter, "followers" "follow" artists who can choose whether or not to follow back. Relationships can be asymmetrical. Musicians may follow potential fans as a way to draw their attention. The power is in each person's hands to make a relationship symmetrical or not. On Facebook, "fans" "like" musicians' pages. The relationships afforded by fan pages are even more asymmetrical than Twitter's, since artists have no mechanism for following fans back. When people's privacy settings are locked down, they can't even learn much about who the fans are by looking at their profiles.

Facebook does let musicians be "friends" with fans if the connection is managed through a personal profile. This can cause complications. Jill Sobule, for example, would prefer that all her fans be "friends" on Facebook, but the company made a design decision that people can only sustain five thousand friendships and put a cap there. Having surpassed the limit, every couple of weeks Sobule turns on the TV, logs on, and rejects friend requests, apologizing as she asks people to be fans instead. This means that for every person she meets in any capacity and would like to be friends with on the site, she would need to "unfriend" someone whose connection she valued less. Another musician accepted friend requests from fans before Facebook created fan pages. Now he'd like to move those people out of his personal feed and over to his official page, but he can't envision a polite way to do it.

Concert halls create boundaries for relationships in part by limiting entry to those willing to pay, thus creating a commodified focus as well as a social foundation of audience commonality and musician superiority. In contrast, musicians' social media profiles are generally public, making them accessible to anyone who uses the platform. This doesn't mean the relationships are unencumbered by capitalism. Having a social media presence is often seen as a means of monetizing audiences. Furthermore, much as venues monetized the artist-audience relationship by selling alcohol, social media platforms monetize the relationship by selling ads.

Unlike the concert hall, though, with very few exceptions, social media platforms do not provide audiences with direct ways to transfer money to artists. You can talk to a band directly on Facebook or Twitter, but try paying them there. With exceptions such as YouTube and Twitch, most sites that offer a monetization option link to other platforms or, more often, ignore whether musicians can make money through the site. Even tip jars are rare. From the platform's perspective, so long as musicians and audiences are there, it really doesn't matter. The way audiences pay on social media, if they pay at all, is with attention and the currencies of likes, favorites, retweets, and other visible displays of popularity, all of which accrue to both the artists and the platform, but none of which pay rent or cover recording costs. The money in social media flows between sites' owners, investors, and advertisers, not musicians and audiences. The business models of all social media sites rely on "manipulating and monetizing social data," something for which "people making connections and constructing communities is a necessary pretext."[45]

Audiences on social media include some of the people who show up at concerts, but also many others. A social media account may reach fans, friends, family, peers, other music professionals, people who don't know the artist or like the music but like the tweets, as well as people who hate the music or artist and take pleasure in being mean to them online. These platforms thus complicate the notion that musicians have a singular audience and raises questions about what counts as an "audience" in the first place. On social media, musicians have "to negotiate a complicated social environment where fans, famous people, and intermediaries such as gossip columnists co-exist. These multiple audiences complicate self-presentation, since people present identity differently based on context."[46] Think of Zoë Keating, an instrumental, new-classical solo cellist with more than a million followers on Twitter. She has nowhere near as many listeners, let alone people who would pay for a ticket to see her play or purchase her music. She's "certainly under no illusions" they are all fans. She also knows that the people who follow her on each platform are different from one another. And it's not clear how any of them map on to who exactly buys her album or shows up to see her live, although some of them certainly do. How is she to know what a million plus people who don't even listen to her music expect from her as a tweeter? Which self is she to put forth?

Audiences may also be missing on social media sites. Høyem is one of Norway's most popular musicians. Yet when we spoke, he had fewer than a thousand Twitter followers. As I write, it is up to nearly twelve thousand, still far fewer than either his Facebook following or his actual fan base. A simple explanation is that not many Norwegians use Twitter. With one out of every seven people on earth now using Facebook on any given day, listeners are more likely to be found there. As Steve Lawson pointed out, "there are a whole lot of people who treat the entire internet like Facebook. And they very rarely go outside of it." Yet some fans may not even use Facebook, and those who do may never click "like."

Goffman describes conversationalists as sorting one another into different categories of listeners through their microactions, creating "participation frameworks" that orient participants toward one another and toward what is being said.[47] Some listeners—like those at a live concert or facing you at the merchandise table, are "ratified," meant to hear the message. "Addressed" recipients are ratified listeners who have the right, and may be expected, to respond. Bystanders, like venue staff and other people waiting in the merchandise line, are ratified. Speakers know they are there, but it is socially inappropriate for them to reply to what's said. On social media, anyone following an account is ratified, although specific recipients can be addressed by name, making the others into bystanders. Nonratified recipients—those who listen while pretending they don't—are what Goffman calls eavesdroppers. People who watch and listen to unauthorized concert recordings and livestreams or look at photos posted online might be considered eavesdroppers on those events. Social media eavesdroppers include people who read without logging in or following and, crucially, automated bots that mine public content for reuse elsewhere. Just as they complicate the general definitions and distinctions of "audience," social media make it extremely hard to know on a moment-to-moment basis who exactly is standing by, who is eavesdropping, and whether the people you are addressing are even going to see your message.

On a site like Facebook, which filters people's feeds algorithmically, messages musicians post for those who have liked their page may never appear in those people's feeds. The algorithms are currently weighted toward "friends" and against "pages," putting musicians at a structural disadvantage in reaching their fans. "Organic reach" is very low. Inorganic reach, the kind you pay for, can be better.[48] Messages posted to social media can also be replicated and spread to audiences other than followers. This is great for publicity purposes, but also means that even as intended recipients may not hear you, unratified audiences may. It can be easy to forget these other audiences. Roger O'Donnell, for example, described "the trouble with Twitter" as "being at the pub, and a subject comes up, and you're standing there with three or four mates, and you're just like, 'oh, blah, blah, blah.' And then you realize there's hundreds of people reading it, and also it comes up in Google." Musicians, like most of us, simply can't imagine all their potential readers every time they post, let alone craft messages that serve them all equally well.[49]

Musicians also take advantage of the presence of eavesdroppers and bystanders. Twitter and Facebook are, as van Dijck argues, ideal for advertising the self. Metrics such as follower counts signal your popularity, and hence your revenue potential, to professionals making decisions about whom to sign to a label or book in a venue.[50] Using simple metrics like follower counts or retweets to make this kind of judgment is naïve, as I've discussed elsewhere.[51] Platform algorithms tend to amplify attention rather than distribute it evenly, simultaneously noticing and creating trends. "Friending, liking, following, trending and favoriting are all subject to their respective site's engineering mechanisms of filtering, selecting, and promoting certain users and content over others," writes van Dijck.[52] Metrics can also be bought. What exactly they measure is ambiguous at best. Nonetheless, their existence and visibility affords social hierarchies based on whose numbers are higher. On Twitter, for instance, "the ability to attract and command attention becomes a status symbol."[53] It doesn't happen to Beyoncé, but normal musicians may have followers with more followers than they have. Fans who might appear to be one of the crowd in an auditorium may thus come across as influential and powerful on social media.

Even as social media blur boundaries between audiences and calls into question whether there is really "an" audience at all, like the merchandise table, the voice they afford audience members can make fans more individualized and real for musicians. Social media sites may feel to some like they reduce people to avatars and cookie-cutter profiles with privacy settings musicians cannot penetrate, but they can also foster the possibility of getting to see, and even know, audience members. This can change artists' perceptions of and relationships with their live audiences. Coleman described her surprise at looking through her Facebook fans and discovering that despite her own perceptions, she didn't already know them all. Ska musician Chris Murray uses his Facebook page to connect names to the faces he sees repeatedly in Zone 1, relying on the site's insistence on a real-names policy, and its emergent norm of using pictures of one's self for avatars. "I have a page on Facebook where there are over 4,000 people," he told me: "I'll see somebody at a show a few times. I'll start to recognize, 'Oh, here's somebody who's coming to shows, becoming a regular,' and then I see their face on Facebook with their name and that really helps me out because it's like, 'Oh, there's that person. Oh, this is their name.' I forgot it the three times I met them in person, but, if they start liking stuff that I'm posting and I see their name and face repeatedly, that helps me out. So, definitely, it strengthens my connection."

If social media blur the participant frameworks that sort listeners into different types of audiences, they also obfuscates what Goffman calls the "production formats" that make clear who is speaking on behalf of whom.[54] Unlike the concert venue, artists can make choices about whether they need to be the ones "authoring" and "animating" their own messages while still appearing to be present and engaged. If you have ever seen a famous person walking down the street or eating in a restaurant somewhere, you know that in face-to-face situations they cannot escape their public personas. On social media, the person who appears to be the musician online may be their manager, an intern in the management office, someone else entirely, or even a bot trained to speak on their behalf. Unless messages are written in third person (as they often are) or signed with something like "Team Greta" (as Emily White's staff does when posting on behalf of Greta Morgan), it can be hard for audiences to know.

Artists with resources often do have staff who handle all or some of their social media. "Having people help update concert dates or things like that that don't have a huge amount of personality in them is very helpful," says D. A. Wallach. But when it comes to messages with personality, he, like many others, insists it come from him. "I just feel pretty strongly about writing those myself, because if you're going to send an email out to fifty thousand people, it's pretty important that it's exactly on message and in the right voice." A manager I know told me how much he enjoys responding as one of his artists. In his view, fans were thrilled to get a response they thought came straight from the musician, the musician was thrilled someone else dealt with it, and he got the thrill of being able to make people happy so easily with just one tweet. Other managers, and some artists, think that's unethical. In an in-between position are stars like Beyoncé, Usher, Taylor Swift, and Mariah Carey who, even as they work with digital strategists, have at least a role in approving all the messages that go out as their own.[55] This can provide a good strategy for finding the middle ground between closeness and distance on which the next chapter will focus.

People unaffiliated with the artists also pretend to be them or, often in acts of fandom but sometimes with nefarious intent, appropriate their names. Social media companies' verification process, which uses blue checkmarks to affirm that accounts really do belong to the person whose name is on it, only go partway toward mitigating this problem. Cowboy Junkies were unable to claim the @cowboyjunkies Twitter handle, for example, having to settle for the verified but nonintuitive @CJmusic. Their Twitter bio reads "The OFFICIAL Cowboy Junkies Twitter feed. Someone took our name." Høyem was never able to get verified on MySpace since a major record label that did not represent him claimed his name first. When it first began verifying accounts, Facebook went through a sweep of musician pages in which they judged many real accounts to be fake and replaced what musicians and their audiences had built together with imported versions of artists' Wikipedia pages. (Amusingly, but indicative of the challenges, when I tried to claim the Facebook page that had been created from importing the Wikipedia page about me,

Facebook replied vaguely and without recourse that I did "not meet the criteria" to claim the Nancy Baym page.) Audiences may also do their own verification. Having been in public places like city streets and restaurants with Michael Stipe and seeing how impossible it was for him to escape his persona, it was more than a little entertaining to see "stipey" grilled when he first appeared in online groups where R.E.M. was being discussed in the 1990s.

Social media architectures thus afford musicians choices about which participation frameworks to invoke. They can treat listeners in different ways, using social media like a stage, broadcasting to all without having to listen to what their audiences post or respond. Musicians can also share the floor with audience members, using social media to interact one-on-one and in group discussions. Ceding the floor or hiding their presence entirely, eavesdropping or bystanding, are also choices. This flexible participant structure offers musicians what Stephen Mason described as "a more controlled conversation" than real-time face-to-face encounters. At the same time, just as having to address too many audiences at once can be overwhelming, since everyone else has equal access to the floor, for those who pay attention, the incoming flow of messages can quickly become overwhelming.

Social media lessen the limits imposed on participation by concert halls, creating more malleability in who can address and listen to whom, and granting audiences as much access to the floor as musicians. Social media also lessen the temporal and spatial participatory limits afforded by platforms like those in the concert hall. Log on any time, wherever you are. There will be messages from and chances for artists and audiences to interact. Social media thus encourage relationships grounded in the everyday and the all day. Audiences go to concerts for a ritualized special event. On social media, artists go to the audiences, "sneaking into their daily routine," as Morgan described it. The relationships social media afford are not about one intense encounter but the open-ended accumulations of message exchanges over time that come to feel like relationship. The opportunity to speak to the audience directly, wherever they may be, whenever you like, is a powerful way to sidestep the gatekeepers of both concert venues and the media. But it also poses challenges. When you can post any time at all, how little is too little? How often is too often? No sooner had one musician gotten into "a rhythm of just constantly putting a little mark in the sand," posting daily to Facebook, than others began telling him "you're just always in my stream, you have to cut down." How is one to judge? And what is one to do when the expectations themselves are constantly evolving?

This question of how often to post is further complicated by site architectures. Frequent posting may let you hit enough feeds to get the likes, comments, and shares that can teach filtering algorithms that your messages are interesting. Sindre Solem, of Norwegian metal band Nekromantheon, described the importance of continuous posting: "It's important to stay active, show that you're alive, and every time I post something like that, you can see that you're getting more likes every time, because it reaches out to more and more people, because people who didn't like you before can see if their friends have pressed Like, or commented on what you posted. So it's a slow but safe way of building your reputation and showing that you're still alive. And perhaps it gets people to check out your music." On Twitter, the messages are so short and frequent, the feed so fast moving, that most users who follow hundreds of people never scroll down far enough to catch every message. Posting often can help mitigate that as well, but the problems of who is talking, who is listening, and whether and how the algorithms help or hurt persist. Some musicians, such as Maroon 5, have begun using bots that work through Facebook Messenger as a means of communicating directly with fans in ways that neither algorithms nor rapidly scrolling timelines can impede. "It's among the most intimate ways that you can connect," Ben Parr of Octane AI, the company that makes bots for Maroon 5 and other celebrities, told me: "there's no algorithm between you and your audience."

Unbounding Behaviors

The ways people act at concerts and the merchandise table, and often other fleeting encounters, are highly ritualized. Social media platforms have norms, but neither artist nor audience behaviors are so tightly bound. By opening participation, social media also afford a much wider range of behaviors. MySpace put music front and center, and encouraged artists to present themselves in their musical personas. In this sense, it shared qualities with the stage that Facebook and Twitter do not. Many musicians still regret the loss of MySpace as a viable venue for showcasing their music (though they do not miss the spam, the porn, or the constant requests from other musicians to help them book gigs). This desire to communicate through sound has helped fuel the rise of the music-sharing platform SoundCloud. Twitter and Facebook privilege verbal and visual exchange over musical exchange. Musicians can communicate in words, pictures, links, retweets, and likes, but there is no standardized official way to communicate in song.

The less a platform is designed to play music, the more questions musicians have to answer about how they should communicate through it. On stage, artists play music and banter between songs. At the merchandise table, when time together is brief, they can take their prompts from their interlocutors. But what do you put in an empty update rectangle that sits before you, ever ready to be filled? Musicians are pushed by design toward covering a wider range of topics than they would in the concert hall. "There's more give and take now," Timmins explained. You still send out your music, but you also talk about songs, about touring, about much more than music. "So I guess there's more chances of reaching people on different levels, not just musically. And so people are reacting not just to songs now but also to what you've written."

The pressure on musicians to produce continuous content so as to be a present and available relational partner can be overwhelming in its demands and underwhelming in its results. Høyem shakes his head. "There's just so much information now, it's just this manic stream of just trivial information that all these celebrities and artists are just spewing out. Most of it is just bullshit, and I don't want to be part of it. It's just information for the sake of information. There was just this feeling that there had to be continuity, there had to be a stream of information, there had to be updates every day, and that was the whole point, and not what I wrote."

Audience behavior, no longer constrained by limits on who can be present and engaging, or by access to the floor, is likewise unbound. Fans continue the practices described in chapter 3, but they, and others who are not fans, also talk to musicians much more often and in many more ways than before. For musicians, this loosening of conventions about how and when audiences can communicate with them can be both more validating and more unpleasant than the interactions afforded by time, space, and behaviorally constrained settings.

The everyday nature of social media interaction means that fans can offer musicians much more mundane affirmation at the moments musicians most need it. Artists often spend time alone, whether between gigs or while writing and recording. During these times, the chance to hop instantly into a ready-made setting where fans are waiting to offer encouragement means that audiences can offer the sort of ongoing, casual social support that we expect of friendship. "When you do music it's hard to get any—I guess any real positive feedback," said one musician. "It's like you do a record and no one hears it and you slave over it. It's really hard to do. You do that for six to nine months. And then people start hearing it. And playing live shows really ties all of that together. But also it's good to see what people are actually thinking about it [on the internet]."

White, manager of the reunited Urge Overkill, described their songwriter's reaction to seeing audience response online: "Eddie would say, 'Yeah, you know, I'll be at home writing songs and does anybody care?' And then he's like, 'But then I post on Twitter and Facebook and all these people respond immediately. And I'm like, wow, people really care.'" Høyem would agree. "I like knowing that there's a lot of people out there who are interested and seeing what their reactions are whenever I'm posting information about a new gig or a new tour or new music."

But just as audiences can invalidate during concerts, whether by talking to one another, switching seats, throwing things, or booing, audiences are critical online too. Now people have easier ways to deliver criticism straight to the source. Artists may also eavesdrop on audience criticism by reading what is posted about them. Fans may note flaws from a place of love,[56] but it can still hurt. "I don't know if anybody likes to hear criticism," Keating reflects. "I like the song but I think it would be better if you had done this and then they list all of the ways that the song could be better." Some develop "thick skin" and take it in stride. "There's always one or two people that aren't happy with whatever it is that's happened or what you're doing," Kelly told me. Some musicians take the long view and laugh. "We've got kind of the best and the worst fans wrapped up in one," said one. "Whenever we put out a new record, they all hate the new record. It goes on forever. And everybody just hates it, and then they start liking it. Then after a while, everybody likes it. We can tell it just is very schematic. Just kind of a mechanism [laughs]. But it's fun. It's all in good spirit."

Furthermore, not all who criticize are fans. As Bragg said, the affordances of social media are "a double-edged sword. How can you use that resource to communicate to people? And how can you allow the openness to not undermine the thing you're trying to do? Because if you do stick your head above the parapet, people are going to have a go. If you allow people to put you on a pedestal, you can't complain when pigeons shit on your head."

Criticism of the music is one thing, but the unbound participation that social media afford leads to far more criticism of the musicians themselves. Sometimes this comes from fans who prefer some band members to others. O'Donnell experiences this with the Cure. "There'll be people that decide they don't like you, as well as people that decide they like certain members of groups. There are camps that don't like certain members, and then it doesn't matter what you do. They'll just talk shit about you, and they'll find the worst. And it can be something, really nothing, and that's all you ever hear about on forums and websites forevermore."

Other times they are not fans at all. There are, as the singer-songwriter Sydney Wayser said, "a lot of angry people online," happy to blur the boundaries between you and your music, or between you as a person and you as a persona. These antagonists might be what Jonathan Gray calls anti-fans, people actively invested in disliking an artist, or they may simply be voicing their opinion without restraint about something they've stumbled upon.[57] YouTube can be particularly difficult, as O'Donnell described: "They can be mean though. It can be really hurtful, I think, especially on YouTube. I think there's something about YouTube. The people that comment on there, I think, if you put them together and gave them weapons and put them in uniform, they could take over the world, because they are the nastiest people I've ever come across. It's just venomous and evil and nasty, no holds barred. And you know if you met them in a bar, they wouldn't say boo to you."

Some, like Sobule, avoid eavesdropping outside of their own sites. "I did for a while and then I stopped doing that," she said, "because you'll get a hundred really great things and then you'll get one like kind of mean thing or you look at YouTube and people are just—people just comment just so they can, you know. They're usually probably like fourteen-year-old kids or damaged ex-frat boys, I don't know, who have nothing better to do but to say negative things. But why put myself through that?"

Finally, we have seen that on occasion people in concert halls are genuinely abusive. They point laser pointers, throw bottles, and on rare occasion stalk, assault, and kill. The bounded nature of the concert hall, both as a physical space and as a limited-time event, can increase the lethal potential of these encounters. "Sometimes I'll get the equivalent of a fan letter from someone who seems particularly confused or needy," says Hersh. "I feel for them, but they can't hurt me from there. The only ones that concern me are when they're really drunk and it's the middle of the night and I'm alone." Online, people may feel physically safer, but the potential for audiences to send abuse never ends, whether it's the kind of off-kilter neediness Hersh describes (and to which I return in the next chapter) or what Bragg called "unsolicited invective." Anti-fans and drive-by insulters have as much access to you as the diehards. Bragg gets emails to "tell you that you're shits and that you should shut up and what an asshole you are." Lawson told me, "I've had people on forums going 'you're such a dick, I hate what you do.' The idea that I am my music and my music is me in that way is really odd. People who come looking for a particular thing don't find it and try to hold me responsible because they don't like it, and I find that really weird. The internet lets them say it in a way they wouldn't otherwise."

People often attribute such cruelty to online anonymity, but it is also common where people post under real names. Lauren Mayberry, front-woman of the band CHVRCHES has been outspoken about the misogynistic abuse she receives. She wrote a 2013 column in the *Guardian* in which she explains that she reads "every message—good and bad—that has come into our inbox" on Facebook. Sometimes it's affirming. Other times it's not. "Maybe the men—and I'm sorry, but they are all men—sending the notifications of impending unsolicited 'anal' bothering don't realise it will actually be me who reads the emails—or maybe they don't care either way," she wrote. "But in order to get to the messages from people who genuinely wish to share something with the band, I must filter through every condescending and offensive message we receive." She describes scrolling through audience messages on her phone, throughout the day, every day. "After a while, despite the positive messages in the majority, the aggressive, intrusive nature of the other kind becomes overwhelming." It makes her cry. But "after all the sniffling had ceased," she asks herself, "why should I cry about this? Why should I feel violated, uncomfortable and demeaned? Why should we all keep quiet?"

Alice Marwick interviewed tech workers in San Francisco who, like many musicians, felt compelled to use social media to have viable careers. Some of them likewise "confessed that negative comments or email flames from audience members had upset them or even made them cry. Even people who claimed that negative comments didn't affect them had developed coping mechanisms," including tagging negative comments and turning to friends to read incoming messages for them.[58] The internet is full of people ready to insult anyone for laughs.[59] And if you're a woman, let alone a woman of color, they're going to go low.

Finding New Relational Boundaries

In the last chapter, we saw how musicians manage the boundaries around how audiences participate with their work. This chapter showed how, by fostering connectivity and ongoing engagement, social media have undone the separation between musician and fan that earlier incarnations of the music business instituted, changing the ways audiences participate not just with their work, but with them. Social media's relational affordances perpetuate dynamics that are found in the concert hall, but they also offer new possibilities of continuous, more equal engagement. Social media offer spatial, temporal, participatory, and behavioral flexibility that the prior settings for musician-audience encounters did not. While concerts fostered highly ritualized, emotionally intense, temporally brief interactions, social media are built to create never-ending interactions that generate an everyday sense of connection. Audiences have as much power as the musicians, perhaps more, as musicians vie for attention with all the other items in audience feeds.

Without participatory limits over who can interact with whom and when or rituals for guiding behaviors, musicians can't count on social media platforms to maintain relational boundaries. Whatever relational boundaries they want, whether close or distant, they must create themselves, platform by platform and turn by turn. With so much interactivity, they have to manage their accessibility in new ways. With social media aggressively affording daily interaction, musicians have to decide how much of their everyday personal selves they are willing to offer relative to their musical personas. The grounds of "authenticity," so often in music tied to genre, look, and race, shift in ways the next chapter will explore. Without rituals for what to say when, there is more uncertainty about how to act. With sites constantly launching, dying, revising their terms of service, reweighting their algorithms, and redesigning their interfaces, there is more work. Musicians face all kinds of choices and questions on social media they didn't have to struggle with in contexts that afforded more distant relationships with audiences. How much should they post? What should it be about? Should they reply to tweets or Facebook comments? All of them? This one? That one? To whom do they want to talk? To whom must they talk? Which people should they follow back or let be "friends" rather than "followers"? Control may feel like a blessing to many, but for others the need to make so many choices can itself feel unmanageable. In the final chapter, I turn to how musicians manage the ramifications of social media's call to closeness.

6

Relational Boundaries

Once upon a time, as this book began, musicians could "disappear into a mansion for years," "dropping out of the sky" on rare occasions to bless their audiences with new records and tours. Now, "they're tweeting about what they had for breakfast." Millennial music fans, raised on social media, expect musicians to be constantly available to them, offering unique, personal glimpses of offstage life. They see musicians as "friends" and "crave intimate glimpses into mundane daily activities." The more musicians are open about who they are, the more connected these fans say they feel.[1] Fans want a "glimpse into inner life," they want "access, intimacy, and affiliation."

Zoë Keating is a musician at ease with these demands. She doesn't distinguish between a private self and her musician self: "I don't see a distinction. It's like I'm an individual and I happen to have this creative life. There is no distinction. I think that's why social media is so—I find it—I'm kind of facile. It's sort of easy for me because I don't have to think up like 'is that my inside voice or my outside voice.' For better or worse they're the same voice." But inside and outside voices are not the same for everyone, and, as this chapter will explore, finding a voice that strikes the right balance between "access, intimacy, and affiliation" and privacy, distance, and autonomy often requires ongoing relational labor.

In many genres, including indie, blues, country, hip-hop, jazz, and soul, musicians have long been judged in terms of whether they are "authentic" and "real," but the standards of realness have changed.[2] Since music became industrialized in the nineteenth century, fans have "sought to understand stars as authentic people, with whom they had an intimate bond."[3] Like the love of "liveness," this fascination with authenticity can be traced to mediation. "'Disembedded' out of their immediate experiential contexts of face-to-face interaction by the modern music media," authenticity became a way to recreate a personal sense of social relationships.[4]

From the earliest days of the music industries, authenticity has been essential to marketing. Musicians have been sold as ordinary people, just like us, except photographed at home by *Life* magazine in somewhat nicer homes. In images and in sound, this kind of authenticity depended on believable performances that came off "as natural and effortless." Musicians have also been sold as larger than life, cultural avatars with whom audiences might identify, to which they might aspire, or whom they might find exotic and alluring. In this sense, an "authentic" musician is one who credibly conforms "to an idealized representation of reality," qualified to speak as a legitimate member of a subculture. Whole genres have been built on such mythologies. In either sense, far from given, authenticity is socially constructed. As Negus argues: "Songs and musical styles do not simply 'reflect, 'speak to' or 'express' the lives of audience members or musicians. A sense of identity is created out of and across the processes whereby people are connected together through and with music." Authenticity "is never an objective quality inherent in things, but simply a shared set of beliefs about the nature of things we value in the world." Its meaning changes as it is "renegotiated in a continual political struggle in which the goal of each contending interest is to naturalize a particular construction of authenticity."[5]

The standards by which authenticity has been judged in music have had little to do with an individual's inner self, but everything to do with social positioning, from the independent label to which one is (or is not) signed to the color of one's skin. As a general rule, the further musicians are from commercial pressures, the more authentic they are seen to be. Audiences of many genres use "demographic profiling" to test for authenticity. It "is said that to play bluegrass a musician must be white, working-class, rural and preferably from the Appalachian Mountains; you must be young, white, and an underachiever to perform punk music; and all salsa musicians must be Latin American."[6] I'm old enough to remember the career-destroying ridicule Vanilla Ice faced when he was revealed to be an affluent kid from the suburbs rather than the streetwise tough guy he sold audiences.

Today, musicians encounter a third sense of being real, which is to communicate with audiences as you would with friends. The aloof-yet-authentic star has been replaced by a new ideal, musicians who openly share their private selves by routinely communicating with audiences about their everyday life. Why settle for a magazine publishing a photograph of you at home when you can pull out your phone at home and invite your audience in? The new standard for "authenticity" is using your inside voice with everyone.

As we will see in this chapter, this demands the relational labor of developing strategies for choosing when and when not to communicate with audiences. Musicians need strategies for deciding which of the continuous incoming stream of invitations to conversation they will engage. They need to learn when and how to shut a conversation down. They also need strategies for managing topics in ways that let them create a presence that feels close but not too close, or, as one musician put it, "having boundaries without having the appearance of having boundaries." Being "real" with audiences can bring life-enriching consequences, especially when musicians express themselves as they want to be and are rewarded with affirmation and affection. But letting audiences in also makes musicians vulnerable. Their identities are at stake, both as professionals, able to accomplish their musical magic, and as they know and want themselves to be in the privacy of their homes.

Being Real

The call to intimacy can be traced to cultural histories of commodifying feeling that transcend music, from flight attendants paid to smile to expectations of casual conversation in service contexts (see introduction). Intimacy, once a private source of refuge from utilitarian pursuits, came to be a tool for accomplishing those pursuits by the 1940s. As it did, cultural ideologies shifted away from maintaining formal distance in public toward engaging in less restrained interactions more like those of private contexts. Richard Sennett describes an ideology of intimacy that arose in the mid-twentieth century premised on the idea that "relationships of all kinds are real, believable, and authentic the closer they approach the inner psychological concerns of each person."[7] This dovetailed with the rise of the "new economy" from the 1970s onward, in which workers, less likely to find lasting employment, felt more pressure to be entrepreneurial, increasing the need to build relationships and create aesthetic, emotional, and social experiences for customers across a wide range of fields.

As the last chapter argued, the new demand for intimacy can also be traced in part to the relational affordances of social media, which favor a norm of "personal authenticity and connection." This norm takes shape in subtle social pressures, as well as explicit messages about how to use social media. Twitter's official advice for musicians, for instance, emphasizes "authenticity": "For performers, connecting with your fans in an authentic way is one key to your success," it reads. "A Twitter connection tells fans how much you appreciate them, and it also enables you to tailor your messages. The fact is, Twitter provides more authenticity and creative control than any other online medium. Tweets come straight from you, and go right to your followers all over the world, in real-time." When maintaining "authentic" connection has become the norm, musicians who don't take advantage of social media to create ongoing relationships with fans seem uncaring and unavailable.

Musicians hear this new call to intimacy. "Twitter and Facebook's microblogging aspect kind of demanded fresh personal content," says singer-songwriter Erin McKeown, "and I have certainly felt the pressure to keep up with that." I asked Laurence "Loz" Colbert, drummer of the 1990s band Ride, who reunited in 2015, how he'd compare interactions with their fans then and now. "People want more of you now, every day," he told me, "and it means less because what you used to do with so few people now you do with so many."

For some, like Keating, meeting these new relational expectations comes easily. Musicians often feel close to their audiences anyway. They feel an intimate connection when they play, or when fans tell their personal stories. They get to know their audiences as groups and individuals, sometimes becoming friends, lovers, and family. Some, like Billy Bragg, who's had a loyal community of fans for decades, may see their audience as friends with whom they're growing old. The Cure's Roger O'Donnell gets emails every day. "I don't like to call them fans," he says, "not anymore. They're more like friends, people that are interested in my music and what I'm doing. I get three or four a day, and I'll answer, and I have good conversations with people."

The more relationships with audiences resemble friendship, the more relational labor may be demanded, both to craft relationships with audiences that feel close and to differentiate those relationships from more personal ones. What does it mean when you disclose the same things to

Figure 6.1. Erin McKeown. Photo by Izzy Berdan.
Used courtesy of Erin McKeown.

friends as you share with crowds of semi-anonymous online followers?
Is that really what they want? Nacho Vegas looks back with nostalgia
on earlier times. "It's much easier now to be in contact with your audience," he says in imperfect yet perfect English, "but it's too much easier."
Musicians are navigating what one called "uncharted waters, where everything is on display." Rituals and routines like those we saw at concerts
and merchandise tables can no longer be relied on to guide interaction.
Without recording technology, the press, or venue architectures to
bound how much and in what ways they interact with audiences, it is up
to each person to find a tolerable balance between being interactive and
being autonomous, being open and showing restraint. And each person
must keep finding that balance, interaction by interaction, day after day,
on platform after platform. Managing this can be more challenging than

a big family holiday. "Unlike pretending to be fond of your Uncle Larry at Thanksgiving dinner," advises Scott Kirsner, "this relationship with your audience cannot be faked."[8]

Friends and family are appealing models, especially if one is trying to manage the dialectic tension between music as communication and music as commodity. Recasting a relationship from economic into friends or family emphasizes its social, moral value. But for the most part, musicians and their audiences are neither friends nor family. The metaphors only stretch so far before beginning to fray. Aristotle distinguished true friendship, which is its own reward, from utilitarian friendship, which exists to serve other ends. True friendship is voluntary, equal, and laden with emotional, communicative, tangible, and behavioral expectations, not least of which is that friends disclose personal information with one another.[9]

Musicians may find some of these qualities of true friendship with their audiences as a whole, and may find all of it with specific individuals who are also audience members, but they cannot find all of it with all of their audience. No one can have that many true friends. Furthermore, relationships between musicians and audiences are inherently utilitarian for musicians, if not for audiences, creating a potentially problematic asymmetry. No matter how sincerely they feel a sense of true friendship, musicians' careers depend on their audiences' feelings toward them. Relationships formed through instrumental and economic origins can still have personal dimensions. Workers in all kinds of contexts, especially care work, "get to know each other as role occupants and sometimes as acquaintances or even friends," developing a shared interaction history over time.[10] But the power dynamics and relational expectations in these relationships differ from friendships in important ways.

Important as it is to create a sense of authenticity and closeness for audiences, it is equally essential to draw lines audiences are not allowed to cross. This relational labor of boundary-setting takes strategy and skill. What separates one kind of relationship from another is not given, but negotiated and subject to change. Viviana Zelizer describes people as implicitly consulting "a grid of relationships arranged by their similarity or dissimilarity and mark[ing] boundaries between adjacent relations." The behaviors and interactions that define a relationship as being on one side of a boundary or another are rarely "universally acceptable or unacceptable in themselves; they depend on context." As a result, we can never get out of the work of "marking the boundaries between the relations at hand and others with which they might easily and banefully be confused," especially, Zelizer argues, when those relationships entail economic transactions.[11]

Offering audiences intimate glimpses of everyday, mundane life may help musicians flourish. Keating attributes her income in part to her openness. It can also be personally enriching. When we present ourselves as we believe ourselves to be to others and those others validate us, they provide the kind of intimate recognition that helps us become the selves we strive to be.[12] Presenting a more accessible, private self to audiences can strengthen our sense of who we are and why we matter. Roger O'Donnell likes "the idea of writing a song in the afternoon and letting people hear it that day; and letting them know what the process is, letting them know what you do in your studio, how it works, how you write music. But I know a lot of people aren't comfortable with that, and like to maintain the mystique." "We're removing some of the mystique of all that used to be," said Stephen Mason, "the music and the engagement with fans has not suffered, it has only gotten better, it has only improved, it's only made the experience on our end as the artist more enjoyable. And I have to say, as a music fan too, who follows a lot of bands on Twitter, and Facebook, it's enhanced my experience of a lot of bands that I love as well." The late Swedish pop genius Gustaf Kjellvander of the Fine Arts Showcase, agreed. "It's important to remember that people who play music are just people," he said. "The internet helps that, it's not this huge iconic book of characters, rock stars. Personally I think the rock star thing is boring and played out."

The Perils of Closeness

Equalizing as it can be, the degree of personal engagement now called for can also threaten musicians' selves and music. It might seem easier to be real when that means expressing your innermost self than when it means meeting immutable external criteria. After all, people in Western cultures generally experience themselves and others as having an authentic core whether they display it to others or not. But selves, like relationships, are dialogic, revolving not "around such a unitary essence of self," so much as "countervailing equally valid versions of one another."[13] Musicians, like us all, play different roles in different situations, each of which may be as real as the next. How we are treated in those roles and situations then feeds back into who we become. People become "real" in relation with one another. Authentic selves never preexist.

The new demands of intimacy can be too much: too commercial, too much time, too much interaction, too much expectation, too much vulnerability, too much risk. In a broader cultural environment where authenticity has been co-opted by brand culture and "artisanal" goods are mass manufactured, artists who simply present themselves as wanting to engage their audience can be viewed cynically as marketing themselves, and thus undermine their own or others' perceptions of their artistic integrity. When, as Sarah Banet-Weiser describes it, "building a brand is about building an affective, authentic relationship with a consumer, one based—just like a *relationship* between two people—on the accumulation of memories, emotions, personal narratives, and expectations," it can be hard to tell the difference between a genuine effort to make human connection and an ad campaign.[14]

When you have to be authentic to be a real artist and also to market yourself, you're walking a fine line. Remember (in chapter 4) Happy Tom's admonition not to confuse having a community with having a sales channel? Musicians often struggle with the paradox between being themselves and selling themselves. Like self-branding more generally, the expectations musicians face are contradictory, promoting "both 'authenticity' and business-targeted self-presentation."[15] As Marwick describes it, the resulting incongruity is a source of stress and emotional labor for practitioners in many fields.

On this matter, though, music audiences are often generous. They recognize that artists work in systems they cannot control. Like Springsteen's fans, they can see a musician as a "human being who has had to deal with commodity-producing institutions like the music business and the media and has had to work through the consequences of having his work mass-produced" without viewing them as tools of that system.[16] An understanding audience can help an artist maintain a sense of both authenticity and integrity, while acknowledging and accepting that intimacy may have some utilitarian aims.

The Last Shards of Mystique

Many musicians, and some fans, worry that knowing too much about the people who make music can detract from audiences' experiences. Noel Gallagher from Oasis complained in 2006 that "all the fantasy's gone out of music, 'cos everything is too fucking real."[17] He explained that he was brought up on icons of mystique, Marc Bolan and David Bowie, "and it was like, 'Do they actually come from fucking Mars?'" The scene in Bowie's movie *The Man Who Fell to Earth* where he eats a bowl of metal seems like a better fit for his musical personas than any breakfast the real man might ever have tweeted.

Sometimes, when you show audiences who you really are, that's just not who they want you to be. That can undermine a career. It can also undermine a self. No matter how "real" musicians try to be, audiences are still likely to project fantasies on to them. Wendy Fonarow describes musicians as tricksters. Though they are "really just an ordinary person with a few tricks up his sleeve, a bass slung at her waist or a pair of sticks in his hand,"[18] they can temporarily make the audience think that their sensory and emotional experience is real, that they are wizards, not salespeople. Blues musicians are often seen as "mournful saints and unabashed sinners, wise sages and innocent fools" who sell their souls to the devil and are nomadic sexual conquerors. This works well for legend, but "can sometimes prevent us from understanding these performers as real human beings."[19]

Musicians know that audiences will hold them accountable both for the "illusion of verisimilitude" they create and for whatever the audience imagines them to be.[20] "When a fan or audience member sees a performer as himself or herself rather than as the character he or she envisioned," Fonarow writes, "it is difficult to go back to believing in the character. When you see how the trick is performed, you can't believe in the trick anymore."[21] "It's a tricky one," explained Mark Kelly,

> because at the end of the day you've got these fans that are into your music and it's almost like you know the musician isn't the music. You've got the message and the messenger, and maybe they should be kept a bit separate because if they find out too much about it, it might interfere with their enjoyment of the music that they listen to. People say they want to

know everything that's going on, but again, when we're in the studio writing and recording, if I was to tweet everything that happened, you know, the things that people say, the arguments that we have, the stuff that goes down, it would probably destroy the magic a little bit, you know?

"I have met some of my heroes," warned Lloyd Cole, "and it's not always a good thing. And I do think that that inequality in the relationship is what keeps it alive. And I think one of the things that's possible with my web presence is that the last shards of my mystique are in danger of being completely obliterated."

A star is usually seen as "an extraordinary fellow who brings excitement and glamour into the lives of his fans, ordinary people," argued Simon Frith, "but the process works the other way around too: stars, dull professionals, are made glamorous by the imagination and wit and excitement of their fans."[22] Cole is right to see that filling gaps in fans' imaginations with details of his everyday life could interfere with their ability to experience the music on its own terms. "I don't necessarily want to know what Tina Turner ate for breakfast," one musician told me, speaking as a fan. "I think that artists should maintain a certain distance."

Mystique, with all of the awe and power it implies, has its virtues. D. A. Wallach argues that to preserve mystique and keep consistent with their image, some musicians should not use social media themselves. "I was on a panel last week about this stuff," he told me. "I said look if you're Jack Johnson and your kind of brand is that everyone likes you because you feel like the guy next door, then it's consistent and on message for you to be very responsive yourself and to be Twittering all of the time. But if you're Ozzy Osbourne you can still engage the medium, but maybe it should be your roadie tweeting about all of the blow that you're doing."

Musicians don't need to actively craft mystique to leave false impressions that can diminish audience affections when absences are replaced with details. Letting audiences see who they "really" are can lead people who like them or their music to change their minds. Sometimes artists cross a line they didn't see coming. Fans burned Beatles records when John Lennon described the band as "bigger than Jesus." Other times, they violate the expectations of the social positions fans expect someone in their genre to hold. Audiences turned against country band the Dixie Chicks when they spoke out against then-President George W. Bush. Fans were mortified when hip-hop's Kanye West declared that he didn't vote, but would have voted for Donald Trump if he had. Many seemed to prefer to interpret it as a sign of mental illness, which is at least in keeping with West's image, than as a sign of real politics that betray who they want West to be. It may also be that the musician a fan loves has personal flaws severe enough to cause audiences to turn. Azealia Banks has managed to get herself banned from both Twitter, for going on a racist tirade against Zayn Malik, and Facebook, for going on a tirade against everyone in Brazil. When I asked people on Twitter if anyone had ever liked a musician less because of how they acted on social media, one response complained about a person with "the ability to both be sincere and incredibly obnoxious," and whose efforts at being vocal about what he believes come across as "petty narcissistic complaints" that reveal his lack of originality. Letting your authentic self out may drive fans away.

Too Much Intimacy

Getting close can also become harmful in a variety of personal ways. The never-ending invitation to interact with your audience may become a habit that distracts you from what your better self would have you do. Not long after she'd run a successful innovative early fan-funding campaign, Jill Sobule found herself online all the time engaging with her audience. She also had a terrible case of writer's block. A friend encouraged her to see a psychiatrist, "because I'm thinking maybe I have ADD, maybe I should get on Ritalin. I was that desperate." The doctor asked her to talk through a typical day. When he took out a pad to write a prescription, Sobule thought, "I'm getting speed." She wasn't. The prescription read, "no internet for two weeks." She made it eight days. It was "fantastic." Coming up with ways to stay away can be critical for those who do relational labor, especially for people who like it.

If you have a lot of fans, the sheer scale of people who want you to engage can also threaten the self, making it hard to sustain the sense of closeness they may seek and you may wish you could provide. Casey Rain explained that Swami's female singer couldn't turn on Facebook's chat feature because too many random people immediately expected her to chat with them. Travers complained that when he got on Facebook, people kept sending him the stickers that were popular on the site at the time and asking why he hadn't reciprocated. It might have made sense with five fans, or with friends, but with "11,000 people signing on, I thought 'no, this is crazy.'"

The threat of too many fans is complemented by the threat of individual fans who want too much. Fans may come to feel entitled and indignant if the artist doesn't respond. They may persistently and repeatedly ask the musician to play on their own record. They may ask them to send birthday cards to their friends. If an artist has met a fan once or twice, the fan's sense of entitlement can be particularly intense. Put them on a guest list, they may take for granted that they will always get in free and have backstage access. "People have unrealistic expectations about what you're going to do for them or what your relationship is to them and they don't know the boundaries," Jon Ginoli sighed.

Fans can also become too adoring. Though he warns us not to be trite in connecting music fandom to religion, Daniel Cavicchi notes that both are "centered around actions of devotion which may create similarities of experience."[23] When music can be a religious experience, it's not a huge stretch to assign God status to the music makers. "I'm not really like the top-of-the-charts level where there are millions and millions of people obsessed," explains Kristin Hersh, "but there are occasionally a few kids who seem very lost, a lot of times come from broken homes, and are really, really looking to find—you know, they really connect with the music, and they think that I'm like their saving grace kind of thing." This sort of adulation, even in its lighter-weight varieties, can feel like a powerful corrupter for musicians who value authenticity and accessibility.[24] When the adoration can manifest through everyday media in addition to infrequent in-person encounters, it can also just be a drag.

For a small but problematic handful of fans, obsession with the music leads to obsession with the artist, and a sense that the relationship is or should be mutual. Stephen Mason referred to this as "false intimacy" (so too did an Instagram celebrity interviewed by Crystal Abidin).[25] Nearly everyone I spoke with raised this topic. Recording may have separated musicians from fans in space, but, as we have seen, the ability to listen on repeat, in high fidelity, in private spaces, and alone made the sense of intimate connection between fan and performer more palpable.[26]

I've probably spent years of my life with the sounds of others' voices and instruments quite literally dwelling inside me, often delivered directly into my body through headphones or earbuds. To pick a favorite example, I've been listening to Sivert Høyem sing for the last decade. He's evoked every emotion I know and many I can't name. I've felt in love. I've felt compassion. I've felt pain, rage, righteous indignation, arousal, melancholy, yearning, sadness, and grief through the textures of his voice. I've had a few moments of being glad I learned the difference between singer and song decades ago, especially as I prepared to interview him for this book. It's not hard to imagine how someone standing on shakier emotional ground to begin with could project all of that onto him.

And they do. I asked Høyem if he'd had interactions with audience members that were upsetting or really bothered him. "Yeah," he answered, "some people pick up on everything I do, and they seem to think that it's all very significant, so they just seem to get a little too much. There's been quite a few who have been a little scary."

The problem is amplified by technology and his internal standards of politeness. "Sometimes, since you're really available to people all the time—if people want to get a hold of me, they can—so some people—you just start communicating with people and they just kind of—it can take up a little bit too much of your time, because they write back all the time, and I don't want to be rude, so."

"So you feel kind of compelled to keep responding?"

"Yeah, and it can get a little too friendly."

I wonder aloud if this is because his voice can feel so intimate living in our bodies as it does.

"Well, I guess some people have really—they have that kind of connection on a really spiritual level or whatever, and they really feel that they know me. That can be pretty scary. For a small country like Norway, that's just not okay." He laughs uncomfortably.

I ask if he's felt physically unsafe.

"No, no, no. It's just that nowadays, it's easy for people to monopolize you if they want to. And I have people just sending me ten emails each day and contacting me and following me on everything I do, sending me text messages and stuff, which is just really tiring and annoying."

It's taken decades to convince the world at large that even if "fan" comes from "fanatic," fandom is not a pathology. The overwhelming majority of music lovers, even if they feel close to musicians, never contact them at all. If they do, they behave entirely appropriately. But the fans who demand musicians' attention are not those who never communicate, or who do so quickly, politely, and then disappear. Social media technologies may create physical distance that leaves musicians' bodies safe from obsessive fans, but the presence of social media in daily life makes obsessive behavior so visible and invasive that it can make them more psychologically vulnerable. "In the past, there was a kind of—I suppose a kind of barrier between you and the public," said Travers, an avid tweeter. "I think Twitter has changed a few things, and Facebook's changed a few things. You can kind of be subject to some kind of crazy people and that could get to you." It only takes a few people who push the boundaries too far to call for developing strategies for managing distance.

Many of the people I spoke with, male and female, had dealt with some degree of stalking. Sydney Wayser recounted a tale of someone who followed her around Europe, telling different stories about where he lived wherever he was. "It's unsettling," she concluded, "because you want to be nice to your fans, you want to welcome them into your camp kind of, but what is that boundary, I don't really know." Another, who is English speaking, has a German stalker. "I got two emails from her today. She usually writes to me in German, and I usually can't be bothered to translate them." The day we spoke she had written in English to ask if he thinks she is hot. I ask how long this has been going on. Five years, he says. And she's not his only stalker. She writes in spates: "it's like once a month, and within the space of a few hours. The first one will start, 'Oh we're supposed to be together. I love you. Why won't you—we should try and make this work.' But by the tenth email she's like, 'I fucking hate you. You're a piece of shit. You're an ugly old man.' She talks herself out of it."

"I sort of have a stalker," another man told me. "This dude that like he used to make me all of these mix CDs and stuff. And then it just got out of control and he kept sending me more and more emails and everything. And I just sort of turned that stuff off. And then you get the email that says like 'oh I hope I didn't piss you off' and it's a really long email apologizing. And then the next email will be angry. You just see all of these different things. I just tend to try to ignore that."

With false intimacy an ever-present possibility, even relatively benign messages from fans, like a message on Twitter saying "I was on a train with you today!" or a Facebook post that says "I saw you in the station last night and I wanted to tell you how much I love your music but I didn't because you were making out with someone" can make people uncomfortable. "It does sort of have its sort of overtones of stalking doesn't it?" Mark Kelly reflects, "but of course it's not. It's just people going about their daily business that see you. And not everybody is the sort of person that would come up to you and go 'Hey, are you Mark Kelly?'"

Nearly every musician I spoke with had fans who communicate too frequently or with too much depth, revealing things musicians don't want to see or know. Several had been sent naked photographs. This can feel invasive enough when you don't want unsolicited nudes. Romantic partners may take offense that you've seen them, even if you didn't want them. When the fans who send photographs are under age eighteen, simply receiving them is a violation of international law. Musicians also hear frightening disclosures. "Occasionally you get people who just won't stop writing you and it turns into crazy shit," said D. A. Wallach, "You end up hearing about their abusive father." Greta Morgan, who you will remember found it deeply validating that her music comforted grieving parents (see chapter 1), has also found herself thrust into the middle of other family dynamics that were far harder to address:

> I've had a few disturbing interactions where—for example, one girl who would come to our shows all the time—her father would start sending me emails about how he couldn't go to the show because he had to spend a night in jail and their mom—and, you know, like all these personal stories. Then I would get another message from this girl, who's a fan, saying "I'm so sorry. Ignore my dad. He's manic-depressive and he's in a bad bout." That kind of thing. Like when a family really, really reaches out to me and I see some of their kind of emotional or personality flaws in that way, like in a very obsessive, scary kind of way, it freaks me out a little bit.

Few of us are prepared for encounters like this. Musicians are no different. They just have to deal with it more often, thanks, in no small part, to social media.

Distancing

In short, even those who like close relationships and want to welcome fans into their camp find they need strategies to set boundaries and create distance. The musicians I interviewed used a variety of bounding strategies. They may explicitly set themselves apart, like Cole:

> It's possible that you get people who are somewhat delusional about their relationship with the artist, and I don't think it's to be encouraged. I still make it quite clear, and I try to reiterate it throughout my presence on my website, that I am the artist and I am onstage, and you're not onstage, and the concert is the concert. And we have a community, and I really appreciate it, but we're not a band together. You're my community, and obviously I appreciate the fact that you keep me in business, so to speak, but our relationship is not like a normal friendship.

Like Sobule, whose therapist told her not to use the internet for two weeks, musicians must also learn strategies for managing when they will be accessible to their audiences. In Sobule's case, she learned that she can take a vacation from social media now and then and her audience will still be there when she returns. In the meantime, she can write songs. Kristen Hersh combats the "noisiness" of social media by choosing silence when she doesn't feel like engaging. Deepchild blocks out time to do social media daily. Wallach does it on the tour bus. Wayser tweets when she's on tour, but not when she's writing. Nacho Vegas and Johan Angergård take their time joining sites, making sure they are interested and will be willing to keep using them before creating profiles.

Musicians also develop strategies for managing how much they respond to their audiences when they are online. Some stick to platforms that let them stay brief. Høyem has finally found a way of using the internet that suits him. When he's on tour or has a new album to promote, he checks Facebook almost daily, answering most of the questions he's asked, and responding to or "liking" many of the comments people leave on his posts. "With Facebook, it just seems very easy. And people don't expect to get a long message whenever they just write, 'Hey, when are you coming to Cologne?' or 'When are you coming to Mexico City?' It's easy for me to just reply with just a sentence or something. It's really superficial. But it's nice, I guess, for people to know that I'm there checking."

Wallach's strategy, motivated less by self-preservation than by his ideas about professionalism, is to be intentionally coy:

> You want to create an exciting experience of being a fan for your audience. And that involves both presenting and concealing information in interesting and surprising ways that make it fun to follow you, fun to wonder what you're up to or whatever. . . . I think there is a virtue on the customer service side of things, if it were a traditional business, in answering every single question on Twitter. But I think as an entertainer there might be kind of a value to answering one out of every ten so that it feels really special if you do, and you're kind of reinforcing some sense of inaccessibility or stardom.

Wallach does respond to fans' emails but has developed a radar for detecting situations like the one where a fan started telling him about her abusive father. His antenna goes up when he sees "trigger phrases like 'I really believe that we need to meet each other,'" or anything that makes him think "under no circumstance would I ever write that email to someone even if I love what they do." When that happens, he doesn't reply, even if he had been interacting with that person before.

One person I spoke with had some "bad experiences in the early days" and developed a simple "policy." She will let people know that she appreciates the story they sent, that she's glad they enjoyed the concert and hopes to see them again, or that she really is coming to Denver in October, but "I don't email someone twice. I just don't respond to the second email. I don't want to have an email conversation one-on-one with fans." She connects this to a general unwillingness to get close to fans that began when she got burned by dating one too many.

> I would hook up with someone and then they would tell all their friends and then they would tell all their friends. I have very very low tolerance

for that. It only had to happen a few times for me to be just like "Ok. Done. Done." I don't need to find a date at my gig. I think some of that went into online boundaries. For me, rather than try to go case-by-case, I just made a decision like "You know what? There's a certain kind of communication that is cool with me in terms of me as a musician you as a fan, and there's a certain kind that isn't." I do draw a pretty strong line between how I communicate with fans and how I communicate with friends.

Travers shuts conversations down with laughter when fans "want to know about your life and things" or "crazy, crazy personal stuff." He figures if he laughs, he's "like a dog wagging his tail. Nobody kicks a dog wagging his tail. They kind of laugh with you and move on. You don't have to point out that they're being a bit too close."

Finally, musicians manage closeness by carefully selecting the topics they discuss. Relationship scholars have long connected self-disclosure to intimacy, arguing that as people become closer, they cover more topics and do so in greater depth. While this is sometimes presumed to lead to liking a person, it doesn't always. Good relationships "are established as much by privacy, secrecy, and deception as by self-disclosure, empathy, and openness."[27] Being available and open may be a good strategy sometimes for some people, but "it may be equally important for individuals to develop skill at restrained remarks and selective disclosure."[28]

We all live in streams of experience, any moment of which could be converted into self-expression. Which moments should be shared with audiences? The social norms guiding "appropriate" disclosure are unclear. How much information is too much information? In friendship and other interpersonal relationships, "appropriate" disclosure is that which is reciprocated, part of an ongoing relationship that builds in small steps, "takes the receiver's feelings and responses into account," "is relevant to the current topic of discussion," and "is intended to improve the relationship."[29] These terms rarely apply to interactions between musicians and audiences, leaving few benchmarks for how to assess what is and is not okay to share. Even in interpersonal relationships, "high levels of disclosure often turn out to be a mixed blessing at best and a deterrent to attraction at worst." Rawlins describes the tension between being open and honest and being closed and protective as one of the most important dialectics in close friendships.[30] Like everyone else who uses social media, musicians "must maintain equilibrium between a contextual social norm of personal authenticity that encourages information-sharing and phatic communication (the oft-cited 'what I had for breakfast' example) with the need to keep information private, or at least concealed from certain audiences."[31]

Information management skills become particularly salient when people's families are involved. It is one thing to put yourself out there for critical evaluation and another to do the same with loved ones. Again, people simply have different tolerances of vulnerability. Stephen Mason has shared photographs of his daughter from when she was a baby bump well into middle childhood. Keating shares her family life with her audience, from her young family's joyous years with their brand-new son through the horror of her husband's illness, cancer diagnosis, death, and into her grief, single parenting, and finding new footing. She may make no divisions between her private and professional selves, but she does make them for her extended family. "If it's Christmas and I'm with my family members at Christmas I won't tweet. I won't talk about other family members. Unless I ask them, like say, 'hey can I post this?' I'll ask them. So I make a division there because it's not just me, it's somebody else. I don't want to impact somebody else's life."

Others make strict rules against mentioning family, often in consultation with them. For as long as he can remember, Lowery has deleted any discussion of his children on his web page. Their mother was "more paranoid about people getting fixated on our kids, or knowing who our kids were, or anything like that. And I think that she was actually pretty smart for establishing that early on." Cole's wife is also "hypersensitive" to his sharing personal information:

I try and keep my wife and children pretty much completely out of it. I might mention the odd thing, like I've got a little band with my children now for fun, playing AC/DC songs and things. But my father recently uploaded a video of it from our basement, which one of the fans got hold of and put it on the forum, and my wife and I don't want my kids really to be recognizable with my work. So we asked that to be taken down, and I made a point of saying, "This is something that shouldn't happen again."

People may keep families out of bounds in their own discussions even when families make themselves public. Høyem never mentions his wife or children on social media, although his wife wrote a book about her postpartum depression. He referred to it in song, but online he's "trying not to just Twitter and blog and stuff about things that don't have anything to do with what I'm supposed to be doing, which is the music."

Part of what makes an interpersonal relationship intimate is that there are some things you only talk about with each other.[32] Sharing information with online audiences can thus threaten the intimacy of close relationships. Kelly, for instance, got in trouble with his wife for "posting stuff that's too personal." He didn't want to have a "corporate" approach where all he did was send out information about the band. He was finding it fun and "just tweeting whatever was going on." But he got "a bit risky with it." The TMI his wife couldn't abide? "Tweeting that I had a vasectomy." He's not sure whether his audience would have found it interesting. He "must admit I haven't done so much lately. Maybe I've gone a bit—gone too far with it now." What feels appropriate changes as the people around you respond to your public presence.

Another way to manage information strategically is to talk openly, but only about topics that are neither deeply personal nor out of keeping with your image. If a musician's image is tied to a topic other than themselves already, like Billy Bragg's is tied to politics, they can avoid personal self-disclosure by talking about things they are known to care about without having to reveal much about themselves that audiences don't already know. Bragg debates politics on his fan sites with relative impunity:

> If you look back on my Facebook page you see me there, not just posting stuff but arguing with people about it as well, and learning stuff from them, and putting ideas out and forming ideas. It helps me too, you know, we're going to have a referendum next year. . . . By the time we get to the referendum I'm going to have so many arguments on Facebook with people I'll be sharp as a pin. I will have seen it from every which way and hopefully I'll be able to sum it down into 140 words and I'll be able to put it on Twitter.

Sobule likens her fan pages to an eighteenth-century salon of which she is the madame, throwing out topics in hopes of getting fans to talk to one another rather than to her. She might post to ask them what they're thinking. She is happiest when her online presence is "not about me. It's just for a community of people to talk to each other, like-minded people. So I'm the madame of my house." Sometimes she will ask innocuous questions like "has anyone got a good dentist in New York?" But, knowing that her audience knows she's "a news junkie," she will also try to get them talking about politics. For instance, she might intentionally rile up her "really rightwing fans" by posting something provocative about the Swedish healthcare system, launching comment threads that go on and on whether she posts to them or not. Other musicians do the same, but with sports.

The ultimate way to create distance when things get too vulnerable is to quit the medium. One musician I met after a concert recently told me he's quit social media entirely because "no matter what you say, people attack you for it." There were several high-profile cases of celebrities walking away from social media platforms in 2016. Justin Bieber, upset at the comments fans were leaving on pictures he posted with his girlfriend to Instagram, left the site. The actress Leslie Jones quit Twitter when she was the target of a coordinated campaign of racist misogyny. Even the Queen of Social Media, Kim Kardashian, quit for a time after she was bound at gunpoint by robbers who took much of the expensive jewelry she had so often made a point of wearing in her selfies. To leave social media, though, is to forego the opportunities you may have to monetize your presence there. Kardashian regained some privacy, and I hope a greater sense of safety, but she lost millions. Few have millions, or even singles, to lose. Musicians who need to reach their fans to fund their careers may feel they don't have that choice to walk away.

Dynamic Limits

The ideology of intimacy would have us all believe that behaviors we once kept for loved ones translate seamlessly to interactions with the public. The ideology promotes "communication which is not dependent on public roles and institutions," without recognizing that "expenditures of time and energy increase dramatically when communication becomes independent of the norms, stereotypes, formalities, and rituals which characterize public roles and institutions." Musicians are at the leading edge of workers caught expending time and energy working out norms for everyday intimacies with audiences that are untethered from the public norms and rituals that previously guided those relationships. When we expect all of our relationships to look like personal ones, with authentic, natural feeling mobilized as a resource within them, we may be asking "more of relationships than they can give, thereby fostering dissatisfaction and alienation."[33]

Even if it weren't the case that publics are filled with anti-fans and antagonists, the kinds of openness and accessibility that fans increasingly expect from musicians can be threatening. Certainly, musicians who open themselves can find validation and meaningful relationships. But they may also find attacks, disillusionment, conflict in their own families, a sense of being overwhelmed, and feelings of discomfort and unease. Not everyone wants intimacy, even in relationships with people they know well. There's no inherent reason to think that musicians who open themselves to more intimate personal relationships with fans will be any happier than those who don't. Given all the issues accessibility and openness can raise, they may be less happy. When causal links between communicating like a friend and making money are so unclear, for some it may simply not be worthwhile.

Artists are almost always urged to learn to get closer to audiences, but what they really need to learn is how to get close enough while staying distant enough to preserve their sense of integrity, of private self, of personal relationships that are different from fan relationships, and of the audience's experience of the music itself, which can be spoiled by too much information about those who make it. To protect themselves and those who love them, musicians develop strategies that help them balance their needs and desires to be open and connected with their needs to preserve their privacy and be autonomous. There is not an all-purpose, correct solution, only correct solutions for individuals in specific moments. What works for them in one interaction may not work in another. They also need to differentiate their own sense of self from that of the musician their audience knows. Especially when the cell phone makes everyplace a workplace, musicians need to know how to "detach and differentiate aspects of themselves from workplace environments."[34] When online workplace environments are filled with not only people you want to reach but also those who hate you and those who love you too much, the need to find a self you can be both at home or at work or a way to keep identities distinct across contexts becomes ever more important.

Conclusion

Staying Human

Musicians were among the first to have their livelihood challenged by digital media. They were also among the first to adapt by using social media to build relationships with audiences hoping it might lead to sustainable revenue in uncertain economic times. Musicians' stories illuminate cultural, historical, economic, and technological forces that transcend them. Their experiences have implications for how we understand the new relational labor of playing to crowds across a variety of fields, especially as it encompasses social media. When more and more people feel that their livelihood depends on how well they self-brand, self-promote, and connect, relational labor becomes less and less optional.

Our most personal time and experience is now always a potential tool for commerce, raising concerns about how to hold on to the best of what makes us human and our capacity to reach our individual potentials while also forming long-lasting bonds that support ourselves and one another. As Viviana Zelizer asks, "what combinations of economic activity and intimate relations produce happier, more just, and more productive lives?"[1] The connections built through relational labor straddle and reconfigure boundaries between personal life, with all of its rewards, pleasures and problems, and work life, with all of the same. This book has identified a variety of relational dynamics and specific strategies artists use to address them. In this brief conclusion, I ask what we can learn from musicians that will help us understand the relationships at the heart of relational labor, and what advice might be gleaned for those who do relational labor, for audiences, and for those creating the platforms through which they interact.

It is essential to keep the concept of *relationships* foremost in our hearts and minds. Too often, it's presented as a gloss based on the assumption that we all know what it means so we needn't unpack it or pay it much sustained attention. When we oversimplify relationships as "connection," we miss that they are processes. We miss the competing demands they place on us, the ways connection always entails disconnection, and how tricky it is to find the sweet spots in between. We too easily assume that relationships that do not feel voluntary and where power is a source of struggle can seamlessly merge with something like "friendship," which is defined by equality and both people's choices to be in relationship.

There are many kinds of relationships at play in relational labor, and the boundaries that differentiate them are blurry. As people navigate the daily waters of interaction, possibilities are always in dynamic flux. One moment you may be a friend, the next an idol. You may be offering comfort or status to one person this minute and under attack from another the next. You may move between speaking as the center of attention, as server, caretaker, collaborator, citizen, and—let us not forget—fan. Sometimes you encounter audiences as individuals, other times as groups or even communities. The people with whom you relate also have relationships with one another. All this happens at once. Anyone who imagines they can use social media, yet focus only on the one kind of audience member they seek, is naïve.

Each of these audiences, whether group or individual, has their own needs and priorities, creating different pushes and pulls in the relationships. These complementary and competing needs are negotiated moment by moment, turn by turn, through communication. It is the ongoing, ever-changing nature of this interaction that creates relationships and keeps them alive. The end of interaction is the end of relationship. Just as the needs of relational laborers and their audiences inevitably may be in tension in any given interaction, so too may laborers' own personal and professional needs.

The multiple, messy, dynamic relationships that come from relational labor offer real opportunities both professional and personal. We've seen people form social ties that are entertaining, pleasurable, enriching, and profoundly validating. Building and sustaining these relationships is a way to participate in and foster relational and communal life for oneself and for others. The chance to interact directly with people who appreciate your work can help you to better understand what your work means, and hence its real value. Professionally, these relationships can support us not just by providing customers for a finished work but also at every stage of the process, from cheering us on along the way to shaping and financing work to distributing and publicizing it and to creating the online and sometimes offline communities and infrastructures to sustain it.

At the same time, these relationships pose personal and professional challenges. Being in touch, as Nacho Vegas said, is "too much easier." It is hard to construct messages that balance so many competing needs when audiences are so diverse and noisy. Sometimes audiences are entitled and want more than you are willing or able to give. Not all are friendly, and some are much too friendly. They can be too much, in too many ways. The learning curve is steep and what's on it is always changing. It takes time, yet it's not always clear how, if at all, it pays off financially. For many people, time spent in many of their relational efforts, including time on social media, may not. We know nothing about what works for which people, when, where, and how.

In each moment of encounter with audiences, different aspects of our selves are called into being. We come to be who we are through ongoing communication with other people. "The very idea of a self requires the idea of an other even as it contrasts with it," writes William Rawlins.[2] As Brian Travers said of the audiences that come to see his band, "they give you permission to be what you're going to be." Onstage and off, others' recognition shapes our personhood.[3] At their best, the relationships and interactions with the audiences people seek for their work, whatever work that may be, are sources of significance, validation, and inspiration that strengthen their understanding of and belief in their own value. But these relationships and encounters also threaten our personhood.[4] At their worst, crowds and the people in them are demoralizing, dehumanizing, and dangerous.

No matter how personally enriching these relationships may be, their creation and maintenance require labor. It is another job layered on top of those for which relational laborers get explicit credit. Much of this labor involves the feminized work of expressing and assisting others with emotion and relationship. It is mundane and domestic, mirroring housework in its multiplicity of tasks, never-ending nature, lack of recognition, and sometimes in the locations from which it is done. Relational work is often seen as "immaterial," in contrast to "productive" labor. "We are still embedded in a masculine model of what is work, what is skilled work, what is productive work," writes Sharon Bolton, "and I think this is what we need to move away from if emotion work is to be recognised as work, not merely as social interaction, caring, embodied and/or women's work."[5] Bolton argues that there are "tragic consequences" of thinking about emotional work as immaterial "because, fundamentally, it misses emotion work's materiality and overlooks the fact that it is hard and productive work that is often unrewarded and unrecognised because of its association with the domestic sphere." Like housework, emotion work "does not quite count as labor but is nonetheless crucial to getting other things done." Having to put your daily, personal self into utilitarian service as a means of building relationships that will offer professional sustenance threatens to transform our selves and one another into vehicles for commerce. A minimal first step toward helping people who do this kind of work flourish is to recognize that it is real, difficult, skilled, ongoing, and that it matters.

People's relationships with audiences are shaped by psychological and sociological dialectics that are at play in all relationships. Each time people stay silent or construct and respond to one another's messages, we are negotiating and managing competing dialectics, though we seldom think of it that way as we do. We seek intimacy and closeness yet also formality and distance. We seek autonomy, yet also interdependence, individualism yet also community. We seek to be open yet also restrained. We seek to dominate, yet also be equal and subservient. We seek the transcendence that can only come from losing ourselves in the flow of experience, yet we seek to control that flow. We seek others for the value they offer in and of themselves, yet also for how they can be used to further other aims. Our relationships are situated in contexts that include other relationships and are in dynamic tension with them, from the microlevel respect for privacy that a spouse demands to the macrolevel shifts among workers and other actors in newly destabilized industries and economies.

Dialectics are always in further tension with one another, and they never really settle. As historical dynamics shift, so too do the pressures. Technologies, the new possibilities they present, and the norms that emerge through and around their use, make some dialectics more relevant, some ends of dialectics easier and others harder, some ends desirable and others out of fashion. Technologies shape contexts, and in so doing reshape the everyday pushes and pulls of our relationships. To an extent, new media of any historical moment enhance and make visible practices that have long histories, whether in musician-audience relationships, friendships, or any other field of human endeavor. But in other ways, new media recalibrate the external pressures on those relationships, altering their potentials as they do.

Social media and the internet more generally have made it possible for people to communicate day in and day out with audiences far and wide. In so doing, they have pushed people's public communication to be more daily, more personal, and, for those used to being positioned as powerful media voices, less dominant and more interactive. By design, social media offer participants equal access to the floor and tremendous flexibility in the social roles they take toward one another and toward the things they communicate. The pendulum swings toward participation and away from control, toward connection and away from autonomy, creating more obligation.

The affordances offered by social media and the devices through which they are accessed, as well as the norms that emerge around and through their use, push people further toward definitions of "authenticity" that focus on revelation of an innermost self rather than fidelity to one's social situatedness or adherence to the manufactured constraints of a genre. Being distant, reserved, and surrounded by mystique is out. Being interpersonal and open is in. There's more potential for validation, but we are more vulnerable too. Connecting through devices ever present in our pockets brings the public into our most private domestic spaces and can turn our most private moments into outward-facing self-commodification. Everything we do or don't do online can send statements about who we are and how we see our relationships with others, including those who may be our customers, clients, or potential employers. Making decisions about where to be present online, setting privacy settings, turning comments on and off, and the myriad other acts that go into setting the boundaries of mediated relationships with audiences are essential parts of relational labor.

Relational labor practices on social media may or may not benefit workers, but they definitely benefit those with stock in the platforms.

Rather than assuming the truth of claims that we need these things to have viable careers, we should look critically, asking what works for which people and when, as well as what we are willing to do ourselves. Social media afford the potential for meaningful relational communication, yet offer no refuge from commodification or from that communication when it goes wrong. With all the push toward utilitarianism, we must work to hold on to the experience of relationships that are their own reward.

Charles Keil argues that music should never be commodified and that musicians should only be rewarded with "happiness and barterlike reciprocities."[6] One could take this argument to its (even further) extreme and argue that anything that was once participatory should be rewarded only with gifts. We've seen many ways the people for whom relational labor is performed offer meaningful gifts as reward. Many of the gifts audiences offer can themselves be seen as labor, replicating work that is paid in other contexts. When we think about fairness and flourishing, artists and platforms alike need to think about whether the work that audiences do is appropriately recognized and rewarded, whether through monetary compensation or other perhaps more socially valuable rewards. Everyone participating in relational labor online is communicating through platforms that profit from the continuing presence of the interactions they generate. Happiness and barter will never be fair compensation when small sets of people profit so immensely from ownership of those platforms. Like Keil, we can dream of reinstating a world before capitalism, but we must be realistic. Those places and days were oppressive for many of the people living in them. Our quest to make this a fair world can't rely on re-creating the past.

If these relationships are going to help people flourish, they need to help them not only meet the minimal conditions of flourishing but also exceed them. We should aim for the following eight goals.

First, if we expect people to engage in relational labor, the relationships they create should provide audiences with what they seek while providing those around whom they gather a predictable income that lets them afford a home, a family, a secure future, the ability to take time off work now and then without guilt, and to retain their sense of dignity in the work that they do.

Second, if we are going to take people out of organizations and leave them on their own to manage the manifold tasks work demands, we need better, more organized ways to get them resources and assistance than relying on their ability to make friends. Unions can be exclusionary and have other shortcomings, as we saw, but the functions they serve remain important. Workers and those who need them must organize to offer support, perhaps especially to the self-employed.

Third, if we are going to push people into gift economies in work contexts, we need to allow them to participate on their own terms so that they can appreciate the pleasures of the social bonds that gift exchange can create without being forced into giving what they believe they should be selling. In these relationships, we should be able to exercise control, while still creating possibilities for participation.

Fourth, the environments in which relational labor is enacted must be safe and, ideally, should be validating. No one, except perhaps soldiers and first responders, should have to venture into terrain where they are under attack while doing their work.

Fifth, relational labor should lead to a better and more valued understanding of the self and its place in the world. The connections relational labor fosters should develop into meaningful relationships. Even if they never become close, the social value of their relationships should exceed the utilitarian.

Sixth, relational labor should promote community so that those around you treat one another well and sustain one another over time. For professionals, having a community that cares about each other will help them care about you. For everyone, strong communities contribute to well-being.

Seventh, the benefits of relational labor should accrue first and foremost to those relating, and only secondarily to the platforms through which they communicate or the organizations that bring them together. We must demand that the riches mined from our actions be fairly distributed.

Finally, each of us should have the power to determine for ourselves how intimate we are willing to be with those who support our work. No one should be monetarily punished for choosing clear boundaries between public and private relationships.

All of this is possible, but none is given. In closing, I offer three brief thoughts for different readers on how to act toward these goals.

Conclusions for Those Trying to Connect

If you take one thing from this book, I hope it is that there is nothing straightforward or simple about relating to audiences. It is work and it requires business savvy, technical skills, and, above all, social skills. Every message you send, whether an announcement, a snapshot from everyday life, or even silence, conveys symbolic meaning about how you see your audience and what kinds of relationships you seek to create. To be a competent communicator, as Leslie Baxter and Barbara Montgomery point out, is to keep the flow of conversation going and to foster ongoing dialogue while being sensitive to other people's logics and their social and relational cultures.[7] To communicate competently, let alone well, with audiences, you must understand both them and yourself.

There is no one right way to communicate, no strategy that works for everyone. Coping with, let alone thriving in, these new contexts requires finding ways to simultaneously attend to needs that are in opposition to one another. Synthesizing both sides of dialectic tensions into a satisfying whole takes wisdom, confidence, and a willingness to see the big picture and live with uncertainty. Even then, what is satisfying at one point may not be at another. The people to whom we relate will change, and so too will our relationships. We are always in motion. We must accept this and work from there.

Though they may change, you need to think through your own moral commitments and ethics regarding relationships with audiences. Perhaps friendship is a model in which you deeply believe. Perhaps you believe in formal distance. Whatever the case, you should be mindful of the choices you make in models for new relationships.

When you approach audiences primarily as markets or customers, you undermine their potential, and hence your own, from the start. Even as we operate in financial realities, we need to remember that economics should be subservient to our need to have meaningful, nonalienated lives in which we can do good work. You don't have to think of audiences as potential friends to think of them as co-participants in creating new social and moral orders through your interactions.

When we discuss audiences, we are referring to people who are dispersed through many sites, yet networked together into subcultures that, as a rule, are far more concerned with themselves and one another than with you. They have their own hierarchies, their own norms, their own standards of what counts as fair and just exchange. They may be kind to you. They may turn on you. You must respect their autonomous needs and their value systems, even when they push against your own. Market systems urge us to control audiences. We can take advantage of audience information and practices to further our own ends, but when we datafy, territorialize, and invoke the law, we must be careful to do so in ways that benefit them as well as ourselves.

Although you cannot control audiences, when they feel respected they can serve as sources of support and assistance. It's all right to ask for more. It's okay to take risks. There is a fine line between honoring and appropriating, though, and you need to be mindful of treating audiences as fairly as you want them to treat you. If you are in a position where others can help with your media presence, you need to think through the ethics of who you will let speak for you, when, and on what, and whether you will make it visible when it is not really you who speaks (you should). Sometimes, though, there will be conflict, just as there is conflict in all relationships. And when there is, let it be a source of growth.

The best we can hope for in our engagement with audiences is a resonant cycle, where our messages go out to them, create meaning and value in their lives, and theirs come back to us and do the same in ours. Each of us has our own interest in forming close relationships with others, tolerance of risk, and degree of identification with our work. We need to become conscious of our own needs and identify our own limits. We need to be attentive to our experience and reflective, observing ourselves so that we can learn what works for us and what doesn't. Know that your limits will change over time, sometimes by the hour. And remember, restraint is also a virtue. There are communication skills you can learn. If you don't have them, perhaps you should. But such training can lead to competence without leading to fulfillment.[8] You may want to curtail the domains in which you focus your social efforts. If it proves more burden than boon, it is okay not to use social media. Adele doesn't.

Conclusions for Audiences

All of us are audiences, and all of us have a responsibility to think about the well-being of those who create what we use and cherish. The power to connect with others through social media means that we can put ourselves into interpersonal relationships with them even if they did not choose to be in relationship with us. We need to be mindful of the ethics of this imposition. To the extent that we think the people around whom we gather should act like friends, accessible and revealing, we must remember that friendships include both "significant privileges and responsibilities."[9] At the very least, if we can afford it, we should pay for what we enjoy and believe is important, even if we can get it for free. If there is need and we can lend a hand, we should.

But we also need to remember that people's work is entangled in people's selves and when we engage them as professionals, we are also engaging them as humans, with all their foibles and vulnerabilities. Being the center of attention does not come with an infinite ability to absorb the relational demands of others. It is always appropriate to be kind. Remember that just finding a public persona interesting does not mean that you are entitled to a person's time, let alone their private life. Just as we want others to respect our autonomy, we need to respect theirs. We must also quit stalking people and heaping abuse upon them just because it's easy. Even virtual slings and arrows cause real suffering.

Conclusions for Platform Developers

There are few people outside of those interacting together who have more power to influence the direction in which communication values and norms flow, and hence their potential to flourish, than those creating the media through which we distribute our creations and communicate with one another. Platforms have moral responsibilities to the well-being of those who use them and the cultures in which they operate. Jodi Dean describes the current platform model as a kind of "communicative capitalism," in which the circulation of messages is more important than their meanings. To the extent this is true, "communicativity hinders communication."[10] I believe that communication, and even communion, happens within systems designed to exploit interactions for profit. But I still urge those with the power of design to consider the ethical responsibilities of their work. You are pushing the line between yin and yang this way and that, and your choices matter. If platform developers are building businesses based on people's relationships, especially those that touch most closely on what matters most to them, they have an ethical responsibility to create conditions for relationships that help those people flourish.

Affordances have material and emotional consequences in people's lives. Social media platforms have relentlessly, and sometimes openly, pushed us further into the ideology of intimacy even as they have exploited that intimacy for profit. This book has shown a range of problems that ensue from the pressure toward closeness. Developers need to start designing social systems based on helping people manage dialectics and social platforms with multiple ways to use them right so that people can find the boundaries that work best for them. Developers should focus more attention on developing sophisticated approaches to letting people scope the scales of their interactions and define and manage boundaries as they see fit, rather than pushing them always toward more connection, more engagement, and more openness.

There are many ways in which musicians and others using platforms feel unfairly treated. Platforms like social media sites tend to focus on making money by selling user data to advertisers, yet they offer users few direct ways to make money themselves. What if they took seriously the call to let those who are already using them for career gain earn money through their practices on site? YouTube and Bandcamp provide some models, but there could be many more. Micropayments have barely been explored. Furthermore, if platforms are going to algorithmically filter messages between people and those who wish to hear them, they need to give people clearer information about how those algorithms work and easier ways to get messages through to those who have chosen to receive them.

I am neither first nor will I be the last to say it, but platforms must work harder to foster more civil environments in which people are less vulnerable to random and coordinated expressions of anger and hate. Ultimately, relationships belong to people, not to platforms. When our ties to one another are converted into currency for others, we have a right to ask that we be safe in those spaces. Those with the ability to shape the relational affordances of the institutions that enable and constrain our interactions have special responsibilities to support us in our quest to flourish.

Final Thought

Work and life are not different domains. The work we do and the self we are produce one another. "Once we recognize that work produces subjects," writes Kathi Weeks, "the borders that would contain it are called into question."[11] From this holistic perspective, we must recognize the material, consequential value of relational labor, and work together across sites and relationships to achieve and expand the material conditions and affective experiences people most value. We must work to create contexts that help us to know that we matter and that what we do meaningfully contributes to others' well-being.

There are many powerful forces that make it difficult to focus on social and emotional well-being before profit, but the more social our media become, the more the former may give rise to the latter. As individuals, we cannot upend entrenched ways of organizing society and culture, but we can shape our experience within it, both through the ways we interpret our interactions and relationships with others and through ways in which we communicate with others. We are in a moment when norms are being redefined. We must all do our parts to create better ones.

ACKNOWLEDGMENTS

This book would not exist without the musicians I interviewed. I have never loved working with any material as much as I have loved working with their words. I hope more than anything that I've done their diverse perspectives justice. Any royalties I earn from this book will go directly to the Future of Music Coalition and CASH Music in the hopes of paying forward a little bit of the generosity you have shown me.

I didn't realize until late in the writing how much this book began when I was a teenager. Thanks to my old friends who appear explicitly or in the background of chapter 3, especially my compatriots in record store hijinks and fandom. Helen and Jamie, I so wish you were still here.

I wrote this book at Microsoft Research New England where members of our Social Media Collective, especially Mary Gray and Tarleton Gillespie, were ideal partners in thought, as were Andrea Alarcon, danah boyd, Sarah Brayne, Kate Crawford, Kevin Driscoll, Megan Finn, Sharon Gillette, Dan Greene, Sarah Hamid, Rebecca Hoffman, Jessa Lingel, Kate Miltner, Dylan Mulvin, Steve Schirra, Lana Swartz, and all the people who have visited to share their work and listened to me talk through mine. Thanks also to Jennifer Chayes and Christian Borgs, and everyone who helps make MSRNE such an extraordinary environment.

Many people helped by introducing me to people I interviewed, pointing me to relevant scholarship and offering feedback, conversation, and opportunities to develop the work further. Our SMC research assistants were invaluable. Thank you John Agnello, Lucy Bennett, Georgina Born, André Brock, Jean Burgess, Klaus Bruhn Jensen, Melissa Click, Jean Cook, Paul Dalen, Paul Dourish, Andrew Dubber, Wendy Fonarow, Jeff Hall, David Hesmondhalgh, Kylie Jarrett, Henry Jenkins, Marj Kibby, Mike King, Steve Lawson, Sonia Livingstone, Annette Markham, Alice Marwick, Joshua McVeigh-Schultz, Jeremy Meyers, Sharif Mowlabocus, Gina Neff, Susanna Paasonen, Ben Parr, Andrea Press, Virginie Sautter, Nick Seaver, Aram Sinnreich, Jonathan Sterne, T. L. Taylor, Kristin Thomson, Katrin Tiidenberg, Trond Tornes, Siva Vaidhyanathan, Anjali Vats, Sarah Banet Weiser, and Emily White.

Thank you, Joel Orff, for illustrating my R.E.M. story and letting me reproduce it here, to Per Ole Hagen for the Sivert Høyem photo (and Anja Nyland Hagen for gifting it to me), and to all the photographers and fans who generously made their work available for reproduction here through Creative Commons licenses. I am sorry I couldn't reach you all to tell you.

Thanks to those whose music has been my soundtrack during the years I've worked on this. You gave me constant opportunities to reflect on what I was writing and made my life more abundantly feelingful. Sivert and Nacho, your songs move me every time. Feelies, you are my grounding wire. Others played on repeat include Arctic Monkeys, Club 8, Courtney Barnett, Iggy Pop, Jenny Wilson, Kitchie Kitchie Ki Me O, Lorde, Madrugada, Peter Bjorn and John, Queens of the Stone Age, R.E.M., Röyksopp, Teleman, the Fine Arts Showcase, and Woodkid. Robert and Gustaf, I will always miss the songs you never got to write.

Thanks to everyone who cheered me on as I worked.

And thanks to you for the reading and responding that will give this book life.

APPENDIX 1

Musicians Interviewed

This includes only those who wished to be identified.

Name (Band)	DOB	Nationality	Genre (as identified on Wikipedia, Spotify, and Apple Music)
Johan Angergård (Club 8/Legends/ Acid House Kings)	1974	Swedish	Scandinavian pop, post-punk, garage rock
Ahmed Best (Cosmic Ghetto/ STOMP!)	1973	American	jazz, electronic, acid jazz, jazz rap
Billy Bragg	1957	British	folk punk/rock, indie folk, Americana
Stuart Braithwaite (Mogwai)	1976	Scottish	post-rock, instrumental rock, art rock
Rick Bull/Deepchild	Unknown	Australian/ German	techno, house, nu-dub electronica
Lloyd Cole	1961	Scottish/ American	rock, pop, indie pop
Honeychild Coleman (Apollo Heights/Pollen)	1967	American	avant-electro-pop, dubstep
Jon Ginoli (Pansy Division)	1959	American	queercore, punk
Richie Hawtin (Plastikman)	1970	Canadian (English born)	house, microhouse, Detroit techno, ambient house, electronica
Nathan Harold (fun.)	Unknown	American	indie pop
Kristen Hersh (Throwing Muses/ 50FootWave	1966	American	alternative rock
Sivert Høyem	1976	Norwegian	rock
Zoë Keating	1972	American (Canadian born)	contemporary classical, cello rock
Mark Kelly (Marillion)	1961	English (Irish born)	art rock, neo-progressive rock, pop rock
Gustaf Kjellvander (The Fine Arts Showcase)	1980	Swedish	indie rock
Steve Lawson	1972	British	jazz fusion, progressive rock, ambient, New Age, experimental, doom metal

Name (Band)	DOB	Nationality	Genre (as identified on Wikipedia, Spotify, and Apple Music)
Rickard Lindgren (Hell on Wheels)	Unknown	Swedish	indie rock
David Lowery (Camper Van Beethoven and Cracker)	1960	American	traditional rock, alternative rock
Erin McKeown	1977	American	alternative rock, indie rock, indie pop, folk, jazz
Jonas Martinsson (Starlet)	Unknown	Swedish	Swedish pop, Åhus scene
Stephen Mason (Jars of Clay)	1975	American	Christian alternative folk rock
Greta Morgan/ Salpeter (The Hush Sound, Gold Motel)	1988	American	indie pop, alternative rock, indie rock, jangle pop
Chris Murray	1966	American (Canadian born)	ska
Roger O'Donnell (The Cure)	1955	English	post-punk, gothic rock, dark wave, alternative rock, new wave, synthpop
Casey Rain (aka S-Endz) (Swami)	1987	British	hip-hop, Desi beats, neo funk
Kate Schutt	1975	American	jazz, folk, adult contemporary, rock, pop
Jonathan Segel (Camper Van Beethoven)	1963	American	alternative/pop/progressive rock, blues, improv, avant-garde, electronica
Thomas Seltzer/ Happy Tom (Turbonegro)	1969	Norwegian (American born)	punk rock, hardcore/glam/death punk, hard rock, thrash metal
Jill Sobule	1961	American	folk rock, indie rock, rock
Sindre Solem (Obliteration and Nekromantheon)	1987	Norwegian	death metal
Chris Stroffolino	Unknown	American	alternative folk, indie
Michael Timmins (Cowboy Junkies)	1959	Canadian	Americana, alternative country, country/ folk/blues/indie/psychedelic rock
Brian Travers (UB40)	1959	British	English reggae, pop
Nacho Vegas	1974	Spanish	indie/folk Rock
Gary Waleik (Big Dipper)	Unknown	American	alternative rock, indie rock, jangle pop
D. A. Wallach (Chester French)	1985	American	classic pop
Sydney Wayser	1986	French-American	folk

APPENDIX 2

Social Media Presence as of January 2017

Johan Angergård, Ahmed Best, Billy Bragg, Stuart Braithwaite, Rick Bull, Lloyd Cole, Honeychild Coleman, Jon Ginoli, Nathan Harold, Richie Hawtin, Sivert Høyem, Zoë Keating, Mark Kelly, Gustaf Kjellvander, Rickard Lindgren, David Lowery, Stephen Mason, Erin McKeown, Chris Murray, Roger O'Donnell, Casey Rain/S-Endz, Greta Salpeter/Morgan, Kate Schutt, Jonathan Segel, Thomas Seltzer, Jill Sobule, Sindre Solem, Chris Stroffolino, Michael Timmins, Brian Travers, Nacho Vegas, Gary Waleik, D. A. Wallach, Sydney Wayser

FACEBOOK (PAGE) (32)
Johan Angergård, Ahmed Best, Billy Bragg, Stuart Braithwaite, Rick Bull, Lloyd Cole, Honeychild Coleman, Jon Ginoli, Richie Hawtin, Sivert Høyem, Zoë Keating, Mark Kelly, Gustaf Kjellvander, Steve Lawson, David Lowery, Stephen Mason, Erin McKeown, Chris Murray, Roger O'Donnell, Casey Rain/S-Endz, Greta Salpeter/Morgan, Jonathan Segel, Thomas Seltzer, Jill Sobule, Sindre Solem, Chris Stroffolino, Michael Timmins, Brian Travers, Nacho Vegas, Gary Waleik, D. A. Wallach, Sydney Wayser

TWITTER (32)
Johan Angergård, Ahmed Best, Billy Bragg, Stuart Braithwaite, Rick Bull, Lloyd Cole, Honeychild Coleman, Jon Ginoli, Nathan Harold, Richie Hawtin, Sivert Høyem, Zoë Keating, Mark Kelly, Gustaf Kjellvander, Steve Lawson, David Lowery, Stephen Mason, Erin McKeown, Chris Murray, Roger O'Donnell, Casey Rain/S-Endz, Greta Salpeter/Morgan, Kate Schutt, Thomas Seltzer, Jill Sobule, Chris Stroffolino, Michael Timmins, Brian Travers, Nacho Vegas, Gary Waleik, D. A. Wallach, Sydney Wayser

SOUNDCLOUD (31)

Ahmed Best, Billy Bragg, Stuart Braithwaite, Rick Bull, Lloyd Cole, Honeychild Coleman, Jon Ginoli, Richie Hawtin, Sivert Høyem, Zoë Keating, Mark Kelly, Steve Lawson, Rickard Lindgren, Jonas Martinsson, Stephen Mason, Erin McKeown, Roger O'Donnell, Casey Rain/S-Endz, Greta Salpeter/Morgan, Kate Schutt, Jonathan Segel, Thomas Seltzer, Jill Sobule, Sindre Solem, Chris Stroffolino, Michael Timmins, Brian Travers, Nacho Vegas, Gary Waleik, D. A. Wallach, Sydney Wayser

YOUTUBE (28)

Billy Bragg, Stuart Braithwaite, Rick Bull, Lloyd Cole, Jon Ginoli, Nathan Harold, Richie Hawtin, Sivert Høyem, Zoë Keating, Mark Kelly, Steve Lawson, Rickard Lindgren, David Lowery, Stephen Mason, Erin McKeown, Chris Murray, Roger O'Donnell, Casey Rain/S-Endz, Greta Salpeter/Morgan, Kate Schutt, Jonathan Segel, Thomas Seltzer, Jill Sobule, Chris Stroffolino, Brian Travers, Gary Waleik, D. A. Wallach, Sydney Wayser

FACEBOOK (PERSONAL) (25)

Johan Angergård, Billy Bragg, Stuart Braithwaite, Rick Bull, Jon Ginoli, Sivert Høyem, Steve Lawson, Rickard Lindgren, David Lowery, Jonas Martinsson, Stephen Mason, Chris Murray, Roger O'Donnell, Casey Rain/S-Endz, Greta Salpeter/Morgan, Kate Schutt, Jonathan Segel, Thomas Seltzer, Jill Sobule, Sindre Solem, Chris Stroffolino, Brian Travers, Gary Waleik, D. A. Wallach, Sydney Wayser

INSTAGRAM (25)

Ahmed Best, Stuart Braithwaite, Rick Bull, Honeychild Coleman, Richie Hawtin, Sivert Høyem, Zoë Keating, Mark Kelly, Steve Lawson, David Lowery, Stephen Mason, Erin McKeown, Chris Murray, Roger O'Donnell, Casey Rain/S-Endz, Greta Salpeter/Morgan, Kate Schutt, Jonathan Segel, Thomas Seltzer, Jill Sobule, Sindre Solem, Michael Timmins, Brian Travers, D. A. Wallach, Sydney Wayser

GOOGLE + (17)

Billy Bragg, Jon Ginoli, Sivert Høyem, Zoë Keating, Steve Lawson, Stephen Mason, Casey Rain/S-Endz, Kate Schutt, Jonathan Segel, Jill

Sobule, Sindre Solem, Chris Stroffolino, Michael Timmins, Brian Travers, Gary Waleik, D. A. Wallach, Sydney Wayser

LINKEDIN (17)
Johan Angergård, Ahmed Best, Rick Bull, Honeychild Coleman, Richie Hawtin, Zoë Keating, Gustaf Kjellvander, Steve Lawson, David Lowery, Jonas Martinsson, Casey Rain/S-Endz, Kate Schutt, Chris Stroffolino, Michael Timmins, Gary Waleik, D. A. Wallach, Sydney Wayser

BANDCAMP (15)
Rick Bull, Honeychild Coleman, Jon Ginoli, Nathan Harold, Zoë Keating, Mark Kelly, Steve Lawson, Erin McKeown, Casey Rain/S-Endz, Greta Salpeter/Morgan, Jonathan Segel, Sindre Solem, Chris Stroffolino, Gary Waleik, Sydney Wayser

FLICKR (10)
Rick Bull, Honeychild Coleman, Steve Lawson, David Lowery, Jonas Martinsson, Casey Rain/S-Endz, Greta Salpeter/Morgan, Brian Travers, D. A. Wallach, Sydney Wayser

TUMBLR (9)
Sivert Høyem, Zoë Keating, Steve Lawson, Erin McKeown, Casey Rain/S-Endz, Greta Salpeter/Morgan, Chris Stroffolino, D. A. Wallach, Sydney Wayser

SNAPCHAT (3)
Casey Rain/S-Endz, Kate Schutt, Brian Travers

NOTES

INTRODUCTION

1 Hillhouse, "MTV's 'Music to the M Power.'"
2 Frith, *Sound Effects*, 43.
3 Keating, "There Is a Light."
4 Torpey and Hogan, "Working in a Gig Economy."
5 Major, *Juba to Jive*.
6 Nunberg, "Goodbye Jobs, Hello 'Gigs.'"
7 Burch, Batchelor, and Humphrey, "Emotional Labor for Entrepreneurs."
8 Gill and Pratt, "Social Factory."
9 Mihm, "Gig Work."
10 Gray and Suri, "Spike in Online Gig Work."
11 Helms, "Presence of Precarity," 41.
12 Frith, *Sound Effects*.
13 Marwick, *Status Update*.
14 Neff, *Venture Labor*.
15 Marwick, *Status Update*.
16 Neff, *Venture Labor*.
17 Marwick, *Status Update*.
18 Hochschild, *Managed Heart*, 12.
19 Muehlebach, "On Affective Labor," 75.
20 Peterson, *Creating Country Music*.
21 Negus, *Popular Music in Theory*, 97.
22 Turino, *Music as Social Life*, 1.
23 Tomlinson, *Million Years of Music*.
24 Albrecht, *Mediating the Muse*; Tomlinson, *Million Years of Music*.
25 Small, *Musicking*.
26 Ibid., 221.
27 Hesmondhalgh, *Why Music Matters*, 146.
28 Born, "On Musical Mediation," 7.
29 Ibid.
30 Tomlinson, *Million Years of Music*, 50.
31 Turino, *Music as Social Life*.
32 Ibid., 28.
33 Negus and Pickering, *Creativity, Communication and Cultural Value*.

34 Hesmondhalgh, *Why Music Matters*, 3.

35 Suisman, *Selling Sounds*, 9.

36 Future of Music Coalition, "Artist Revenue Streams: Population of Study."

37 Lena, *Banding Together*, 41.

38 Ibid., 13.

39 Future of Music Coalition, "Artist Revenue Streams."

40 I've written in some depth about an enduring friendship that blossomed from a fan email I sent in 2005 in Baym, *Personal Connections*.

41 Hesmondhalgh and Baker, *Creative Labour*.

42 Stopera, "Rihanna Meet and Greet."

43 Hochschild, *Managed Heart*, 5.

44 Ibid.

45 Tracy, "Becoming a Character," 98.

46 Adkins, "New Economy"; Hochschild, *Outsourced Self.* See also Fortunati, "Immaterial Labor"; Jarrett, *Feminism, Labour, Digital Media*; Weeks, "Life Within."

47 Hochschild, *Managed Heart*, 106.

48 Grazian, *Blue Chicago*, 6–7.

49 Peterson, *Creating Country Music*.

50 Adkins, "Cultural Feminization"; Adkins and Jokinen, "Introduction."

51 Adkins, "Cultural Feminization," 605.

52 Veijola and Jokinen, "Hostessing Society," 176.

53 Gill and Pratt, "Social Factory."

54 Tracy, "Locking Up Emotion."

55 Hochschild, *Managed Heart*, 86.

56 Aronson and Neysmith, "Depersonalizing Home Care Labor."

57 Gregg, "Learning to (Love) Labour."

58 Hochschild, *Managed Heart*; Tracy, "Locking Up Emotion."

59 Bellous, "Classroom Activities," 100.

60 Muehlebach, "Affective Labor."

61 Zelizer, *Purchase of Intimacy*, 35.

62 E.g., Beebe, Beebe, and Redmond, *Interpersonal Communication*.

63 On mentoring and teaching, see Bell et al., "To All the Girls"; Bellous, "Classroom Activities"; Fenwick, "Tidying the Territory"; Wood, "Teachers' Learning Communities." On care work, see Morini and Fumagalli, "Life Put to Work"; Verkerk, "Care as Process." On sex work, see Garofalo, "Feminist Critique of Trafficking." On romantic and domestic work, see Becker and Marecek, "Positive Psychology History"; Casey and Alach, "Just a Temp?"; Sabatini and Crosby, "Ceilings and Walls"; Schull, "Escape Mechanism."

64 Zelizer, *Purchase of Intimacy*, 105.

65 Prager, *Psychology of Intimacy*.

66 Sexton and Sexton, "Intimacy," 1.

67 Zelizer, *Purchase of Intimacy*, 14.

68 Beebe, Beebe, and Redmond, *Interpersonal Communication*, 253.

69 Sennett, *Fall of Public Man.*

70 Gadlin, "Private Lives."

71 Levinger and Raush, "Close Relationships," viii.

72 Parks, "Ideology in Interpersonal Communication."

73 Levinger and Raush, "Close Relationships," vii.

74 Parks, "Ideology in Interpersonal Communication," 83.

75 E.g., Bakhtin, *Speech Genres*; Baxter and Montgomery, *Relating*; Buber, *I and Thou*; Montgomery and Baxter, *Dialectical Approaches*; Rawlins, *Compass of Friendship.*

76 Buber, *I and Thou*, 55.

77 Ibid., 84–85.

78 Ibid., 68.

79 Ibid., 85.

80 Rawlins, *Compass of Friendship.*

81 Baxter and Montgomery, *Relating*, 26.

82 Ibid., 4.

83 Bakhtin, *Speech Genres*, 276.

84 Tracy, "Dialectic, Contradiction, or Double Bind?"

85 Baxter and Montgomery, *Relating*, 66.

86 Born, "On Musical Mediation," 8.

87 Reimer et al., "Why Do Humans Value Music?"

88 Ibid.

89 Hesmondhalgh, *Why Music Matters*, 120.

90 Ibid.

91 Zelizer, *Purchase of Intimacy*, 40.

92 Ibid., 298.

93 Hesmondhalgh and Baker, *Creative Labour.*

CHAPTER 1. MUSIC AS COMMUNICATION

1 Frith, *Sound Effects*, 101.

2 Tomlinson, *Million Years of Music.*

3 Lutgen-Sandvik, Riforgiate, and Fletcher, "Work as a Source."

4 Bakhtin, *Speech Genres.*

5 Buber, *I and Thou*, 90.

6 Ibid., 66–67.

7 Suisman, *Selling Sounds*, 125.

8 Small, *Musicking*, 214.

9 Cavicchi, *Tramps Like Us.*

10 Hesmondhalgh and Baker, *Creative Labour*, 200.

11 Ibid.

12 Cills, "David Bowie."

13 Musicians are usually fans: "in most popular music genres music-making emerges from obsessive music listening; a certain sort of 'fandom' is thus built into the process" (Frith, *Performing Rites*, 55).

14 Polanyi, *Telling the American Story*.

15 Lauer, *Intimacy*; Rawlins, *Compass of Friendship*.

16 Rawlins, *Compass of Friendship*. 43.

17 Ibid.

18 E.g., Albrecht, *Mediating the Muse*; DeNora, *Music in Everyday Life*; DeNora, *After Adorno*; Hesmondhalgh, *Why Music Matters*.

19 Frith, *Performing Rites*; Tagg, "'Universal' Music"; Reimer et al., "Why Do Humans Value Music?"

20 Frith, *Performing Rites*, 73.

21 Steven Feld quoted in Keil and Feld, *Music Grooves*, 91.

22 Reimer et al., "Why Do Humans Value Music?"

23 Lena, *Banding Together*.

24 Nussbaum, *Upheavals of Thought*.

25 Reimer et al., "Why Do Humans Value Music?"

26 Lena, *Banding Together*, 170.

27 Neal, *What the Music Said*, 8.

28 Ibid., 30.

29 Davis, *Miles*, 23.

30 Ibid., 347.

31 Mitchell and Snyder, "Narrative Prosthesis," 49.

32 Siebers, "Introduction," 9.

33 Tagg, "'Universal' Music."

34 Small, *Musicking*, 13.

35 Ibid., 183.

36 Palmer, *Art of Asking*, 122.

37 Sarbanes, "Musicking and Communitas," 17.

38 Bourdieu, *Distinction*; Frith, *Sound Effects*; Hebdige, *Subculture*; Thornton, *Club Cultures*.

39 Turino, *Music as Social Life*, 2.

40 Lena, *Banding Together*, 169.

41 Baulch, "Gesturing Elsewhere," 197.

42 Ibid.

43 Fox, *Real Country*; Peterson, *Creating Country Music*.

44 Fox, *Real Country*, 21.

45 Kot, *Ripped*, 99.

46 Hyde, *Gift*.

47 Palmer, *Art of Asking*.

48 Zelizer, *Purchase of Intimacy*, 1.

49 Ibid., 288.

50 Blau, *Exchange and Power*.

51 Hesmondhalgh and Baker, *Creative Labour*, 25.

52 Hyde, *Gift*, 357.

CHAPTER 2. MUSIC AS COMMODITY

1 Goldman, "Music's Lost Decade."
2 Wikström, *Music Industry*, 93.
3 Hughes and Lang, "If I Had a Song," 181.
4 Anderson, *Popular Music*, 174.
5 Albrecht, *Mediating the Muse*, 140.
6 Suisman, *Selling Sounds*.
7 Cavicchi, "Loving Music," 237.
8 Ibid.
9 Born, "On Musical Mediation," 10.
10 Albrecht, *Mediating the Muse*; Suisman, *Selling Sounds*; Théberge, *Any Sound You Can Imagine*.
11 Albrecht, *Mediating the Muse*, 117.
12 Attali, *Noise*; Small, *Musicking*.
13 Attali, *Noise*; Small, *Musicking*.
14 Small, *Musicking*.
15 Haynes, *End of Early Music*.
16 Tremain, *Music and Silence*.
17 Haynes, *End of Early Music*, 132.
18 Small, *Musicking*, 159.
19 Ibid.
20 Peterson, *Creating Country Music*.
21 Kraft, *Stage to Studio*.
22 Frith, *Performing Rites*.
23 Small, *Musicking*.
24 Kraft, *Stage to Studio*.
25 Ibid.
26 Suisman, *Selling Sounds*.
27 Kraft, *Stage to Studio*, 33.
28 Peterson, *Creating Country Music*.
29 Kraft, *Stage to Studio*, 109.
30 Hughes and Lang, "If I Had a Song," 180.
31 Suisman, *Selling Sounds*, 271.
32 Albrecht, *Mediating the Muse*; Frith, *Sound Effects*; Small, *Musicking*.
33 Suisman, *Selling Sounds*, 240–41.
34 Small, *Musicking*, 8.
35 Albrecht, *Mediating the Muse*, 177.
36 Keil and Feld, *Music Grooves*, 228.
37 Ibid.
38 Suisman, *Selling Sounds*.
39 Quoted in ibid., 128.
40 Ibid., 40.

41 Stahl, *Unfree Masters*, 2.

42 Peterson, *Creating Country Music*, 107.

43 Albrecht, *Mediating the Muse*, 150.

44 Suisman, *Selling Sounds*, 148.

45 Horton and Wohl, "Mass Communication," 156.

46 Cavicchi, *Tramps Like Us*.

47 Kraft, *Stage to Studio*, 59.

48 Ibid., 135.

49 Grazian, *Blue Chicago*.

50 Neal, *What the Music Said*, 17.

51 Ibid., 160.

52 Grazian, *Blue Chicago*, 97.

53 Kraft, *Stage to Studio*, 6.

54 Ibid., 200.

55 Sterne, "There Is No Music Industry," 50.

56 Wikström, *Music Industry*.

57 Suisman, *Selling Sounds*.

58 Stahl, *Unfree Masters*.

59 Hughes and Lang, "If I Had a Song," 182.

60 Lena, *Banding Together*.

61 Quoted in Kot, *Ripped*, 35.

62 Ibid., 44.

63 Stahl, *Unfree Masters*.

64 Witt, *How Music Got Free*.

65 Sinnreich, *Piracy Crusade*.

66 IFPI, "Global Music Report 2016."

67 Ibid.

68 Morris, "Artists as Entrepreneurs"; Wikström, *Music Industry*.

69 Napoli, *Audience Evolution*.

70 Duffy and Wissinger, "Cultural Work"; Duffy, *(Not) Getting Paid*; Wissinger, "Glamour Labour"; Phillips, *This Is Why*.

71 Morris, "Artists as Entrepreneurs."

72 Quoted in Kot, *Ripped*, 233.

73 Anderson, *Popular Music*, 155.

74 Ibid., 169.

75 Hesmondhalgh and Baker, *Creative Labour*, 110.

76 Veijola and Jokinen, "Hostessing Society," 168.

77 Becker, *Art Worlds*.

78 Lena, *Banding Together*.

CHAPTER 3. AUDIENCES

1 Small, *Musicking*, 44.

2 Ang, *Desperately Seeking the Audience*, 52.

3 Livingstone, "Challenge of Changing Audiences."
4 Ang, *Desperately Seeking the Audience.*
5 Livingstone, "Challenge of Changing Audiences," 79.
6 Rosen, "People Formerly Known."
7 Anderson, *Popular Music*, 15.
8 Gray, "New Audiences."
9 Cavicchi, "Loving Music."
10 Ibid., 242.
11 Quoted in ibid., 244.
12 Booth, *Playing Fans.*
13 Grossberg, "Is There a Fan?"; Jenkins, *Convergence Culture.*
14 Cavicchi, "Loving Music," 236.
15 Ehrenreich, Hess, and Jacobs, "Beatlemania."
16 Cavicchi, "Loving Music," 236.
17 Brownstein, *Hunger Makes Me.*
18 Cavicchi, *Tramps Like Us*, 38.
19 Jenkins, Ford, and Green, *Spreadable Media*; Reagin and Rubenstein, "I'm Buffy."
20 Reagin and Rubenstein, "I'm Buffy."
21 Jenkins, Ford, and Green, *Spreadable Media*; Reagin and Rubenstein, "I'm Buffy."
22 Cavicchi, "Loving Music."
23 Reagin and Rubenstein, "I'm Buffy."
24 Ibid.
25 Ibid.
26 Jenkins, Ford, and Green, *Spreadable Media.*
27 Cavicchi, "Loving Music," 248.
28 Reagin and Rubenstein, "I'm Buffy."
29 E.g., Dayan, "Peculiar Public of Television"; Livingstone, "On the Relation."
30 Théberge, "Everyday Fandom," 488.
31 Ibid.
32 Hills, *Fan Cultures.*
33 Jenkins, Ford and Green, *Spreadable Media.*
34 Banet-Weiser, *Authentic^{TM}*, 5.
35 Fiske, "Cultural Economy of Fandom."
36 Jenkins, Ford, and Green, *Spreadable Media.*
37 Gray, Sandvoss, and Jenkins, "Introduction," 2.
38 Jenkins, Ford, and Green, *Spreadable Media.*
39 Gray, Sandvoss, and Jenkins, "Introduction," 4. See also Milner, "Working for the Text."
40 Watson, "Why We Argue."
41 Cavicchi, *Tramps Like Us.*
42 Mihelich and Papineau, "Parrotheads in Margaritaville," 176–79.
43 Ehrenreich, Hess, and Jacobs, "Beatlemania."
44 Crowe, "Harry Styles."
45 Cline, "Essays from *Bitch*," 71.

46 Ibid.

47 Kruse, *Site and Sound*.

48 Sullivan, *R.E.M.*

49 See Hellekson, "Fannish Field of Value."

50 Condry, "Cultures of Music Piracy."

51 Hills, *Fan Cultures*, 46.

52 E.g., Bennett, *Thinking Fans*; Cavicchi, *Tramps Like Us*; Thornton, *Club Cultures*.

53 Théberge, "Everyday Fandom."

54 Woolley, "PLATO."

55 Doub, "Community Memory."

56 Computer History Museum, "Computer History Museum."

57 Jarnow, *Heads*.

58 Ibid.

59 Driscoll, "Hobbyist Inter-Networking."

60 Rheingold, *Virtual Community*.

61 Ibid., 49.

62 Ibid.

63 Théberge, "Everyday Fandom," 492.

64 Cavicchi, *Tramps Like Us*.

65 Watson, "Why We Argue."

66 Whittaker, "Dark Webs," 42.

67 See Baym, *Tune In, Log On*, for an in-depth discussion of a television fan USENET group.

68 Pew Research Center, "Internet/Broadband Fact Sheet."

69 Bennett, *Thinking Fans*; Bennett, "Music Fandom Online"; Bennett, "Discourses of Order."

70 Théberge, "Everyday Fandom," 492.

71 Strauss, "Rolling Stones Live."

72 Ibid.

73 Ibid.; Shah, "Poor Lonely Computer."

74 Strauss, "Rolling Stones Live."

75 Ibid.

76 Ibid.

77 Shah, "Poor Lonely Computer."

78 Baym, " New Shape of Online Community"; Baym and Burnett, "Amateur Experts."

79 Working up the nerve to phone their singer, Sivert Høyem, when he agreed to be interviewed for this book was one of the most intimidating parts of this project. He put me immediately at ease, doing the rapport building I was too nervous to start. His voice was as soothing on the phone as it is on the record, and familiar from listening to so many live recordings.

80 Bergquist and Ljungberg, "Power of Gifts."

81 Whittaker, "Dark Webs."
82 Kot, *Ripped.*
83 Burgess, "Hearing Ordinary Voices."
84 Théberge, "Everyday Fandom."

CHAPTER 4. PARTICIPATORY BOUNDARIES

1 Hersh, "What Is a Strange Angel?"
2 Hersh, "Thoughts on Sustainability."
3 Buber, *I and Thou.*
4 Théberge, "Everyday Fandom."
5 Ibid., 496.
6 Ibid.
7 Ibid.
8 Fiske, "Cultural Economy of Fandom."
9 Ingram, "Prince Was an Early Fan."
10 Gershman, "Prince of Copyright Enforcement."
11 Higgins, "Prince Inducted."
12 Napoli, *Audience Evolution.*
13 Beniger, *Control Revolution.*
14 Ang, *Desperately Seeking the Audience.*
15 Bermejo, *Internet Audience.*
16 Napoli, *Audience Evolution.*
17 Johnson, "Historical Analysis."
18 Scott and Halligan, *Marketing Lessons.*
19 Ibid.
20 Topspin, "Average Fan Value."
21 Baym, "Data Not Seen."
22 Théberge, "Everyday Fandom," 486.
23 Fonarow, *Empire of Dirt.*
24 Wikström, *Music Industry.*
25 Kot, *Ripped,* 97.
26 Regner and Barria, "Do Consumers Pay Voluntarily?"
27 Bandcamp, "What Pricing Performs Best?"
28 Ibid.
29 Wikström, *Music Industry.*
30 Ibid., 162.
31 Palmer, *Art of Asking,* 13.
32 Lauer, *Intimacy.*
33 Randolph, "Free Words," 69.
34 Hochschild, *Managed Heart,* 81.
35 Terranova, "Free Labor," 48.
36 Hesmondhalgh and Baker, *Creative Labour,* 206.

CHAPTER 5. PLATFORMS

1 Hann, "Bruce Springsteen."
2 See appendix 2 for a list of the main websites on which the artists I interviewed are present.
3 Gibson, "Theory of Affordances."
4 Postigo, " Socio-Technical Architecture."
5 Hochschild, *Managed Heart*, 50.
6 Goffman, *Forms of Talk*.
7 Lena, *Banding Together*, 11.
8 Ibid.
9 Small, *Musicking*, 74, 196–97.
10 Ibid., 27.
11 Ibid., 35–36.
12 Gillespie, "Politics of 'Platforms.'"
13 Gibson, "Theory of Affordances"; McVeigh-Schultz and Baym, "Thinking of You."
14 Small, *Musicking*.
15 Fonarow, *Empire of Dirt*.
16 Auslander, "Against Ontology," 55.
17 Small, *Musicking*; Fonarow, *Empire of Dirt*.
18 See chapter 1 and Turino, *Music as Social Life*.
19 Small, *Musicking*, 27.
20 Fonarow, *Empire of Dirt*, 196.
21 Auslander, "Musical Personae."
22 Frith, *Performing Rites*.
23 Boyd, *Musicians in Tune*, 161.
24 Ibid., 147–48.
25 Ibid., 146.
26 Small, *Musicking*, 197.
27 Goffman, *Forms of Talk*, 138.
28 Turino, *Music as Social Life*, 64.
29 Fonarow, *Empire of Dirt*, 294–95.
30 Bauman, *Verbal Art as Performance*.
31 Fonarow, *Empire of Dirt*, 193.
32 Ibid.
33 Kot, *Ripped*, 104.
34 Ehrenreich, Hess, and Jacobs, "Beatlemania," 87.
35 Hesmondhalgh and Baker, *Creative Labour*, 207.
36 Boyd, *Musicians in Tune*, 147.
37 Grazian, *Blue Chicago*, 143.
38 Fonarow, *Empire of Dirt*.
39 Ibid., 131.

40 Hesmondhalgh, *Why Music Matters*, 110.

41 Fonarow, *Empire of Dirt.*

42 Ibid., 225.

43 Ibid., 198.

44 Friedlander, "Grimes in Reality."

45 Van Dijck, *Culture of Connectivity*, 162.

46 Marwick and boyd, "To See and Be Seen," 144.

47 Goffman, *Forms of Talk.*

48 In what could be interpreted as a bit of a bait and switch on Facebook's part, after creating fan pages with easy access to newsfeeds, the site reduced page reach and began encouraging page owners to buy sponsored posts in order to reach more people.

49 See Litt, "Knock, Knock."

50 Van Dijck, *Culture of Connectivity.*

51 Baym, "Data Not Seen."

52 van Dijck, *Culture of Connectivity*, 129.

53 Marwick and boyd, "I Tweet Honestly," 127.

54 Goffman, *Forms of Talk.*

55 Collins, "Why Beyoncé."

56 Jenkins, *Textual Poachers.*

57 Gray, "New Audiences." See also Pinkowitz, "Rabid Fans."

58 See Marwick, *Status Update*, 196.

59 Phillips, *This Is Why.*

CHAPTER 6. RELATIONAL BOUNDARIES

1 Hillhouse, "MTV's 'Music.'"

2 Kruse, *Site and Sound*; Grazian, *Blue Chicago*; Neal, *What the Music Said*; Lena, *Banding Together.*

3 Cavicchi, "Loving Music," 249.

4 Negus, *Music Genres*, 130; Peterson, *Creating Country Music*, 220.

5 Negus, *Music Genres*, 113.

6 Lena, *Banding Together*, 51.

7 Sennett, *Fall of Public Man*, 259.

8 Kirsner, *Fans, Friends, and Followers*, 5.

9 Bigelow and La Gaipa, "Development of Friendship"; Fehr, "Intimacy Expectations"; Hall, "Sex Differences."

10 Gutek et al., "Distinguishing between Service Relationships," 219.

11 Zelizer, *Purchase of Intimacy*, 57, 99, 117.

12 Lauer, *Intimacy.*

13 Baxter and Montgomery, *Relating*, 159.

14 Banet-Weiser, *Authentic*, 66.

15 Marwick, "Status Update," 167.

16 Cavicchi, *Tramps Like Us*, 65.

17 "Noel Gallagher."
18 Fonarow, *Empire of Dirt*, 189.
19 Grazian, *Blue Chicago*, 128.
20 Fonarow, *Empire of Dirt*, 238.
21 Ibid., 188.
22 Frith, *Sound Effects*, 265.
23 Cavicchi, *Tramps Like Us,* 51.
24 Fonarow, *Empire of Dirt*.
25 Abidin, "Aren't These?"
26 Suisman, *Selling Sounds*.
27 Parks, "Ideology in Interpersonal Communication," 90.
28 Rawlins, *Compass of Friendship*, 130.
29 Parks, "Ideology in Interpersonal Communication," 81.
30 Rawlins, *Compass of Friendship*, 85.
31 Marwick and boyd, "I Tweet Honestly," 124.
32 Parks, "Ideology in Interpersonal Communication."
33 Ibid., 96–97.
34 Adkins and Lury, "Labour of Identity," 610.

CONCLUSION

1 Zelizer, *Purchase of Intimacy*, 298.
2 Rawlins, *Compass of Friendship*, 27.
3 Lauer, *Intimacy*.
4 Kaplan, "Life of Dialogue."
5 Bolton, "Lady Vanishes," 76.
6 Keil and Feld, *Music Grooves*, 228.
7 Baxter and Montgomery, *Relating*.
8 Parks, "Ideology in Interpersonal Communication."
9 Rawlins, "Openness as Problematic," 47.
10 Dean, "Communicative Capitalism," 58.
11 Weeks, "Life Within," 246.

REFERENCES

Abidin, Crystal. "'Aren't These Just Young, Rich Women Doing Vain Things Online?': Influencer Selfies as Subversive Frivolity." *Social Media + Society* 2, no. 2 (April–June 2016): 1–17. doi:10.1177/2056305116641342.

Adkins, Lisa. "Cultural Feminization: 'Money, Sex and Power' for Women." *Signs* 26, no. 3 (2001): 669–95.

———. "The New Economy, Property and Personhood." *Theory, Culture and Society* 22, no. 1 (February 1, 2005): 111–30. doi:10.1177/0263276405048437.

Adkins, Lisa, and Celia Lury. "The Labour of Identity: Performing Identities, Performing Economies." *Economy and Society* 28, no. 4 (November 1, 1999): 598–614. doi:10.1080/03085149900000020.

Adkins, Lisa, and Eeva Jokinen. "Introduction: Gender, Living and Labour in the Fourth Shift." *NORA-Nordic Journal of Feminist and Gender Research* 16, no. 3 (September 1, 2008): 138–49. doi:10.1080/08038740802300947.

Albrecht, Robert. *Mediating the Muse: A Communications Approach to Music, Media and Cultural Change.* Cresskill, N.J.: Hampton Press, 2004.

Anderson, Tim J. *Popular Music in a Digital Music Economy: Problems and Practices for an Emerging Service Industry.* New York: Routledge, 2014.

Ang, Ien. *Desperately Seeking the Audience.* London: Routledge, 1991.

Aronson, Jane, and Sheila M. Neysmith. "You're Not Just in There to Do the Work: Depersonalizing Policies and the Exploitation of Home Care Workers' Labor." Gender and Society 10, no. 1 (February 1996): 59–77.

Attali, Jacques. *Noise: The Political Economy of Music.* Translated by Brian Massumi. Minneapolis: University of Minnesota Press, 1985.

Auslander, Philip. "Against Ontology: Making Distinctions between the Live and the Mediatized." *Performance Research* 2, no. 3 (January 1, 1997): 50–55.

———. "Musical Personae." *TDR: The Drama Review* 50, no. 1 (April 20, 2006): 100–119.

Badhwar, Neera K. "Friendship and Commercial Societies." *Politics, Philosophy and Economics* 7, no. 3 (August 1, 2008): 301–26. doi:10.1177/1470594X08092105.

Bakhtin, Mikhail M. *Speech Genres and Other Late Essays.* 2nd ed. Edited by Caryl Emerson and Michael Holquist. Translated by Vern W. McGee. Austin: University of Texas Press, 1986.

Bandcamp. "What Pricing Performs Best?" *Bandcamp.* https://bandcamp.com. Accessed January 23, 2017.

Banet-Weiser, Sarah. *Authentic™: The Politics of Ambivalence in a Brand Culture.* New York: New York University Press, 2012.

Barreto, Manuela da Costa, Michelle K. Ryan, and Michael T. Schmitt, eds. *The Glass Ceiling in the 21st Century: Understanding Barriers to Gender Equality.* Washington, D.C.: American Psychological Association, 2009.

Baulch, Emma. "Gesturing Elsewhere: The Identity Politics of the Balinese Death/ Thrash Metal Scene." *Popular Music* 22, no. 2 (May 2003): 195–215.

Bauman, Richard. *Verbal Art as Performance.* Prospect Heights, Ill.: Waveland, 1984.

Baxter, Leslie A. *Voicing Relationships: A Dialogic Perspective.* Thousand Oaks, Calif.: SAGE, 2010.

Baxter, Leslie A., and Barbara M. Montgomery. *Relating: Dialogues and Dialectics.* New York: Guilford Press, 1996.

Baym, Nancy K. "Data Not Seen: The Uses and Shortcomings of Social Media Metrics." *First Monday* 18, no. 10 (September 29, 2013). doi:10.5210/fm.v18i10.4873.

———. "The New Shape of Online Community: The Example of Swedish Independent Music Fandom." *First Monday* 12, no. 8 (August 6, 2007). doi:10.5210/ fm.v12i8.1978.

———. *Personal Connections in the Digital Age.* Cambridge: Polity, 2010.

———. *Tune In, Log On: Soaps, Fandom, and Online Community.* Thousand Oaks, Calif.: SAGE, 1999.

Baym, Nancy K., and Robert Burnett. "Amateur Experts International Fan Labour in Swedish Independent Music." *International Journal of Cultural Studies* 12, no. 5 (September 1, 2009): 433–49. doi:10.1177/1367877909337857.

Becker, Dana, and Jeanne Marecek. "Positive Psychology History in the Remaking?" *Theory and Psychology* 18, no. 5 (October 1, 2008): 591–604. doi:10.1177/0959354308093397.

Becker, Howard S. *Art Worlds.* 25th anniversary ed., updated and expanded ed. Berkeley: University of California Press, 2008.

Beebe, Steven A., Susan J. Beebe, and Mark V. Redmond. *Interpersonal Communication: Relating to Others.* 6th ed. Boston: Pearson, 2010.

Bellous, Joyce. "Five Classroom Activities for Sustaining a Spiritual Environment." *International Journal of Children's Spirituality* 11, no. 1 (April 1, 2006): 99–111. doi:10.1080/13644360500504389.

Beniger, James R. *The Control Revolution: Technological and Economic Origins of the Information Society.* Cambridge, Mass.: Harvard University Press, 1986.

Bennett, Lucy. "Delegitimizing Strategic Power: Normative Identity and Governance in Online R.E.M. Fandom." *Transformative Works and Cultures* 7 (July 16, 2011). http:// journal.transformativeworks.org.

———. "Discourses of Order and Rationality: Drooling REM Fans as 'Matter Out of Place.'" *Continuum* 27, no. 2 (2013): 214–27.

———. "Music Fandom Online: REM Fans in Pursuit of the Ultimate First Listen." *New Media and Society* 14, no. 5 (2012): 748–63.

———. "Thinking Fan's Rock Band: REM Fandom and Negotiations of Normativity in Murmurs.com." Cardiff University, 2009. http://orca.cf.ac.uk.

Bergquist, Magnus, and Jan Ljungberg. "The Power of Gifts: Organizing Social Relationships in Open Source Communities." *Information Systems Journal* 11, no. 4 (October 1, 2001): 305–20. doi:10.1046/j.1365-2575.2001.00111.x.

Bermejo, Fernando. *The Internet Audience: Constitution and Measurement.* New York: Peter Lang, 2007.

Bigelow, Brian J., and John J. La Gaipa. "The Development of Friendship Values and Choice." In *Friendship and Social Relations in Children,* edited by Hugh C. Foot, Anthony J. Chapman, and J. R. Smith, 15–44. New York: John Wiley, 1980.

Blau, Peter M. *Exchange and Power in Social Life.* New York: John Wiley, 1964.

Bolter, Jay David, and Richard Grusin. *Remediation: Understanding New Media.* Cambridge, Mass.: MIT Press, 2000.

Bolton, S. C. "The Lady Vanishes: Women's Work and Affective Labour." *International Journal of Work Organisation and Emotion* 3, no. 1 (2009): 72–80. doi:10.1504/IJWOE.2009.025400.

Booth, Paul. *Playing Fans: Negotiating Fandom and Media in the Digital Age.* Iowa City: University of Iowa Press, 2015.

Born, Georgina. "On Musical Mediation: Ontology, Technology and Creativity." *Twentieth-Century Music* 2, no. 1 (March 2005): 7–36. doi:10.1017/S147857220500023X.

Bourdieu, Pierre. *Distinction: A Social Critique of the Judgement of Taste.* London: Routledge, 1986.

Boyd, Jenny. *Musicians in Tune: 75 Contemporary Musicians Discuss the Creative Process.* New York: Fireside, 1992.

Brownstein, Carrie. *Hunger Makes Me a Modern Girl: A Memoir.* New York: Riverhead Books, 2015.

Bryson, Mary, Lori MacIntosh, Sharalyn Jordan, and Hui-Ling Lin. "Virtually Queer? Homing Devices, Mobility, and Un/Belongings." *Canadian Journal of Communication* 31, no. 4 (December 21, 2006). http://www.cjc-online.ca.

Buber, Martin. *I and Thou.* Translated by Walter Kaufmann. New York: Charles Scriber's Sons, 1970.

Burch, Gerald F., John H. Batchelor, and Ronald H. Humphrey. "Emotional Labor for Entrepreneurs: A Natural and Necessary Extension." *Entrepreneurship Research Journal* 3, no. 3 (January 12, 2013). doi:10.1515/erj-2012-0022.

Burgess, Jean. "Hearing Ordinary Voices: Cultural Studies, Vernacular Creativity and Digital Storytelling." *Continuum* 20, no. 2 (June 1, 2006): 201–14. doi:10.1080/10304310600641737.

Casey, Catherine, and Patricia Alach. "'Just a Temp?' Women, Temporary Employment and Lifestyle." *Work, Employment and Society* 18, no. 3 (September 1, 2004): 459–80. doi:10.1177/0950017004045546.

Cavicchi, Daniel. "Loving Music: Listeners, Entertainments, and the Origins of Music Fandom in the Nineteenth Century." In *Fandom: Identities and Communities in a Mediated World,* edited by Jonathan Alan Gray, Cornel Sandvoss, and C. Lee Harrington. New York: New York University Press, 2007.

———. *Tramps Like Us: Music and Meaning among Springsteen Fans.* New York: Oxford University Press, 1998.

Cills, Hazel. "How David Bowie Predicted Internet Fandom." *MTV News.* http://www.mtv.com. Accessed January 23, 2017.

Cline, C. "Essays from *Bitch*: The Women's Rock Newsletter with Bite." In *The Adoring Audience: Fan Culture and Popular Media,* edited by Lisa A. Lewis, 69–83. London: Routledge Press, 1992.

Collins, Katie. "Why Beyonce Has Only Tweeted Eight Times." *WIRED UK.* http://www.wired.co.uk. Accessed November 8, 2016.

Computer History Museum. "Computer History Museum: Guide to the Community Memory Records." 2005. http://archive.computerhistory.org.

Condry, Ian. "Cultures of Music Piracy an Ethnographic Comparison of the US and Japan." *International Journal of Cultural Studies* 7, no. 3 (September 1, 2004): 343–63. doi:10.1177/1367877904046412.

Crowe, Cameron. "Harry Styles' New Direction: Singer Opens Up about Famous Flings, Honest New LP." *Rolling Stone,* April 18, 2017. http://www.rollingstone.com.

Davis, Miles. *Miles.* New ed. New York: Simon and Schuster, 2011.

Dayan, Daniel. "The Peculiar Public of Television." *Media, Culture and Society* 23, no. 6 (November 1, 2001): 743–65. doi:10.1177/016344301023006004.

Dean, Jodi. "Communicative Capitalism: Circulation and the Foreclosure of Politics." *Cultural Politics* 1, no. 1 (March 1, 2005): 51–74. doi:10.2752/174321905778054845.

De Micheli, Carlo, and Andrea Stroppa. "Twitter and the Underground Market." *Nexa Center for Internet and Society.* Turin, 2013. http://nexa.polito.it.

DeNora, Tia. *After Adorno: Rethinking Music Sociology.* Cambridge: Cambridge University Press, 2003.

———. *Music in Everyday Life.* Cambridge: Cambridge University Press, 2000.

Doub, Bo. "Community Memory: Precedents in Social Media and Movements." *Computer History Museum,* February 23, 2016. http://www.computerhistory.org.

Driscoll, Kevin. "Hobbyist Inter-Networking and the Popular Internet Imaginary: Forgotten Histories of Networked Personal Computing, 1978–1998." University of Southern California, 2014. http://digitallibrary.usc.edu.

Duffy, Brooke Erin. *(Not) Getting Paid to Do What You Love: Gender, Social Media, and Aspirational Work.* New Haven, Conn.: Yale University Press, 2017.

Duffy, Brooke Erin, and Elizabeth Wissinger. "Cultural Work in the Social Media Age: Lessons from the Insta-Glam." *International Meeting of the Association of Internet Researchers.* October 2016, Berlin.

Ehrenreich, Barbara, Elizabeth Hess, and Gloria Jacobs. "Beatlemania: Girls Just Want to Have Fun." In *The Adoring Audience: Fan Culture and Popular Media,* edited by Lisa A. Lewis, 84–106. London: New York: Routledge, 1992.

Fehr, Beverley. "Intimacy Expectations in Same-Sex Friendships: A Prototype Interaction-Pattern Model." *Journal of Personality and Social Psychology* 86, no. 2 (February 2004): 265–84. doi:10.1037/0022-3514.86.2.265.

Fiske, John. "The Cultural Economy of Fandom." In *The Adoring Audience: Fan Culture and Popular Media*, edited by Lisa A. Lewis, 30–49. London: Routledge, 1992.

Fonarow, Wendy. *Empire of Dirt: The Aesthetics and Rituals of British Indie Music.* Annotated ed. Middletown, Conn.: Wesleyan University Press, 2006.

Fortunati, Leopoldina. "Immaterial Labor and Its Machinization." *Ephemera* 7, no. 1 (January 1, 2007): 139–57.

Fox, Aaron A. *Real Country: Music and Language in Working-Class Culture.* Durham, N.C.: Duke University Press, 2004.

Friedlander, Emilie. "Grimes in Reality." *FADER*, July 28, 2015. http://www.thefader.com/2015/07/28/grimes-cover-story-interview.

Frith, Simon. *Performing Rites: On the Value of Popular Music.* Cambridge, Mass.: Harvard University Press, 1998.

———. *Sound Effects.* New York: Pantheon, 1981.

Future of Music Coalition. "Artist Revenue Streams: A Multi-Method, Cross-Genre Examination of How US Based Musicians and Composers Are Earning a Living." http://money.futureofmusic.org.

Gadlin, Howard. "Private Lives and Public Order: A Critical View of the History of Intimate Relations in the United States." In *Close Relationships: Perspectives on the Meaning of Intimacy*, edited by George Klaus Levinger and Harold L. Raush, 33–72. Amherst, Mass.: University of Massachusetts Press, 1977.

Gershman, Jacob. "The Prince of Copyright Enforcement." *Wall Street Journal*, April 21, 2016. http://blogs.wsj.com.

Gibson, James J. "The Theory of Affordances." In *Perceiving, Acting, and Knowing: Toward an Ecological Psychology*, edited by Robert Shaw, John Bransford, and James J. Gibson, 127–43. Hillsdale, N.J.: Lawrence Erlbaum, 1977.

Gill, Rosalind, and Andy Pratt. "In the Social Factory? Immaterial Labour, Precariousness and Cultural Work." *Theory, Culture and Society* 25, no. 7–8 (2008): 1–30. doi:10.1177/0263276408097794.

Gillespie, Tarleton. "The Politics of 'Platforms.'" *New Media and Society* 12, no. 3 (May 1, 2010): 347–64. doi:10.1177/1461444809342738.

Goffman, Erving. *Forms of Talk.* Philadelphia: University of Pennsylvania Press, 1981.

Goldman, David. "Music's Lost Decade: Sales Cut in Half." *CNN Money*, February 3, 2010. http://money.cnn.com.

Grandey, Alicia, James Diefendorff, and Deborah E. Rupp, eds. *Emotional Labor in the 21st Century: Diverse Perspectives on Emotion Regulation at Work.* New York: Routledge, 2012.

Gray, Jonathan. "New Audiences, New Textualities: Anti-Fans and Non-Fans." *International Journal of Cultural Studies* 6, no. 1 (March 1, 2003): 64–81. doi:10.1177/1367877 903006001004.

Gray, Jonathan, Cornel Sandvoss, and Henry Jenkins. "Introduction." In *Fandom: Identities and Communities in a Mediated World*, edited by C. Lee Harrington. New York: New York University Press, 2007.

Gray, Mary, and Siddharth Suri. "Spike in Online Gig Work: Flash in the Pan or Future of Employment?" *In the Crowd*, November 17, 2016. http://www.inthecrowd.org.

Grazian, David. *Blue Chicago*. Chicago: University of Chicago Press, 2003.

Gregg, Melissa. "Learning to (Love) Labour: Production Cultures and the Affective Turn." *Communication and Critical/Cultural Studies* 6, no. 2 (June 1, 2009): 209–14. doi:10.1080/14791420902868045.

———. *Work's Intimacy*. Cambridge: Polity, 2011.

Grossberg, Lawrence. "Is There a Fan in the House? The Affective Sensibility of Fandom." In *The Adoring Audience: Fan Culture and Popular Media*, edited by Lisa A. Lewis. London: Routledge, 1992.

Gutek, Barbara A., Anita Bhappu, Matthew A. Liao-Troth, and Bennett Cherry. "Distinguishing between Service Relationships and Encounters." *Journal of Applied Psychology* 84, no. 2 (1999): 218–33. doi:10.1037/0021-9010.84.2.218.

Gutek, Barbara A., Bennett Cherry, Anita D. Bhappu, Sherry Schneider, and Loren Woolf. "Features of Service Relationships and Encounters." *Work and Occupations* 27, no. 3 (August 1, 2000): 319–52. doi:10.1177/0730888400027003004.

Hall, Jeffrey A. "Sex Differences in Friendship Expectations: A Meta-Analysis." *Journal of Social and Personal Relationships* 28, no. 6 (December 2010): 723–47. doi:10.1177/0265407510386192.

Hann, Michael. "Bruce Springsteen: 'You Can Change a Life in Three Minutes with the Right Song.'" *Guardian*, October 30, 2016. https://www.theguardian.com/music.

Haynes, Bruce. *The End of Early Music: A Period Performer's History of Music for the Twenty-First Century*. Oxford: Oxford University Press, 2007.

Hebdige, Dick. *Subculture: The Meaning of Style*. Rev. ed. London: Routledge, 1979.

Hellekson, Karen. "A Fannish Field of Value: Online Fan Gift Culture." *Cinema Journal* 48, no. 4 (September 27, 2009): 113–18. doi:10.1353/cj.0.0140.

Helms, Gesa. "The Presence of Precarity: Self-Employment as Contemporary Form." *Variant* 41 (Spring 2011): 39–42.

Hersh, Kristin. "Thoughts on Sustainability." August 30, 2007. https://www.kristin-hersh.com.

———. "What Is a Strange Angel?" https://www.kristinhersh.com.

Hesmondhalgh, David. *Why Music Matters*. Chichester, West Sussex: Wiley-Blackwell, 2013.

Hesmondhalgh, David, and Sarah Baker. *Creative Labour: Media Work in Three Cultural Industries*. London: Routledge, 2011.

———. "Creative Work and Emotional Labour in the Television Industry." *Theory, Culture and Society* 25, no. 7–8 (December 1, 2008): 97–118. doi:10.1177/0263276408097798.

Higgins, Parker. "Prince Inducted into Takedown Hall of Shame with New Lifetime Aggrievement Award." *Electronic Frontier Foundation*, May 7, 2013. https://www.eff.org.

Hillhouse, Alison. "Study: MTV's 'Music to the M Power.'" *Viacom Corporate: Blog. Viacom*. June 5, 2013. http://blog.viacom.com.

Hills, Matt. *Fan Cultures*. London: Routledge, 2002.

Hochschild, Arlie Russell. *The Managed Heart: Commercialization of Human Feeling*. 1983. 3rd ed. Berkeley: University of California Press, 2012.

———. *The Outsourced Self: What Happens When We Pay Others to Live Our Lives for Us*. 2012. Reprint, New York: Picador, 2013.

Honan, Mat. "How to Use Social Media to Juice Your Story's Popularity." *WIRED*, July 16, 2013. https://www.wired.com.

Horton, Donald, and R. Richard Wohl. "Mass Communication and Para-Social Interaction." *Psychiatry* 19, no. 3 (August 1, 1956): 215–29. doi:10.1080/00332747.1956.11023049.

Hughes, Jerald, and Karl Reiner Lang. "If I Had a Song: The Culture of Digital Community Networks and Its Impact on the Music Industry." *International Journal on Media Management* 5, no. 3 (January 1, 2003): 180–89. doi:10.1080/14241270309390033.

Hyde, Lewis. *The Gift: Creativity and the Artist in the Modern World*. New York: Vintage, 1983.

IFPI. "IFPI Global Music Report 2016." http://ifpi.org.

———. "Recorded Music Sales 2008." London: International Federation of the Phonographic Industry, 2009. http://www.ifpi.org.

Ingram, Mathew. "Prince Was an Early Fan of the Internet, but Grew to Hate What It Did to Artists." *Fortune*, April 22, 2016. http://fortune.com.

Jarnow, Jesse. *Heads: A Biography of Psychedelic America*. Philadelphia: Da Capo Press, 2016.

Jarrett, Kylie. *Feminism, Labour and Digital Media: The Digital Housewife*. New York: Routledge, 2015.

———. "The Relevance of 'Women's Work': Social Reproduction and Immaterial Labour in Digital Media." *Television and New Media* 15, no. 1 (May 15, 2013): 14–29. doi:10.1177/1527476413487607.

Jenkins, Henry. *Convergence Culture: Where Old and New Media Collide*, 2006. Rev. ed. New York: New York University Press, 2008.

———. *Textual Poachers: Television Fans and Participatory Culture*. 1992. 2nd ed. New York: Routledge, 2012.

Jenkins, Henry, Sam Ford, and Joshua Green. *Spreadable Media: Creating Value and Meaning in a Networked Culture*. New York; London: New York University Press, 2013.

Johnson, Maurice. "A Historical Analysis: The Evolution of Commercial Rap Music." Unpublished master's thesis. Florida State University, 2011. http://diginole.lib.fsu.edu/etd/3486.

Kaplan, A. "The Life of Dialogue." In *Communication: A Discussion at the Nobel Conference*, edited by J. D. Roslansky, 87–108. Amsterdam: North Holland, 1969.

Keating, Zoë. "There Is a Light at the End of the Tunnel. My Son Just Got Up and Poured a Bowl of Cereal and Milk without Me." *@zoecello*. June 7, 2017. https://twitter.com/zoecello.

Keil, Charles, and Steven Feld. *Music Grooves: Essays and Dialogues*. 2nd ed. Tucson, Ariz.: Fenestra Books, 2005.

Kirsner, Scott. *Fans, Friends and Followers: Building an Audience and a Creative Career in the Digital Age*. Cambridge, Mass.: CreateSpace Independent Publishing Platform, 2009.

Kot, Greg. *Ripped: How the Wired Generation Revolutionized Music*. New York: Scribner, 2010.

Kraft, James P. *Stage to Studio: Musicians and the Sound Revolution, 1890–1950*. Baltimore: Johns Hopkins University Press, 2003.

Kruse, Holly. *Site and Sound: Understanding Independent Music Scenes*. New York: Peter Lang, 2003.

Kusek, Dave. "10 Secrets of Social Media for Musicians." *Hypebot.com*. http://www.hypebot.com. Accessed November 8, 2016.

Lauer, Christopher. *Intimacy: A Dialectical Study*. London: Bloomsbury Academic, 2016.

Lena, Jennifer C. *Banding Together: How Communities Create Genres in Popular Music*. Princeton, N.J.: Princeton University Press, 2014.

Levinger, George Klaus, and Harold L. Raush. Preface to *Close Relationships: Perspectives on the Meaning of Intimacy*, edited by George Klaus Levinger and Harold L. Raush. Amherst: University of Massachusetts Press, 1977.

Litt, Eden. "Knock, Knock. Who's There? The Imagined Audience." *Journal of Broadcasting and Electronic Media* 56, no. 3 (July 1, 2012): 330–45. doi:10.1080/08838151.2012.705195.

Livingstone, Sonia. "The Challenge of Changing Audiences: Or, What Is the Audience Researcher to Do in the Age of the Internet?" *European Journal of Communication* 19, no. 1 (March 1, 2004): 75–86. doi:10.1177/0267323104040695.

———. "On the Relation between Audiences and Publics." In *Audiences and Publics: When Cultural Engagement Matters for the Public Sphere*, edited by Sonia Livingstone, 17–41. Bristol: Intellect, 2005.

Lutgen-Sandvik, Pamela, Sarah E. Riforgiate, and Courtney Fletcher. "Work as a Source of Positive Emotional Experiences and the Discourses Informing Positive Assessment." *Western Journal of Communication* 75, no. 1 (January 31, 2014): 2–27. doi:10.1080/10570314.2010.536963.

Major, Clarence, ed. *Juba to Jive: A Dictionary of African-American Slang*. London: Puffin, 1994.

Marwick, Alice E. *Status Update: Celebrity, Publicity, and Branding in the Social Media Age*. New Haven, Conn.: Yale University Press, 2013.

Marwick, Alice E., and danah boyd. "I Tweet Honestly, I Tweet Passionately: Twitter Users, Context Collapse, and the Imagined Audience." *New Media and Society*, July 7, 2010. doi:10.1177/1461444810365313.

———. "To See and Be Seen: Celebrity Practice on Twitter." *Convergence: The International Journal of Research into New Media Technologies* 17, no. 2 (May 1, 2011): 139–58. doi:10.1177/1354856510394539.

Mauss, Marcel. *The Gift: Forms and Functions of Exchange in Archaic Societies*. Translated by W. D. Hall. New York: W. W. Norton, 2000.

Mayberry, Lauren. "Chvrches' Lauren Mayberry: 'I Will Not Accept Online Misogyny.'" *Guardian*, September 30, 2013. https://www.theguardian.com/music.

Mayer-Schönberger, Viktor, and Kenneth Cukier. *Big Data: A Revolution That Will Transform How We Live, Work, and Think*. Boston: Eamon Dolan/Mariner Books, 2014.

McVeigh-Schultz, Joshua, and Nancy K. Baym. "Thinking of You: Vernacular Affordance in the Context of the Microsocial Relationship App, Couple." *Social Media + Society* 1, no. 2 (September 22, 2015). doi:10.1177/2056305115604649.

Mihelich, John, and John Papineau. "Parrotheads in Margaritaville: Fan Practice, Oppositional Culture, and Embedded Cultural Resistance in Buffett Fandom." *Journal of Popular Music Studies* 17, no. 2 (August 1, 2005): 175–202. doi:10.1111/j.1524-2226.2005.00041.x.

Mihm, Stephen. "Gig Work Used to Just Be Called 'Work.'" *Bloomberg View*, July 16, 2015. https://www.bloombergview.com.

Milner, R. M. "Negotiating Text Integrity." *Information, Communication and Society* 13, no. 5 (August 1, 2010): 722–46. doi:10.1080/13691180903456538.

———. "Working for the Text: Fan Labor and the New Organization." *International Journal of Cultural Studies* 12, no. 5 (September 1, 2009): 491–508. doi:10.1177/1367877909337861.

Mitchell, David T., and Sharon L. Snyder. "Narrative Prosthesis and the Materiality of Metaphor." *Narrative Prosthesis*. Ann Arbor: University of Michigan Press, 2001.

Montgomery, Barbara M., and Leslie A. Baxter, eds. *Dialectical Approaches to Studying Personal Relationships*. Mahwah, N.J.: Psychology Press, 2013.

Morini, Cristina, and Andrea Fumagalli. "Life Put to Work: Towards a Life Theory of Value: Digital Labour—Workers, Authors, Citizens." *Ephemera: Theory and Politics in Organization* 10, no. 3/4 (2010): 234–52.

Morris, Jeremy Wade. "Artists as Entrepreneurs, Fans as Workers." *Popular Music and Society* 37, no. 3 (May 27, 2014): 273–90. doi:10.1080/03007766.2013.778534.

Muehlebach, Andrea. "On Affective Labor in Post-Fordist Italy." *Cultural Anthropology* 26, no. 1 (February 1, 2011): 59–82. doi:10.1111/j.1548-1360.2010.01080.x.

Napoli, Philip M. *Audience Evolution: New Technologies and the Transformation of Media Audiences*. New York: Columbia University Press, 2010.

Neal, Mark Anthony. *What the Music Said: Black Popular Music and Black Public Culture*. New York: Routledge, 1999.

Neff, Gina. *Venture Labor: Work and the Burden of Risk in Innovative Industries*. Cambridge: MIT Press, 2015.

Negus, Keith. *Music Genres and Corporate Cultures*. London: Routledge, 1999.

———. *Popular Music in Theory: An Introduction*. Hanover, N.H.: Wesleyan University Press, 1996.

Negus, Keith, and Michael Pickering. *Creativity, Communication and Cultural Value*. London; Thousand Oaks, Calif.: SAGE, 2004.

"Noel Gallagher—'The Fantasy's Gone Out of Making Music.'" *NME*, November 8, 2006. http://www.nme.com.

Nunberg, Geoff. "Goodbye Jobs, Hello 'Gigs': How One Word Sums Up a New Economic Reality." *NPR.org*, January 11, 2016. http://www.npr.org.

Nussbaum, Martha C. *Upheavals of Thought: The Intelligence of Emotions*. Cambridge: Cambridge University Press, 2003.

O'Hara, Kenton, and Barry Brown, eds. *Consuming Music Together: Social and Collaborative Aspects of Music Consumption Technologies*. Berlin: Springer, 2006.

O'Reilly, Daragh, and Kathy Doherty. "Music B(r)ands Online and Constructing Community: The Case of New Model Army." In *Cybersounds: Essays on Virtual Music Culture*, edited by Michael D. Ayers. New York: Peter Lang, 2006.

Paine, Andre. "IFPI: $1 Million to Break an Act." *Billboard*, March 9, 2010. http://www.billboard.com.

Palmer, Amanda. *The Art of Asking: How I Learned to Stop Worrying and Let People Help*. New York: Grand Central, 2015.

Parks, Malcolm R. "Ideology in Interpersonal Communication: Off the Couch and into the World." In *Communication Yearbook 5*, edited by M. Burgoon, 79–107. New Brunswick, N.J.: Transaction, 1981.

Perlroth, Nicole. "Researchers Call Out Twitter Celebrities with Suspicious Followings." *Bits Blog*, 1366923467, April 25, 2013. http://bits.blogs.nytimes.com.

Peterson, Richard A. *Creating Country Music: Fabricating Authenticity*. Chicago: University of Chicago Press, 1999.

Pew Research Center. "Internet/Broadband Fact Sheet." *Pew Research Center: Internet, Science and Tech*, January 12, 2017. http://www.pewinternet.org.

Phillips, Whitney. *This Is Why We Can't Have Nice Things: Mapping the Relationship between Online Trolling and Mainstream Culture*. Cambridge, Mass.: MIT Press, 2016.

Piepmeier, Alison. "Why Zines Matter: Materiality and the Creation of Embodied Community." *American Periodicals* 18, no. 2 (2008): 213–38.

Piercy, K. W. "When It Is More Than a Job: Close Relationships between Home Health Aides and Older Clients." *Journal of Aging and Health* 12, no. 3 (August 2000): 362–87.

Pinkowitz, Jacqueline Marie. "'The Rabid Fans That Take [*Twilight*] Much Too Seriously': The Construction and Rejection of Excess in *Twilight* Antifandom." *Transformative Works and Cultures* 7 (September 20, 2010). doi:10.3983/twc.2011.0247.

Polanyi, Livia. *Telling the American Story*. Cambridge, Mass.: MIT Press, 1989.

Postigo, Hector. "The Socio-Technical Architecture of Digital Labor: Converting Play into YouTube Money." *New Media and Society*, July 3, 2014. doi:10.1177/1461444814541527.

Prager, Karen J. *The Psychology of Intimacy*. New York: Guilford Press, 1995.

Randolph, Sal. "Free Words to Free Manifesta: Some Experiments in Art as Gift." *Ethics and the Environment* 8, no. 1 (2003): 61–73.

Rawlins, William K. *The Compass of Friendship: Narratives, Identities, and Dialogues*. Los Angeles: SAGE, 2008.

———. "Openness as Problematic in Ongoing Friendships: Two Conversational Dilemmas." *Communication Monographs* 50, no. 1 (March 1, 1983): 1–13. doi:10.1080/03637758309390150.

Reagin, Nancy, and Anne Rubenstein. "'I'm Buffy, and You're History': Putting Fan Studies into History." *Transformative Works and Cultures* 6 (December 31, 2010). http://journal.transformativeworks.org.

Redmond, Sean, and Su Holmes, eds. *Stardom and Celebrity: A Reader.* Thousand Oaks, Calif.: SAGE, 2007.

Regner, Tobias, and Javier A. Barria. "Do Consumers Pay Voluntarily? The Case of Online Music." *Journal of Economic Behavior and Organization* 71, no. 2 (2009): 395–406.

Reimer, Bennett, Anthony J. Palmer, Thomas A. Regelski, and Wayne D. Bowman. "Why Do Humans Value Music?" *Philosophy of Music Education Review* 10, no. 1 (March 30, 2011): 41–41.

Rethink Music Initiative. "Fair Music: Transparency and Payment Flows in the Music Industry." July 3, 2015. https://www.berklee.edu.

Rheingold, Howard. *The Virtual Community: Homesteading on the Electronic Frontier.* Reading, Mass: Addison-Wesley, 1993.

Rosen, Jay. "The People Formerly Known as the Audience." *Press Think: Ghost of Democracy in the Media Machine,* June 27, 2006. http://archive.pressthink.org.

Sabattini, Laura, and Faye J. Crosby. "Ceilings and Walls: Work-Life and 'Family Friendly' Policies." In *The Glass Ceiling in the 21st Century: Understand Barriers to Gender Equality,* edited by Michelle K. Ryan, Michael T. Schmitt, and Manuela Barreto, 201–23. Washington, D.C.: American Psychological Association, 2009.

Sarbanes, Janet. "Musicking and Communitas: The Aesthetic Mode of Sociality in Rebetika Subculture." *Popular Music and Society* 29, no. 1 (February 1, 2006): 17–35. doi:10.1080/03007760500142738.

Schmandt-Besserat, Denise. "The Evolution of Writing." January 25, 2014. https://sites.utexas.edu.

Schull, Natasha Dow. "Escape Mechanism: Women, Caretaking, and Compulsive Gambling." 2002. http://dlib.bc.edu/islandora/object/bc-ir:100084.

Scott, David Meerman, and Brian Halligan. *Marketing Lessons from the Grateful Dead: What Every Business Can Learn from the Most Iconic Band in History.* Hoboken, N.J.: Wiley, 2010.

Sennett, Richard. *The Fall of Public Man.* New York: W. W. Norton, 1992.

Sexton, Richard E., and Virginia Staudt Sexton. "Intimacy: A Historical Perspective." In *Intimacy,* edited by Martin Fischer and George Stricker, 1–20. New York: Plenum Press, 1982.

Shah, Hasit. "Poor Lonely Computer: Prince's Misunderstood Relationship with the Internet." *NPR.org,* March 8, 2016. http://www.npr.org.

Siebers, Tobin. *Disability Theory.* Ann Arbor: University of Michigan Press, 2008.

Sinnreich, Aram. *The Piracy Crusade: How the Music Industry's War on Sharing Destroys Markets and Erodes Civil Liberties.* Amherst: University of Massachusetts Press, 2013.

Small, Christopher. *Musicking: The Meanings of Performing and Listening*. Hanover, N.H.: Wesleyan University Press, 1998.

Stacey, Clare L. "Finding Dignity in Dirty Work: The Constraints and Rewards of Low-Wage Home Care Labour." *Sociology of Health and Illness* 27, no. 6 (September 2005): 831–54. doi:10.1111/j.1467-9566.2005.00476.x.

Stafford, Laura. "Measuring Relationship Maintenance Behaviors: Critique and Development of the Revised Relationship Maintenance Behavior Scale." *Journal of Social and Personal Relationships* 28, no. 2 (March 1, 2011): 278–303. doi:10.1177/0265407510378125.

Stahl, Matt. *Unfree Masters: Popular Music and the Politics of Work*. Durham, N.C.: Duke University Press, 2012.

Sterne, Jonathan. "There Is No Music Industry." *Media Industries*, no. 1 (May 15, 2014). http://www.mediaindustriesjournal.org.

Stopera, Matt. "A Rihanna Meet and Greet vs. an Avril Lavigne Meet and Greet." *BuzzFeed*, May 5, 2014. http://www.buzzfeed.com.

Strauss, Neil. "Rolling Stones Live on Internet: Both a Big Deal and a Little Deal." *New York Times*, November 22, 1994. http://www.nytimes.com.

Suisman, David. *Selling Sounds: The Commercial Revolution in American Music*. Cambridge, Mass.: Harvard University Press, 2012.

Sullivan, Denise. *R.E.M.-Talk about the Passion: An Oral History*. Lancaster, Pa.: Charles F. Miller, 1994.

Tagg, Philip. "'Universal' Music and the Case of death1." *Critical Quarterly* 35, no. 2 (June 1, 1993): 54–85. doi:10.1111/j.1467-8705.1993.tb00469.x.

Terranova, Tiziana. "Free Labor: Producing Culture for the Digital Economy." *Social Text 63* 18, no. 2 (2000): 33–58.

Théberge, Paul. *Any Sound You Can Imagine: Making Music/Consuming Technology*. Hanover, N.H.: Wesleyan University Press, 1997.

———. "Everyday Fandom: Fan Clubs, Blogging, and the Quotidian Rhythms of the Internet." *Canadian Journal of Communication* 30, no. 4 (January 10, 2006). http://www.cjc-online.ca.

Thornton, Sarah. *Club Cultures: Music, Media, and Subcultural Capital*. Hanover, N.H.: Wesleyan University Press, 1996.

Tomlinson, Gary. *A Million Years of Music: The Emergence of Human Modernity*. New York: Zone Books, 2015.

Topspin. "Average Fan Value: Methodology and Best Practices." *Topspin Tumblr*. http://topspinmedia.tumblr.com. Accessed January 23, 2017.

Torpey, Elka, and Andrew Hogan. "Working in a Gig Economy: Career Outlook: U.S. Bureau of Labor Statistics." *United States Department of Labor: Bureau of Labor Statistics*, May 2016. https://www.bls.gov/careeroutlook/2016.

Tracy, Sarah J. "Becoming a Character for Commerce: Emotion Labor, Self-Subordination, and Discursive Construction of Identity in a Total Institution." *Management Communication Quarterly* 14, no. 1 (August 1, 2000): 90–128. doi:10.1177/0893318900141004.

———. "Locking Up Emotion: Moving beyond Dissonance for Understanding Emotion Labor Discomfort." *Communication Monographs* 72, no. 3 (September 1, 2005): 261–83. doi:10.1080/03637750500206474.

Tremain, Rose. *Music and Silence.* New York: Washington Square Press, 2001.

Turino, Thomas. *Music as Social Life: The Politics of Participation.* Chicago: University of Chicago Press, 2008.

Twitter. "Twitter for Musicians and Artists." N.d. https://dev.twitter.com/media/ music.

van Dijck, José. *The Culture of Connectivity: A Critical History of Social Media.* Oxford: Oxford University Press, 2013.

Veijola, Soile, and Eeva Jokinen. "Towards a Hostessing Society? Mobile Arrangements of Gender and Labour." *NORA-Nordic Journal of Feminist and Gender Research* 16, no. 3 (September 1, 2008): 166–81. doi:10.1080/08038740802279901.

Verkerk, Marian. "Care as Process and the Quest for Autonomy." *Asian Bioethics Review* 3, no. 2 (June 9, 2011): 150–54.

Watson, Nessim. "Why We Argue about Virtual Community: A Case Study of the Phish.Net Fan Community." In *Virtual Culture: Identity and Communication in Cybersociety*, 102–32. London: SAGE, 2002.

Weeks, Kathi. "Life within and against Work: Affective Labor, Feminist Critique, and Post-Fordist Politics." *Ephemera* 7, no. 1 (2007): 233–49.

Whittaker, Jason. "Dark Webs: Goth Subcultures in Cyberspace." *Gothic Studies* 9, no. 1 (May 2007): 35–45.

Wikström, Patrik. *The Music Industry: Music in the Cloud.* 2nd ed. London: Polity, 2013.

Wiseman, Jacqueline P. "Friendship: Bonds and Binds in a Voluntary Relationship." *Journal of Social and Personal Relationships* 3, no. 2 (June 1, 1986): 191–211. doi:10.1177/0265407586032005.

Wissinger, Elizabeth. "Glamour Labour in the Age of Kardashian." *Critical Studies in Fashion and Beauty* 7, no. 2 (2016): 141–52.

———. "Modelling a Way of Life: Immaterial and Affective Labour in the Fashion Modelling Industry." *Ephemera: Theory and Politics in Organization* 7, no. 1 (2007): 250–69.

Witt, Stephen. *How Music Got Free: A Story of Obsession and Invention.* New York: Penguin Books, 2016.

Woolley, David R. "PLATO: The Emergence of Online Community." January 10, 1994. http://thinkofit.com.

Zappavigna, Michele. "Ambient Affiliation: A Linguistic Perspective on Twitter." *New Media and Society* 13, no. 5 (August 1, 2011): 788–806. doi:10.1177/1461444810385097.

Zelizer, Viviana A. *The Purchase of Intimacy.* Princeton, N.J.: Princeton University Press, 2005.

INDEX

ABOUT THE AUTHOR

Nancy K. Baym is a Principal Researcher at Microsoft in Cambridge, Massachusetts. She is the author and co-editor of three previous books about audiences, relationships, and the internet, including *Personal Connections in the Digital Age*. More information, most of her articles, and some of her talks are available at nancybaym.com.